RACING CARS
MASTERPIECES OF ENGINEERING

RACING CARS
MASTERPIECES OF ENGINEERING

JOHN TIPLER

Published by

Brown Books
An imprint of Amber Books Ltd
Bradley's Close
74-77 White Lion Street
London N1 9PF

ISBN: 1-897884-64-8

Editor: Helen Wilson
Design and computer artwork: Richard Burgess
Picture research: Lisa Wren

Printed in Italy

ACKNOWLEDGEMENTS

I want to thank the following people for their help in producing this book, which has without doubt been one of the most enjoyable to do.

Thanks go to Tony Matthews for providing his fine cutaway illustrations that feature throughout the book; Donington Park Circuit Museum for giving access to illustrator Richard Burgess to do his excellent cutaways of F3 Cooper, Lotus 25 and Indy roadster; likewise, Ben Samuelson at TVR for permission to draw the TVR Speed Twelve, and Alastair Florance, Andrew Davis and Sue Bagnall at Lotus for organising pictures of the Sport Elise and opening the door to do a cutaway illustration. Others that I want to mention who were helpful with my research and when sourcing pictures include Angie Voluti and Elvira Ruocco at Alfa Romeo Centro Storico; Jens Torner of Porsche's Historical Archive; Jim Fowler and Fran of Ford Motor Company's Photographic Services; and Linzi Smart of LS Design for Anglo American Challenge TransAm shots from Sebring. Ian Catt, my erstwhile colleague from the John Player Special Team Lotus days, delved into his personal picture treasure chest. The list goes on: Mary Harvey, Andy Robinson, Laurie Caddell, Adam Porter of *Wheels* magazine, Bob Dance, Clive Chapman of Classic Team Lotus, Giancarlo Baccini of Scuderia Ferrari, Martin Pass of Audi, Maria Elena Munoz of Marlboro, Graham Jones at Edelman Public Relations Worldwide for BAR Team, Emma Owen of Jordan Grand Prix, Paula Webb of McLaren Cars, Vanna Skelley of Burmah Castrol picture archive, Miles Johnson of Ford General Media, Greg Rubenstein of SCCA Pro Racing, Julia Horden at Benetton Formula 1, Alison Hill of Reynard Motorsport, Ellen Kolby of TAG McLaren, Jacquie Groom – ELMS Press Officer, Tim Bowles of the Classic Camaro Club, Jamie Campbell-Walter at Lister Cars, TWR-Arrows and Sir John Whitmore. And thanks too to Helen Wilson, Lisa Wren, Richard Burgess and Daniel Balado for handling the production side at Amber Books.

CONTENTS

INTRODUCTION

People have raced horses since time immemorial, so with the coming of the motor car it was natural they would race them too, to see who was faster and which was the quicker car. The sport has metamorphosed through countless evolutions in terms of engine chassis and suspension configuration, body type and construction material, brought about by successive rule changes and economic and political influence. Today there is a bewildering plethora of categories. No matter what kind of vehicle you care to suggest, there will almost certainly be someone somewhere racing it – and probably there is a whole series devoted to it.

The purest form of racing is the single-seater car, exemplified by the Formula 1 machines that contest the F1 World Championship Grand Prix series, and which best represent the pinnacle of technical excellence and innovation. Single-seater racing is essentially European-based, but there are races all over the world, including in the USA where the CART Champ cars are top single-seaters.

Formula 1 World Champion Mika Hakkinen's McLaren-Mercedes is refuelled mid-race. In most major categories of the sport, rapid pit stops are crucial, and the crews are drilled to a peak of efficiency. Sophisticated tactics are employed to gain track position, and races are won and lost on such strategies.

The 5.0-litre (305-cubic-inch) flat-12 engined Porsche 917 dominated endurance racing between 1970 and 1971. Here is the JW Automotive-run Gulf 917 of Jo Siffert/Brian Redman at Brands Hatch during the BOAC 1000 in 1970 – the sister car of Rodriguez/Kinnunen was the winner.

The Indy Racing League is the rival attraction here, with the Indy Lights Series the proving ground for top-notch aspirants. We shall be looking at the cars that contest these championships in the single-seater section, along with the stepping-stone cars of F3000 and Formula 3, and there are myriad lesser formulae for young drivers to winch themselves up the ladder, with Formula Ford the first step up on the nursery slopes from karting. Some drivers progress one formula at a time, spending two or three seasons in each; others – like Jenson Button, Williams' recruit for the 2000 Formula 1 season – have the rare talent to leapfrog the interim formulae.

TIN-TOPS

Beginning in the post-war years, touring car racing quickly grew into one of the most exhilarating categories on the competition calendar, and some of the most memorable duels were fought out by saloon car drivers. Touring cars are just saloon cars by another name, and should not be confused with grand touring cars, which have a much more exalted pedigree, even though they are equally

Among the myriad forms of motor sport are one-make championships. Some cater for single models, like this Renault Sport Spider Trophy series, running at Imola in 1996. The Alpine-built cars are powered by 180bhp 2.0 Clio Williams engines.

dramatically modified for racing. Touring car racers are, externally at any rate, the same mass-produced vehicles you find in dealers' showrooms. Stock car racing in the USA – the NASCAR category – meant just that: they were cars taken out of the dealers' stock and then seriously tweaked to make them handle and perform like race cars.

Touring car racing became popular for several reasons. Spectators could identify with the car they drove to work or the shops every day, while the inter-class competition of years gone by threw up all kinds of David-and-Goliath confrontations, such as Mini-Cooper versus Ford Galaxie. Also, because the drivers are much better protected than in open-wheel single-seater racers, deliberate barging confrontations are inevitable and frequent, and this makes touring cars excellent TV, especially with in-car cameras monitoring the action. Like the other categories, the drivers tend to specialise in touring car racing, although it is not unusual to find ex-Formula 1 drivers competing in tin-tops.

The cars campaigned in most rallying events tend to be saloon cars, and they are adapted in similar ways to their circuit-racing cousins, but with different specification criteria to match the rigours of that particular discipline. Given the nature of the World Rally Championship and its long, fast, special stages through forest and wilderness tracks, rally cars require equally robust

chassis and suspension, and internal roll-cages to protect the occupants. A separate category called 'rallycross' was developed in the 1960s, combining the rally car with the circuit racer. In the UK these events were staged at circuits like Lydden Hill and Brands Hatch, combining tarmac with grass track, and spectators could thrill to the sideways antics of the rally stars without having to hike through forests and moorland to see the action. Rallycross developed into a haven for pensioned-off rally cars like the Metro 6R4, although far more prosaic machines like the VW Beetle could be just as successful.

Over the years there have been various championships for every kind of circuit-racing saloon car, from the most highly modified – like the Super Saloon silhouette cars of the mid-1970s, which gave the world the Skoda-Chevrolet, and the high-tech Class 1

Taking part in motor sport need not be prohibitively expensive, although sponsorship undoubtedly helps. Here at a Brands Hatch club meeting in 1990, the author in his mildly modified Alfa Romeo GTV6 skirmishes with an Alfasud during a round of the AROC series.

World Touring cars from Alfa, Mercedes and Opel seen in the mid-1990s – to virtually bog-standard Group N cars with roll-cages, fire extinguishers and slightly tweaked suspension.

Each country has its own brand of touring car racing, although it has become much more homogenised in Europe in the last 20 years and looks like becoming even more so. Still, each country continues to run its own national series. In Australia and New Zealand, for instance, the locally produced Ford Falcons vie with the domestic Holden Commodores, and the classic event in Australia is the Bathurst 500. As well as NASCAR, the USA has the TransAm series, which started off in the mid-1960s with the Pony cars – Mustangs and Camaros – but evolved into a much more exotic race series for silhouette cars in 2000.

SPORTS AND GT RACING

Historically, sports car racing has gone down two distinct roads. There were sports racing cars derived from their single-seater counterparts as far back as the 1920s and 1930s, such as the Alfa Romeo 6C 1750, and these highly-strung thoroughbreds became the prototypes that vied for the World

Championship of Makes in the 1960s and 1970s. Some cars straddled both camps: in stripped-down form the big 4.5-litre (275-cubic-inch) Bentley raced as a Grand Prix car in 1930. The authorities have always sought to rein in the big, powerful cars, and to that end there have been events and classes specifically for cars that correspond more or less to their road-going siblings. In addition, separate classes sprang up for grand touring cars, which raced alongside sports cars and prototypes, questing not just for overall victory but class distinctions too.

Traditionally, the highlight of the sports car calendar is the Le Mans 24-Hour endurance race in north-western France, but other events have achieved similar status, such as the Mille Miglia in Italy and the Targa Florio in Sicily. In the UK the Tourist Trophy had the longest pedigree, while events such as the Nürburgring 1000km (620 miles) and Sebring 12-Hour were equally taxing for men and machinery.

As with the single-seater categories, a series of races makes up a championship, and the championships current in the year 2000 were the Sports Car Racing World Cup, the American Le Mans Series (ALMS), and the FIA GT

Championship that grew out of GT1 and GT2, which provided the highlights during the 1990s. Within these series were divisions for engine capacity and degrees of modification from standard – less complex now than in the 1950s, 1960s and 1970s – so that the grand touring category is broken down into GT1, GT2 and GT3. The cars are often quite as high-tech as Formula 1 machines, and in the past

The Jordan pit crew refuels Frentzen's car, with three mechanics to change each wheel, three on the fuel hose and one with a fire extinguisher, a man at either end on the jacks, plus one with the 'brakes on' sign. Times vary according to fuel quantities, but seven-second stops are not unknown.

As the sport has progressed and grown more sophisticated, the circuits and trackside facilities have expanded or been modified accordingly. The Brands Hatch pits evolved from little more than a series of primitive sheds to clinically clean garages, with a separate pit wall and signalling platforms.

have been quicker – the Porsche 917, for example – partly because of advantageous regulations and also because all-enveloping bodywork is far better aerodynamically than open-wheel.

One thing is certain: competition in sports GT racing is a lot less frantic than in Formula 1, even though it is nowadays highly professional. Many protagonists – like Derek Bell, Jacky Ickx and Bob Wolleck – specialise in

the long-distance races common to this category, and it is also something of a haven for retired Grand Prix stars.

CLUB RACING

You do not have to be rich or sponsored up to the hilt to go racing (although it helps). Lower down the scale there are flourishing race series run by most of the dedicated car clubs, with different classes for varying engine sizes, and these thrive as a result of enthusiasts competing just for the fun of it. In the late 1980s I raced an Alfa Romeo GTV6 in the British Alfa Romeo Owners' Club Championship, and although I usually ended up among the back markers, it was excellent fun. However, when arriving at the first corner after the start of a race it is alarming to discover that you are surrounded by a group of psychopathic madmen – and women.

Getting started was relatively straightforward. Preparation of the car consisted of removing the seats and trim and installing a Sparco race seat and full racing harness. The safety-devices steel-frame roll-cage consisted of a made up of what would pass for scaffolding poles that ran around the top of the windscreen, the roof of the car, and along the doors, and was diagonally braced from the rear. Also fitted was a fire extinguisher and an external ignition switch (in case I was trapped

Front suspension of the Williams FW18 F1 car of 1996 consisted of carbon-fibre upper and steel lower wishbones with pushrod arms going from the bottom of the wheel upright to act on the inboard horizontal damper system. The more aerodynamic pullrods common in the 1980s were revived by Arrows in 2000.

inside). A sheet of aluminium pop-riveted across the back of the cabin was necessary to isolate the fuel tank from the cabin, and Dzus fasteners were fitted to secure the bonnet and tailgate. The suspension was lowered with shorter springs at the rear and by adjusting the torsion bars at the front, and special adjustable dampers were fitted. If you tried to push down on the car it was rock-hard, with about three inches' ground clearance. Harder competition brake pads were installed and specified control tyres fitted, in this instance B.F. Goodrich Comp T/As. Designated race numbers were also slapped on the sides and bonnet.

Like all racing cars, you had to have it scrutinised prior to every race to ensure that it was completely safe and complied with the regulations. It was also possible to drive to and from the circuit, although a crash would have meant a long walk home. The majority of racing cars travel in transporters or trailers, even at club racing level, because they are either too highly tuned to use on the road or, if single-seaters or sports racers, not clearly road-registered.

JOINING UP

Should you fancy your chances, getting started in racing is simply a matter of joining your local motor club or the owners' club of your chosen make or model. You do not even have to build the racing car yourself; it is much more economical to buy one that someone else has spent large sums of money on. Clearly you must buy something with a proven track record rather than a no-hoper, and there are plenty advertised in a magazine like *Autosport*, or your own club mag.

Once you are a member of the relevant motor club you can try your hand at dedicated track days or practice evenings, and then it is just a short hop into your first race meeting. If you are serious about it there are several racing-driver schools based at the main race circuits to give you a professional grounding. On the way you will have talked to as many people as possible who have experience of running your kind of car, mixing their advice with your own aspirations. But cheap it is not. Race entry fees are high, even at club racing level, and bills are expensive if you shunt or blow the engine up. You also have to budget for tyres, maintenance, travelling and accommodation, so even a modicum of sponsorship is desirable. In order to get the most out of the car and explore its (and your own) limits you must not care if the car is damaged when you go off, so do not race your pride-and-joy as you will be inhibited from giving it your best shot. If you do not give it a good go, you could end up being a mobile chicane, which is alarming and dangerous in its own way when the really quick guys come round to lap you.

My own experience in an Alfa Romeo ranks just about at the bottom of what is possible; given a sponsored budget, a higher standard of preparation is possible, and engines can be tuned to provide much higher performance than standard equipment. But from the highest echelons of Formula

Fans of classic car racing thrill to the sight and sound of Ferrari GTO, Daytona Cobra, E-type Jaguar, Corvette and Aston Martin at the start of the RAC TT Celebration race at the 1999 Goodwood Revival meeting. All were driven by international stars, and the Jaguar emerged the winner.

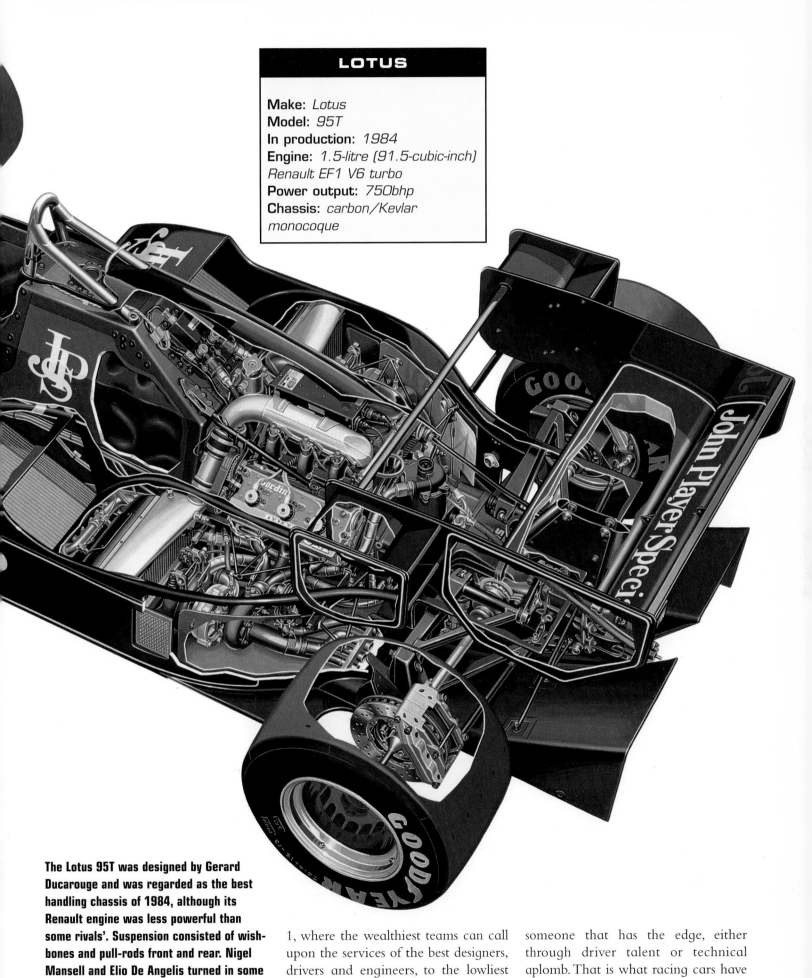

LOTUS

Make: *Lotus*
Model: *95T*
In production: *1984*
Engine: *1.5-litre (91.5-cubic-inch)
Renault EF1 V6 turbo*
Power output: *750bhp*
Chassis: *carbon/Kevlar
monocoque*

The Lotus 95T was designed by Gerard Ducarouge and was regarded as the best handling chassis of 1984, although its Renault engine was less powerful than some rivals'. Suspension consisted of wishbones and pull-rods front and rear. Nigel Mansell and Elio De Angelis turned in some impressive performances, but no wins.

1, where the wealthiest teams can call upon the services of the best designers, drivers and engineers, to the lowliest Mini series, there will always be someone that has the edge, either through driver talent or technical aplomb. That is what racing cars have always been about.

FORMULA 1

Single-seater racing cars are commonly held to be the purest form of motor racing, but it was not until the arrival of the monoposto or single-seater racer of the early 1930s that the format became the norm for Grand Prix events. Prior to that, racing cars in general had evolved as two-seat machines, and had passed through several stages since the early days of the motor car.

The 1894 Paris to Rouen Reliability Trial is regarded as the first big-time motor race, followed by the Paris–Bordeaux–Paris in 1895 and the Paris–Berlin of 1901. The first race held on a closed circuit was in the Ardennes in 1902 – 86km (53.5 miles) long. This was won by Charles Jarrott in a Panhard. By 1903 these hugely ambitious inter-city races had come to an end with the tragic Paris–Madrid event (in which Marcel Renault was killed), and were superseded by the Gordon Bennett Trophy series held on closed circuits comprising dusty public roads.

In the USA, the first series to get going was the Vanderbilt Cup, held on Long Island in 1906, and the French Le Mans and Sicilian Targa Florio circuits were also first used in 1906. The Brooklands Motor Course opened in 1907 at Weybridge in Surrey, England – the first 'superspeedway' in the world. It remained active until the outbreak of the Second World War.

With 16 rounds worldwide, Formula 1 is the pinnacle of international motor sport. One of the most successful teams is Williams, with seven World Champions to its credit. The youngest British driver to compete in a Grand Prix was 20-year-old Jenson Button, pictured here in the Williams BMW FW22 in 2000.

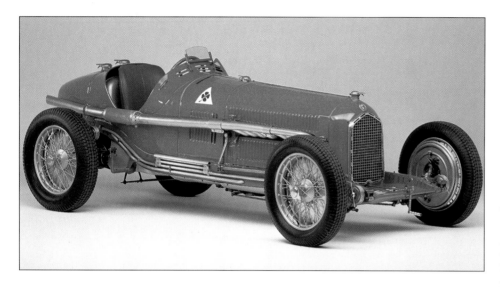

A group of American businessmen were impressed by the project and built the Indianapolis Motor Speedway, which opened in 1909 and hosted the first Indy 500 in 1911.

Titans of these early struggles included Camille Jenatzy, François Szisz, Albert Clement, Louis Wagner, Vincenzo Florio, Felice Nazzaro and Vincenzo Lancia, to name but a few. There were three different classes in those early days, rather than formulae. Heavy class cars were topped by the 10.0-litre (610-cubic-inch) Mors, a 3.3-litre (201-cubic-inch) Panhard typified the Light class, and the Voiturette category featured, among others, a single-cylinder Renault at just 500cc (30.5 cubic inches). The cars were, for the most part, massive by today's standards, towering on chassis directly descended from the horse-drawn carriages that were still in production, with crude transmissions and chain drive. Notable among them were the products of Renault, Darracq, Hotchkiss, Panhard, Napier, Mercedes, Opel, Minerva, Isotta, Itala and Fiat. The constructors of these fledgling racers knew very well that the lighter the car the faster it went, so as a concession to their competitive role they were stripped of all the creature comforts customer cars would normally enjoy, such as hoods and mudguards. They were thus particularly spartan, and the driver and his riding mechanic totally unprotected.

By 1910, the contenders included S.F.

The 215bhp, 2.65-litre (162-cubic-inch), supercharged, straight-eight Alfa Romeo P3 Tipo B monoposto Grand Prix car swept all before it in 1932, and as late as 1935 Nuvolari defeated the Silver Arrows at the Nürburgring with a 3.8-litre (232-cubic-inch) version.

Edge, Rene De Kniff, Leon Théry and Christian Lautenschlager, and cars in contention included Mors, Benz, Lorraine-Dietrich, Bayard-Clément and, in the USA, the Buick. In 1913, the Le Mans programme included events for the Voiturette class, and the dominant makes in that category between 1911 and 1913 were Peugeot and Sunbeam. The basic design comprised, broadly, the engine clad in rudimentary panelling, a cockpit offering the barest protection from flying stones and the elements, and a lateral fuel tank at the back with two or three spare tyres strapped on. As ever, rules and regulations shifted, with the superchargers pioneered by Hispano Suiza outlawed in 1912, and a 3.0-litre (183-cubic-inch) capacity limit imposed the same year. Voiturettes effectively became the new generation of Grand Prix cars, marking the end of the 'Heroic Age' of motor racing.

It was the Ernest Henry-designed 1912 Peugeot that set the trend for the next decade. Up to then, European makes had been dominant, even in US racing, but in 1920 home-grown cars triumphed at Indianapolis and took the fight to Europe too, winning at Le

Mans. The cars that were victorious were the Monroe driven by Gaston Chevrolet to win at Indianapolis, and the Duesenberg driven into third place by Miller at Indianapolis and into first place at Le Mans. The French circuit in the inter-war years enjoyed increasingly exalted status, and was the battleground for Ballot, Talbot and Sunbeam in the early 1920s.

VINTAGE PERIOD
The decade from 1922 to 1933 is known as the 'Vintage Period', and racing cars became more stylish with more attention being paid to aerodynamics. There was a 3.0-litre (183-cubic-inch) engine capacity limit and minimum fuel consumption of 6.37km per litre (18mpg). New standards were set by Fiat, who produced reliable engines that could rev at 5200rpm, which was high for those days. The first supercharged car to appear at a European Grand Prix was the Mercedes 28/95, which won the 1921 Targa Florio, and the forced-induction concept was taken up by Fiat. The next year, Italy staged the first Grand Prix outside France, and later in the 1920s most of the other European countries founded their own Grands Prix (new circuits were created at Nürburgring, Spa-Francorchamps, Reims and Monaco).

As the factory teams participated less and less during the Depression, the V12 Delage became the dominant Grand Prix machine, with private entrants running Alfa Romeos, Bugattis and Maseratis. The drivers who came to the fore at that time were Antonio Ascari, Enzo Ferrari, Sir Henry Segrave (also the world land- and water-speed record holder), Kenelm Lee-Guinness, Robert Benoist, Tazio Nuvolari, Achille Varzi, Rudolf Caracciola, Luigi Fagioli and Louis Chiron. In many events riding mechanics were still carried, which was always a hazardous occupation.

In 1923, a separate category was set up for sports cars. Le Mans was the first circuit to stage a major international sports car race, followed by the Mille Miglia in 1927, and the RAC Tourist

During the second half of the 1930s the German Mercedes-Benz and Auto Unions were dominant in Grand Prix racing. Pictured is a Mercedes-Benz W125 in a demonstration run at Silverstone in 1971. The cars were known as the Silver Arrows after their paint was removed to achieve lighter weight.

Trophy was revived in 1928. The cars that participated were basically Grand Prix cars from manufacturers Sunbeam, Alfa Romeo, Maserati, Bugatti and Mercedes. A new generation of drivers was appearing too, including Tim Birkin (one of the 'Bentley Boys'), René Dreyfus, Raymond Sommer, Phi-Phi Etancelin, Count Trossi, Whitney Straight and Antonio Brivio. There was interest from the USA at Le Mans, with the Bentleys vying with Chevrolet and Stutz.

The Bentley victory at Le Mans heralded a renaissance of the exciting racing that characterised the early 1930s. Key participants were Alfa Romeo's P2 and 1750 6C models,

Bugatti's Type 35, Maserati's Tipo 8CM, and the colossal Mercedes (Rudolf Caracciola won an early Monaco Grand Prix on an implausibly large Mercedes – they used to say 'on' then, rather than 'in', which was apposite as you sat on the car rather than within it, as became the case in the late 1950s). By the end of the 1930 season Bugatti had followed Alfa's example and gone over to twin

camshafts for the 2.3-litre (140-cubic-inch) Type 51.

A new set of rules for 1931 dictated that Grands Prix were to be of ten

BUGATTI TYPE 35

Make: *Bugatti*
Model: *Type 35A/B/C/T*
In production: *1924–1930*
Engine: *2.26-litre (138-cubic-inch) ohc straight eight, three valves per cylinder, Roots-type super-charger*
Power output: *150bhp*
Chassis: *ladder type*

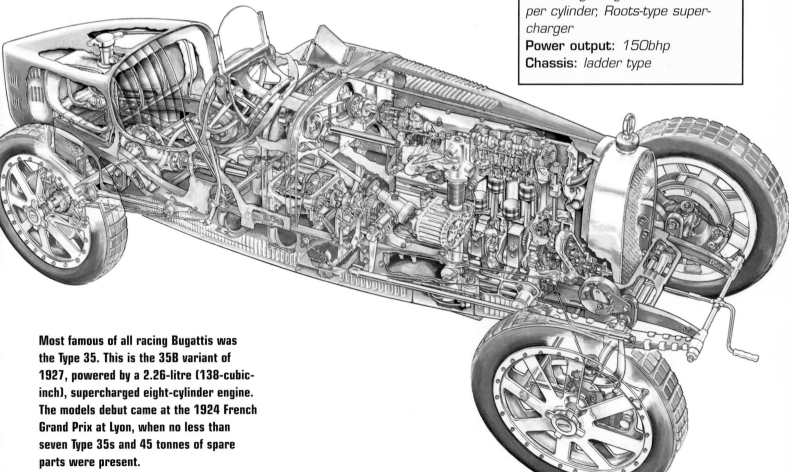

Most famous of all racing Bugattis was the Type 35. This is the 35B variant of 1927, powered by a 2.26-litre (138-cubic-inch), supercharged eight-cylinder engine. The models debut came at the 1924 French Grand Prix at Lyon, when no less than seven Type 35s and 45 tonnes of spare parts were present.

hours' duration, and riding mechanics were forbidden. In fact it was virtually a free formula – *formule libre* – and the top designers, Ettore Bugatti and Vittorio Jano at Alfa Romeo, introduced new machines: the 12-cylinder P3 Alfa Romeo and the Type 51 Bugatti, which had a 2.3-litre (140-cubic-inch) engine. Maserati was still the principal rival, and in 1931 it ran a 16-cylinder car. By this stage engine power had outstripped chassis technology. Alfa Romeo was dominant in Grands Prix until the German revival began in 1934 with the state-sponsored Mercedes and Auto Union teams. But in the second half of the decade only Nuvolari could make any impression on the Silver Arrows, and that was all the more remarkable because he was driving largely obsolete Alfas.

GERMAN ASCENDANCY

The Mercedes squad that contested the 750kg (1653lb) formula was initially led by Caracciola, with Manfred von Brauchitsch and Hans Geier. It would also include the talented Englishman Dick Seaman and, latterly, Maserati star Goffredo Zehender. At Auto Union, Hans Stuck, Achille Varzi, Ernst von Delius and Berndt Rosemeyer formed the nucleus of driving talent. Later on, Nuvolari was drafted in after Rosemeyer was killed making a land-speed record attempt. The German

marques were the largest cars to race since 1912, and the mighty Auto Union – designed by Dr Ferdinand Porsche until 1937 – was all the more spectacular because of its engine being located behind the driver, a format we have taken for granted since the 1960s in single-seater racing.

Halfway through the 1935 Grand Prix season, the four-car German teams were almost completely dominant, putting on ever greater displays of speed and power. Stuck left the lap record at the Berlin race track Avus at 260.46km/h (161.88mph), which gives an impression of the speed capability. At high-speed circuits such as this, the Mercedes and Auto Unions were clad in streamlined all-enveloping bodywork. The Alfas, Bugattis and Maseratis were virtual also-rans – apart, that is, from Nuvolari's legendary victory over the Silver Arrows at the daunting Nürburgring when he drove the Alfa as a man inspired.

Mid-season, Mercedes-Benz introduced the slimmer 4.7-litre (287-cubic-inch) 456bhp short-wheelbase model

The Alfa Romeo Alfetta Tipo 158 and 159 notched up a total of 25 Grand Prix wins. Nino Farina won the first Formula 1 World Championship in 1950 in a 1.5-litre (91.5-cubic-inch) supercharged straight-eight 158, and team-mate Juan-Manuel Fangio took the title in 1952.

better suited to the shorter, twisty circuits in vogue at the time; they took nine wins to Auto Union's four in 1935, Alfa just the one. The positions were reversed in 1936, with Auto Union taking seven wins, Mercedes-Benz just two and Alfa Romeo four. Thereafter Mercedes-Benz proved the dominant team, and the Italians failed to win any more Grands Prix pre-war, although Alfas were dominant in sports car events like the Mille Miglia. By 1937 independent drivers were non-existent in Grand Prix racing.

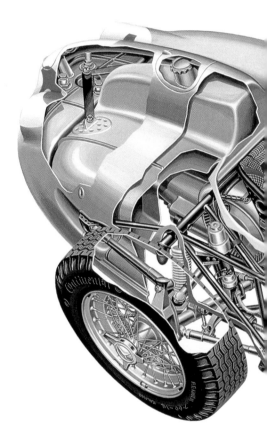

MERCEDES-BENZ W196
Make: *Mercedes-Benz*
Model: *W196*
In production: *1954-5*
Engine: *2.5-litre (152.5-cubic-inch) straight-eight Mercedes-Benz*
Power output: *280bhp*
Chassis: *multi-tubular spaceframe*

Over in the States, the Vanderbilt Cup was revived in 1936, and the European teams travelled over to compete. The following year the American Rex Mays in an Alfa became the only driver to bring a non-German car to finish in the first three places in any Grand Prix. Although the three most consistent contenders – Maserati, Alfa Romeo and Bugatti – were still on the scene and other marques such as ERA, Delahaye and Talbot made a showing, there was little they could do seriously to challenge the Silver Arrows. Rudolf Caracciola emerged the driver with the most wins of the era, while Nuvolari was the most talented.

Leaving the Germans to win as they pleased, Alfa Romeo and Maserati turned to the Voiturette class in 1939 with their new 1.5-litre (91.5-cubic-inch) supercharged Alfa 158 model and the 4 CLT Maserati. Many of these cars were hidden away during the Second World War, and emerged after 1945 to form the backbone of post-war motor sport.

THE WORLD CHAMPIONSHIP

The Grands Prix of the late 1940s were dominated at the top-class level by the Alfa Romeo 158s, driven largely by pre-war aces like Luigi Fagioli and Achille Varzi, and rising talents Giuseppe Farina and Juan Manuel Fangio. Formula 1 was for supercharged cars of 1.5 litres (91.5 cubic inches), or 4.5 litres (275 cubic inches) unsupercharged. There were no fuel or weight restrictions, and tyre technology was still in its infancy; the driver was putting some 400bhp through very narrow treads. The 4CLT/48 Maserati was always a force to be reckoned with, and the six-cylinder C-type ERA, although long in the tooth, was the reliable mainstay of the independent driver. Equally reliable, though not quite as fast, was the 4.5-litre Talbot, similarly developed from pre-war days. Britain's great hope was the BRM, engineered by Raymond Mays, powered by a 1.5-litre supercharged 16-cylinder engine and driven by Reg Parnell and Duncan Hamilton.

In 1949 the Alfas did not appear, and the new Ferrari, Talbot and Maserati led the field. By 1950, Enzo Ferrari had abandoned the supercharged route and his chief engineer, Aurelio Lampredi, designed a 4.5-litre engine to power the Ferrari Grand Prix cars – and their drivers: Luigi Villoresi, Froilan Gonzales and Alberto Ascari – in an attempt

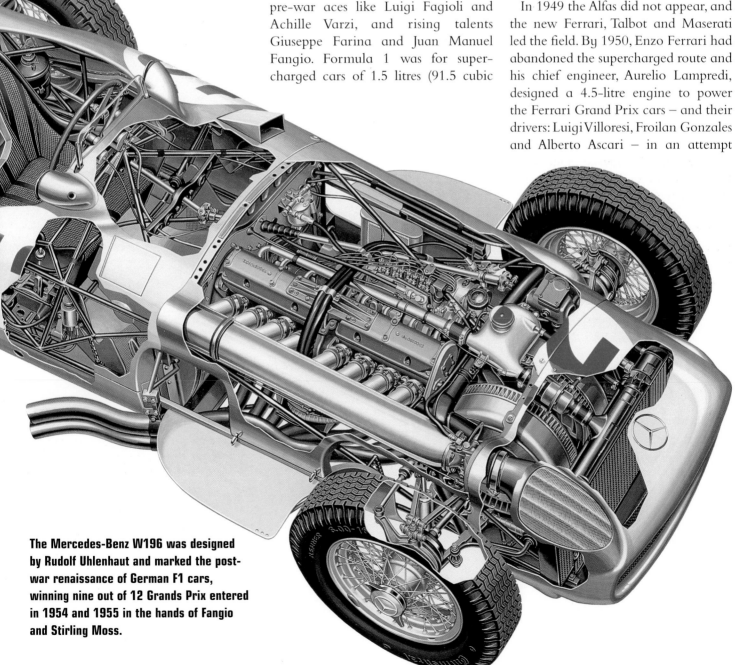

The Mercedes-Benz W196 was designed by Rudolf Uhlenhaut and marked the post-war renaissance of German F1 cars, winning nine out of 12 Grands Prix entered in 1954 and 1955 in the hands of Fangio and Stirling Moss.

finally to topple the Alfa Romeos. However, the Alfas returned for 1950 and 1951 and won everything in sight.

Five of these Alfa 158 Alfettas had been hidden away during the war, and because of a dearth of new cars complying with the new formula, the 158 was still very much state-of-the-art when the championship commenced. Designed by chief engineer Gioacchino Colombo, it remains the most successful Grand Prix car of all time, with 47 wins from 54 Grands Prix

entered. The Tipo 158 Alfa Romeos had made their debut at Livorno in 1938, where they finished first and second, run by Enzo Ferrari's team. The Alfetta was powered by a 1.5-litre straight-eight with a triple-choke up-draught Weber carburettor and a twin-stage supercharger. After the war, development continued under Alfa's chief engineer Dr Orazio Satta Puliga, with changes to the exhaust system and magneto. The gear lever was on the left, and, somewhat alarmingly, the trans-

mission passed between the driver's legs.

While Guiseppe Farina drove a 158 to win the inaugural world championship in 1950, Fangio's 1951 title was won in the Tipo 159. The bodywork of this car was identical to the 158, but the more powerful 420bhp motor had a prodigious thirst for methanol fuel, drinking 4.24 litres per kilometre (1.5 gallons per mile). The fuel tank was enlarged accordingly, and the extra weight it carried affected the handling adversely. Nevertheless it was still able

The Colombo-designed Maserati 250F was the mainstay of Formula 1 during the late 1950s, and was driven to the World title by Fangio in 1957, while 250Fs were also raced by Moss, Behra, Bonnier and Schell, among others.

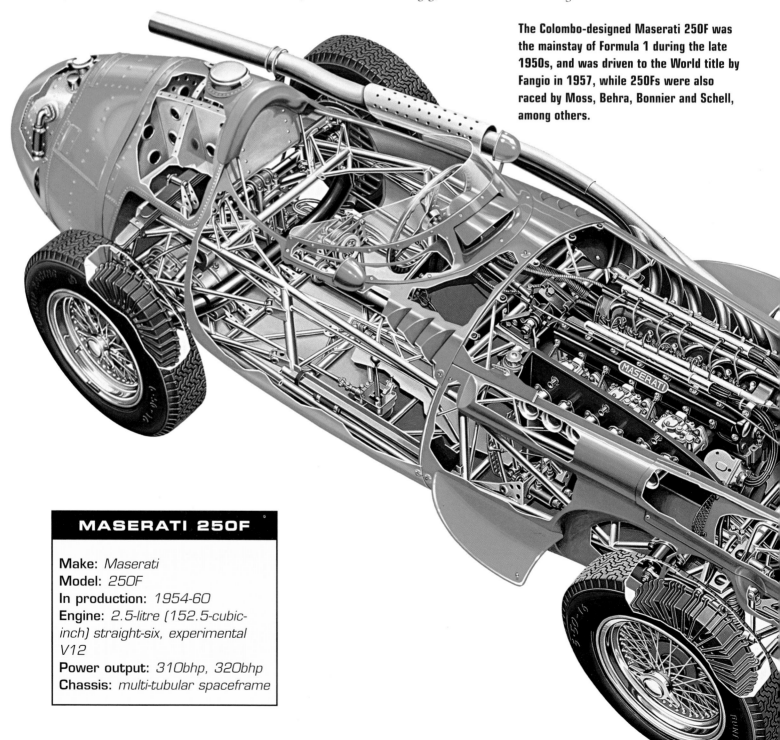

MASERATI 250F

Make: *Maserati*
Model: *250F*
In production: *1954-60*
Engine: *2.5-litre (152.5-cubic-inch) straight-six, experimental V12*
Power output: *310bhp, 320bhp*
Chassis: *multi-tubular spaceframe*

Dan Gurney in the Porsche F1 rounds Station hairpin at Monaco in 1961. It was powered by a 170bhp mid-mounted, 1498cc (91 cubic inches), four-cylinder engine, and in 1962 the American gave Porsche its first GP win at Rouen in the flat-8 engined car.

to attain speeds of 273.5km/h (170mph) at power circuits like Reims and Silverstone.

The Voiturette class, which came to be known as Formula 2, was for 2.0-litre (122-cubic-inch) cars, and was the province of the little Simca Gordinis. Formula 3 was for 500cc (30.5-cubic-inch) cars, which came to be the province of rear-engined Coopers running Norton or JAP motorcycle engines. It was in this arena that the great British driver Stirling Moss cut his teeth. (In 2000, the Brands Hatch circuit staged a commemorative meeting as a celebration of 50 years of Formula 3, which was appropriate since it was originally the home of the 500cc F3).

Inaugurated in 1950, the world championship calendar listed fewer than half the number of races that count for the title today. But those Grands Prix were interspersed with many non-championship races, often titled 'Grand Prix' and not lacking much in terms of atmosphere compared to a proper GP. In addition, the Grand Prix aces drove a wide variety of models, from F1 and F2 cars to sports racing cars and saloons. They even took part in rallies. Go to an historic event today, like the Coy's meeting at Silverstone or the Goodwood Revival in Britain, and watch the 1950s Grand Prix cars in action, and you will be astonished at just how quick they are. And they needed to be: Grand Prix race distances in the 1950s were a minimum 300km (186 miles), or three hours in length, rising in 1954 to a 500km (310 miles) minimum, again for three hours' duration. In 1958, the requirement fell back to 300km, or two hours' duration.

The team that came to prominence in the early 1950s was Ferrari, and in no time at all it had become the most evocative name in motor racing.

FERRARI

Formerly Alfa Romeo's team manager, Enzo Ferrari built his first car in 1940, although the first Ferrari was introduced in 1946. Enzo's priority was with

the engine rather than the chassis, but Ferraris were always on the pace, if not out in front. The first Ferrari to contest the world championship was the Colombo-designed V12-engined 125. Ferrari did not have to wait long for his moment of glory. Having seen off the Alfa Romeos, Alberto Ascari was champion in 1952 and 1953 driving the Lampredi-designed four-cylinder 500 (the models were identified by the displacement size of each cylinder in the early days). In 1956 Ferrari 'inherited' the distinctive side-tank Lancia D50s from the bankrupt company, and these effectively became Ferraris powered by the Jano-designed V8 engine, which Fangio drove to win the world championship in 1956. The most prolific Ferrari of the second half of the decade was the 246 Dino (named after Enzo's late son), and driven to the world title by Mike Hawthorn in 1958. Thereafter Ferrari successes declined until Enzo espoused rear-engined cars. The shark-nosed 156 was the vehicle in which American ace Phil Hill took the championship in 1961.

Not counting the whirlwind Grand Prix successes of the Mercedes-Benz of Fangio and Moss in 1955, plus the British Vanwall in 1957 and 1958, the 1950s was the decade of the Italian manufacturers. Although Alfa Romeo and Lancia withdrew, Ferrari's greatest rival was Maserati, and Fangio drove the Colombo-designed 250F to win the world championship in 1954 and 1957. Not so much a technological trend-setter as the yardstick of the 1950s, the Maserati 250F went on to become the mainstay of privateers during the latter half of the decade. The 250F saw action in the first race of the 2.5-litre (153-cubic-inch) Formula 1 in 1954, and in the last one in 1960. It was such a good car that as early as 1965 it was being raced in historic events.

The mysteries of 250F development and individual chassis are the subject of much scholarship and debate. For example, of the 28 cars built in five years, 17 appear to have been given new chassis numbers at some point. The Maserati 250F was principally the work of Colombo and Alberto Massimino. The 2493cc (152.1-cubic-inch) straight-six engine produced over 220bhp, and the suspension was transverse leaf rear and twin wishbone front, with tubular spaceframe chassis clad in aluminium panels. Maserati ran a works team in 1954, with Fangio accumulating enough points for the title. In 1955, Jean Behra was team leader, and Stirling Moss was his successor in 1956, followed by Fangio in 1957. In 1960 the trident logo of Bologna's finest was still going strong, and the 250F is now raced extensively in historic racing.

THE REAR-ENGINED REVOLUTION

Racing car designers have always striven for the optimum configuration of chassis, engine, and suspension according to the prevailing set of rules. Dr Porsche had shown that a mid-engined layout was possible with the Auto Unions of the late 1930s, and after the war Charles Cooper and his son John were the principal exponents of the little Formula 3 cars with their motorcycle engines behind the driver. Their front-engined Cooper Bristol Formula 2 cars were effective enough in the early 1950s, but in 1957 the

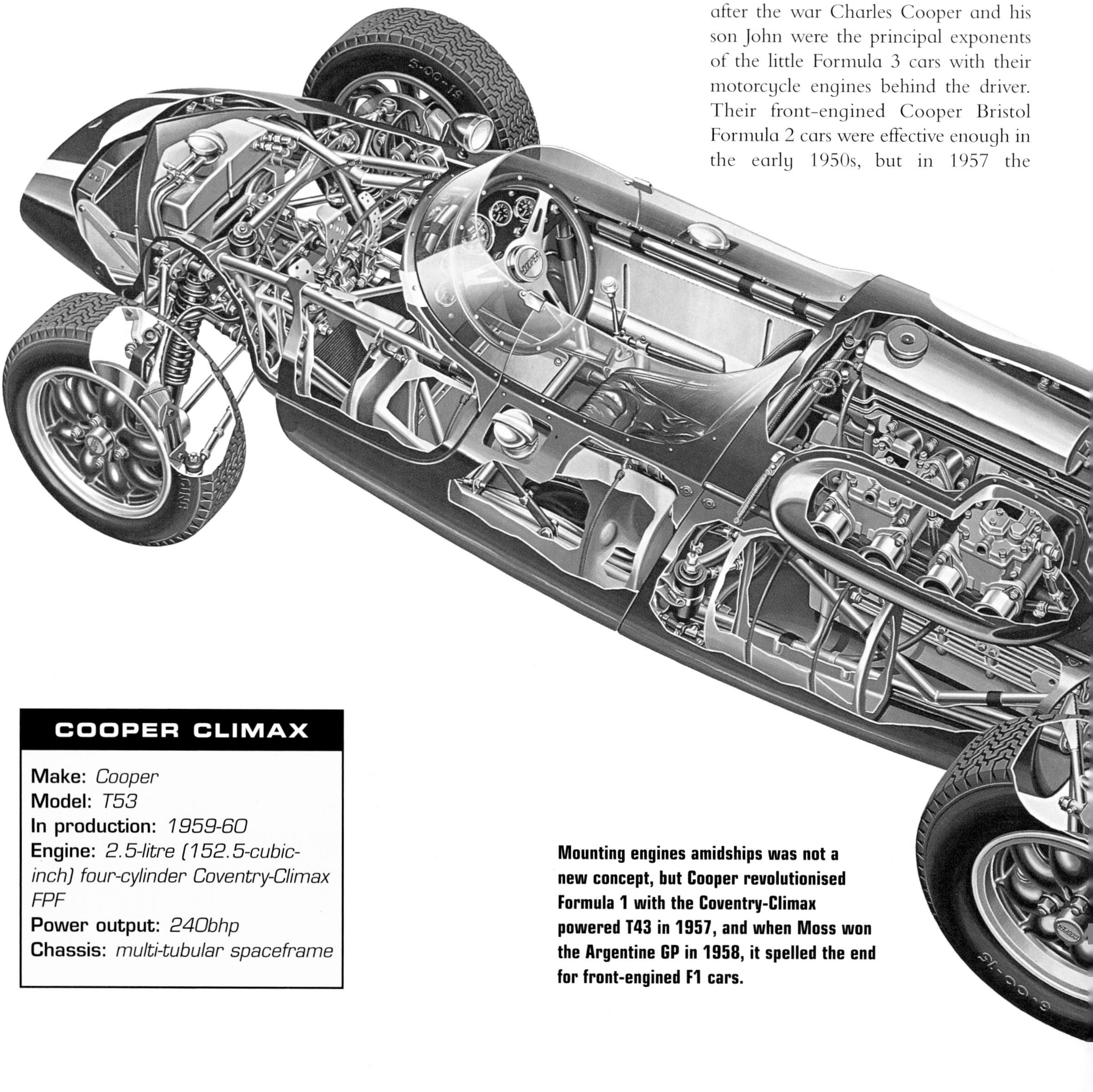

COOPER CLIMAX

Make: *Cooper*
Model: *T53*
In production: *1959-60*
Engine: *2.5-litre (152.5-cubic-inch) four-cylinder Coventry-Climax FPF*
Power output: *240bhp*
Chassis: *multi-tubular spaceframe*

Mounting engines amidships was not a new concept, but Cooper revolutionised Formula 1 with the Coventry-Climax powered T43 in 1957, and when Moss won the Argentine GP in 1958, it spelled the end for front-engined F1 cars.

Dan Gurney drives his Len Terry-designed, 3.0-litre (183-cubic-inch), Weslake-engined, V12 Eagle to victory at Spa in 1967, averaging 235km/h (146mph) on the daunting Belgian circuit. An engineering masterpiece, the Eagle was one of the most elegant F1 cars of the period.

Surbiton-based marque debuted in Formula 1, essentially with a Maddock-designed rear-engined F2 car.

When Stirling Moss won Cooper's first Grand Prix in 1958 in Buenos Aires, the writing was on the wall. Essentially, the simple tubular space-frame chassis with coil-spring and wishbone front suspension Cooper T41 was more nimble and could be cornered faster than the relatively large front-engined Ferraris, Maseratis, and Vanwalls of the day. Having only a 2.2-litre (134-cubic-inch) Coventry-

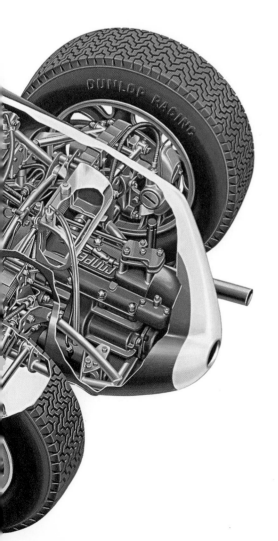

Climax FPF engine developing 176bhp, however, it was slower in a straight line than the Ferrari's Lancia-derived V8 that produced 285bhp. In 1958, Grand Prix regulations stipulated 130-octane Av-Gas aviation fuel, and the Climax engine ran well on this whereas the previously alcohol-fuelled Ferraris and Maseratis had problems adapting. The 1959 Cooper T53 had much cleaner lines, and later in the season was powered by the new 2495cc (152.2-cubic-inch) Wally Hassan-designed Coventry-Climax FPF twin-cam engine, developing 240bhp. Jack Brabham took the championship with it that year, and from then on it was clear that the days of the front-engined Grand Prix car were over.

Significantly, Cooper was the first of the European contingent to try his luck in the Indianapolis 500, and Jack Brabham drove a T53 powered by a 2.7-litre (165-cubic-inch) Coventry-Climax FPF engine (sponsored by Kleenex!) in the 1961 Indy 500. He did not exactly clean up, but he gave the Indianapolis fraternity pause for thought. The Cooper was giving away 1500cc (91.5 cubic inches) to the big front-engined roadsters, yet it was quicker through the turns – all left-handers on an oval – and Brabham finished a creditable ninth. Other drivers to be successful with Grand Prix Coopers during the late 1950s and early 1960s were Roy Salvadori, Tony Brooks, Bruce McLaren, Masten

Gregory, Tony Maggs and Maurice Trintignant.

While Cooper started the rear-engined trend, Lotus's Colin Chapman was quick to see the advantage. A brilliant engineer and innovator, Chapman had risen to prominence with his aerodynamic sports racing cars campaigned through the mid- to late 1950s, and his Mark 16 of 1959 was seen as a miniature version of the Vanwall that he and Frank Costin had largely designed. It was front-engined, however, and over-complex, so Chapman saw in the rear-engined car the potential to simplify the car's powertrain. Accordingly, he came out with the Mark 18 Lotus in 1960, and once again it was Stirling Moss who provided the marque's first world championship success, this time at Monaco in 1960. With its triangulated tubular spaceframe chassis, the 18 was versatile enough to be used in F1, F2 and Formula Junior, which was the equivalent of F3 in the early 1960s, and several up-and-coming drivers rose to prominence in FJ 18s, including Jim Clark, Trevor Taylor, Peter Ashdown and Peter Arundell.

By 1962 BRM was building competitive cars, and Graham Hill took the world title that year in the Tony Rudd-designed P57 V8. Rudd later went to work at Team Lotus, but it was Chapman and his designer Len Terry who came up with the next revolution in racing car design. This was the Lotus

25, which had an aluminium monocoque unitary chassis, known as a 'tub' rather than a tubular spaceframe, which was normal practice at this point. Where Lotus led, it seemed, the rest followed. But the key weapon in Chapman's arsenal was the genius of his lead driver, Jim Clark.

The Lotus 25 monocoque consisted of twin pontoons either side of an undertray, with front and rear bulkheads, while a stressed panel incorporated the instrument panel. Front suspension was by upper cantilever rocking arms, lower wishbones, and inboard coil-springs and dampers; rear suspension was by upper links, twin radius rods, reversed lower wishbones, and outboard coil-springs and dampers. The 25 was powered by the Coventry-Climax FMW V8 engine, and along with its successor, the Lotus 33, and the V8 BRM P57, it was the most successful car of the 1500cc (91.5 cubic inches) Formula 1 period, giving Jim Clark the championship in 1963. For much of 1964 Clark and Arundell used the 25B with revised rear suspension, and after Lotus began using its successor, the 33, in 1965, privateers continued to race the 25. The 33 was raced by the Lotus works team into 1967, when it was superseded by the 49.

DRIVERS BECOME CONSTRUCTORS

The 1960s witnessed the rise of the small team and the driver-turned-constructor, exemplified by Jack Brabham, Bruce McLaren, Dan Gurney (Eagle) and John Surtees. BRM remained in contention with its P261, and Ferrari remained the leading Italian standard

bearer. Maserati returned briefly mid-decade as the purveyor of V8 engines for the Cooper T81 and T86, while Alfa Romeo concentrated on touring cars and sports prototypes.

There were two major changes of engine capacity in Formula 1 during the 1960s: the 1.5-litre (91.5-cubic-inch) limit took effect from 1961, and from 1966 all the way to 1987 the formula was for 3.0 litres (183 cubic inches) normally aspirated or 1.5 litres with forced induction (supercharged or turbocharged). When the 3.0-litre Formula came in, the constructor best placed to take advantage of it was Jack Brabham, who had acquired a stock of 3.0-litre Repco engines from his native Australia. Jack was champ in 1966, and his New Zealander team-mate Denny Hulme took the title the following year in the Ron Tauranac-designed BT19 and BT20.

In 1967 the Ford Motor Company financed the production of the 3.0-litre Cosworth-Ford DFV V8 engine. It was initially harnessed to the Lotus 49 – the first F1 car in which the engine was treated as an integral part of the chassis – and another new era dawned. This engine was the most successful F1 unit of all time, powering 157 cars to Grand Prix victories between 1967 and 1983. Commercial pump fuel with a maximum 100-octane rating had to be used, no oil could be added during a pit stop, and there was a minimum weight limit of 450kg (992lb).

Team Lotus introduced the first F1 monocoque car in 1962, the type 25. Jimmy Clark took the World Championship in 1963 and in 1965 with the derivative Lotus 33. Chassis numbers for the two models ran consecutively, and GP victories totalled 19 from 76 starts.

LOTUS CLIMAX

Make: *Lotus*
Model: *25/33*
In production: *1962-67*
Engine: *1.5-litre (91.5-cubic-inch) Coventry-Climax V8 BRM V8*
Power output: *205bhp*
Chassis: *aluminium monocoque*

Graham Hill's Lotus 49 features the pedal/cable-operated, strut-mounted, rear aerofoil, which could be feathered on the straights. Catastrophic failures to Rindt's and Hill's cars at Barcelona in 1968 caused these high wings to be banned.

WINGS AND SAFETY CONCERNS

Engineers and designers began to experiment with aeronautical aerodynamics, and the wing cars began to appear in 1967. The principle was the reverse of an aeroplane wing, which is shaped to provide lift. Upside down, a wing produces the reverse effect, and the airstream exerts downforce on the vehicle it is mounted on. Aerofoil wings started to sprout from the cars' rear suspension uprights and on top of the engines in the quest for greater downforce in the corners. This was clearly at the expense of outright speed when travelling down the straight, but on balance the wing made for faster lap times. But there is no gain without pain, and a series of high-speed accidents – notably to the Lotus 49s of

Jackie Oliver, Graham Hill and Jochen Rindt – led to a calming down of the lofty aerofoils and an adoption of more realistic spoilers located above the gearbox and fins either side of the nosecone.

And it was not just wings that were the focus of safety measures in the late 1960s. During the previous decade there had been little progress in creating safer cars, although tyre technology had certainly improved. The first trend towards tightening up the safety aspect for the drivers themselves was the wearing of crash helmets, as opposed to the tight-fitting linen headgear universally used until around 1950. By the mid-1960s, drivers were beginning to take seatbelts seriously too, but they still were not compulsory. Prior to that, accidents involving drivers being flung out of their cars happened regularly, and the attrition rate was lamentably high.

The volatility of the fuels used in racing meant fires were more likely in crashes, so on-board fire extinguishers were introduced in the late 1960s, and trackside marshals were instructed in how to combat fires. By the early 1970s, racing driver Herbert Linge had a fleet of specially equipped 2.2-litre (134-cubic-inch) Porsche 914/6s positioned all round the Nürburgring to rush to the scene of a fire and deal with it. An extension of this facility is the course car, an American concept, which is despatched from the pits to lead the pack round in the event of a crisis on the track, until such time as

The most successful F1 car of the early 1970s was the Lotus 72, driven here in 1973 at Brands Hatch by reigning World Champion Emerson Fittipaldi. He and team-mate Ronnie Peterson won the Constructors' title for Team Lotus in 1973.

the obstacle is cleared and racing can resume. By the end of the 1960s, flame-retardant overalls, underwear, bala-clavas, gloves and boots were coming in, both for drivers and mechanics. Full-face helmets replaced the open-face variety in single-seaters, so the driver began to look like a sort of knight in armour. By the mid-1980s, the driver had a breather tube going into his helmet to supply oxygen for a few vital seconds in the event of his becoming trapped in a blazing wreck.

As the new generation of 3.0-litre (183-cubic-inch) cars came in for 1966, aircraft-type rubber-bag fuel tanks started to be incorporated, and as the monocoque chassis evolved from an aluminium construction to a carbon-fibre composite structure it became stronger and stronger. Two decades later it had become a reality. Max Mosley, president of the sport's governing body, the Federation International Auto-mobile (FIA), stated in the mid-1990s that his aim was to make it 'extremely difficult to hurt yourself in a Formula 1 car'. In 1975, an 80km/h (50mph) crash in an F1 car could wreck it, whereas in 1995 the tub could withstand a 240km/h (150mph) impact. Gradually all these changes were enshrined in FIA law, and scrutineers who pore over the cars before and after races got tougher.

The move towards serious safety pre-cautions was started by Jackie Stewart in 1967 and quickly taken up by the Grand Prix Drivers' Association, led by Swedish driver Jo Bonnier. They were seen as crusaders, and attacked as such by purists who disliked the idea of circuits being lined with Armco metal barriers. But too many drivers had died or been injured through a lack of ele-mentary protection. In the wake of his frightening accident at Spa-Francorchamps, where he had lain in a ditch unable to extract himself from his overturned BRM, Jackie campaigned for Armco barriers to line the circuits.

After Armco lined the vast majority of circuits, those with decent run-off areas needed something to prevent contact with the steel barrier. So in the mid-1970s a glut of netted catch fencing popped up outside every corner worth the name. When drivers got injured by the fence posts that sup-ported the netting, the circuit owners introduced sand and gravel traps to help decelerate errant cars.

WIDER MARGINS

While public road circuits dwindled (Monaco's city streets being a lucrative exception), a succession of purpose-built circuits like the new Nürburgring were constructed so that wider margins and run-off areas alongside the track could be incorporated. In the old days, road circuits featured all the typical trackside obstacles: kerbs, lamp stan-dards and letter-boxes, protected only by straw bales (go to an Isle of Man TT race and see how racing used to be set).

The transformation was a slow process anywhere outside the regularly used commercial tracks. As late as the Player's Grand Prix at Dublin's Phoenix Park in 1974, the spectators were restrained by nothing more than a rope, with the additional hazard of the odd stray dog and child. All the

familiar hazards of the 1950s remained, from park benches and lamp-posts to high kerbs, and at the end of the two-day meeting hardly a car was left undamaged. And if you think that is bad, picture the 1971 Mexican Grand Prix, where spectators were actually lying on the track with their cameras, trying to get dramatic pictures of the cars.

Spectators have always been vulnerable. The worst accident in motor racing history was the well-documented 1955 Le Mans tragedy, when over 80 spectators died in the stand opposite

Jackie Stewart pictured in 1973, his final season in F1, in the Tyrrell 006, with which he won the World Drivers' Championship. Stewart won five GPs that year in the Derek Gardner-designed Tyrrell, while team-mate François Cevert was 2nd five times.

the pits. All that separated them from Levegh's doomed Mercedes was an earth bank. Things improved only marginally in the wake of that disaster. Similarly, the response to the Marquis de Portago's crash on the 1957 Mille Miglia – as a result of which he, co-driver Ed Nelson and ten spectators were left dead – was to ban the race. When Farina accidentally slew eleven spectators in Argentina, nothing was done either, but in the 1970s, safety measures to protect drivers went hand in hand with spectator protection.

Today, there are excessively high mesh fences, Indy-style, separating the stands and certain enclosures from the action. But how high is high enough? At Imola in 1994, a wheel from the J.J. Lehto/Pedro Lamy incident flew into the stand, injuring five. Even Armco is not necessarily enough. Indeed,

improperly installed it has been responsible for a number of driver fatalities (Rindt and Cevert), and sometimes cars have simply gone over the top of it, like Rolf Stommelen at Montjuich in 1975, or Elio de Angelis, terminally, at Paul Ricard.

BIG-TIME SPONSORS

The introduction of the Lotus 49 in 1967 coincided with the patronage of big-name, big-time sponsors. In Lotus's case it was the tobacco giant John Player & Son, and from 1968 all Team Lotus cars appeared in the red, white and gold of the Gold Leaf cigarette brand. In the United States, of course, this was nothing new – cars had been named after their sponsors since the 1950s – but in Europe in the 1950s and most of the 1960s, racing cars were painted in their country's national

Several F1 teams flourished in the late 1960s as successful drivers became constructors. One was McLaren, featured here with Denny Hulme driving the M23 at Barcelona's picturesque Montjuich Park in 1973, ahead of Cevert's Tyrrell.

racing colour. Thus you had British racing green, Italian corso rosso, French blue, Belgian yellow, German silver or white, and American white with blue stripes. In 1968, the red, white and gold Lotuses were followed by white-and-brown-striped BRMs sponsored by Yardley cosmetics. The sponsors had arrived, bringing with them the open cheque books which throughout the 1970s and 1980s brought about major technological changes, driver retainers and transfer fees, which had never previously been seen in motor sport. Egos blossomed – and were just as quickly dashed. The pressures these changes wrought took racing into another league. Formula 1 began to be packaged as an exalted travelling circus.

In the early part of the 1970s, though, the climate in F1 was still reasonably relaxed. The major players carried on much as they had during the 1960s – with no contractual pressure, for instance, to limit themselves to just the one formula – but they could now rely on being able to afford engine rebuilds and tyres as

required, while hiring the best drivers. All that was required of them in return was to turn their cars into mobile advertising hoardings. Everyone and everything connected to the teams now displayed the sponsors' logos as prominently as possible. Drivers gave press conferences and referred to the cars not simply as Lotuses or McLarens, but as John Player Specials or Marlboro-McLarens. As the decade progressed, sponsorship mushroomed. More funds meant bigger and better facilities, the teams and the governing bodies became wealthier, and the cars evolved more quickly. Trackside facilities improved accordingly, which in the case of the bleaker 'airfield' circuits was no bad thing.

JOHN PLAYER SPECIALS

In 1972, Team Lotus went all the way with their tobacco giant, and the cars themselves were known as John Player Specials. The PR office (in which I worked) expended a great deal of effort trying to persuade hardened journalists that they were not Lotus 72s any more (usually to no avail). In Formula 2, the Lotus 74 was called the Texaco Star, in deference to its sponsor, and the French fuel company Elf had its name writ large on the Tyrrells. Motul Oil sponsored BRM when Marlboro left, Universal Oil Products sponsored the Shadow F1 and the

thundering Group 7 CanAm cars, while Brooke Bond, Oxo and Fina backed Team Surtees. The oil and tyre companies' logos have remained a constant presence too, and it was Shell that kept organisations like Team Lotus going during the 1950s and 1960s.

But it was the tobacco companies that profited most. The industry was beginning to feel the first vibes of the anti-smoking lobby, and saw in the untapped motor racing world a visible means of offsetting taxes as well as gaining a promotional foothold on the marketing front. Thus Marlboro took over at BRM where Yardley left off in 1973, and other teams subsequently attracted other brands, including Gitanes, Rothmans, Embassy, Camel and Mild Seven. Marlboro began its long-running association with McLaren in 1974; with Marlboro backing, the team won the world championship seven times between 1974 and 1991. Senna's 1993 victory in Adelaide brought the team's total GP tally to 104, making it the most successful in the history of the championship. Marlboro also sponsors some of the top drivers, and over the years other teams have received its support: Ferrari, Alfa Romeo, Williams, Iso and Merzario, for example. Both Player's and Marlboro have sponsored F3 championships too, which bring on new talent, but when racing in Germany and in Britain the teams are obliged to mask the names of their tobacco-purveying sponsors because of government restrictions on tobacco advertising.

Diversity among sponsor names naturally increased. Since the mid-1970s we have seen Olympus and Canon cameras, ICI chemicals, Beta tools, Olivetti office hardware, LEC fridges, Candy washing machines, Saudia airlines, Parmalat dairy products, Martini, Warsteiner beer, Barclays International, Pagnossin ceramics, Denim after-shave, First National City Bank and Benetton clothes, to name just a few – myriad companies vying with one another for the available space on bodywork, overalls and helmets.

Formula 1 is big business. Budgets are a thorny subject, not to say a closely guarded secret in many cases. Sums have escalated quite dramatically. Player's put around a million pounds into the sport in 1973; five million might have got a team on to the middle of the grid in the mid-1980s; today, that sum has easily doubled. The top teams now need £25 to £30 million to budget for a whole Grand Prix season, while the second-rank teams like Minardi and Arrows manage to get by with £10 million. In 1995, Michael Schumacher was signed to Ferrari for the 1996 season for the princely sum of £12 million. Despite his accident in 1999, some sources suggest you could double that figure today.

LOTUS ET AL
Back in the early 1970s, the trend-setting Lotus 49, the first big-name-sponsored car, was replaced by the wedge-shaped Lotus 72, or John Player Special, which had been designed by

Designed by Michel Tétu, the Renault RS10 was powered by Renault's 1.5-litre V6 engine with twin KKK turbochargers. Jean-Pierre Jabouille's win and Rene Arnoux's 2nd place at Dijon in 1979 made the RS10 the first successful turbocharged F1 car.

Maurice Phillipe. Lotus experimented with gas-turbine power in the type 56 and 56B, which ran in F1 and at Indianapolis in 1968. They also tried four-wheel-drive with the type 63, but neither concept endured. Meanwhile, Graham Hill had revived the team's morale in the wake of Jim Clark's death by taking the 1968 championship in the 49B. Then there was a degree of overlap with the incoming type 72 as the fearless Austrian Jochen Rindt used both models to win the title in 1970.

What was at issue here was straight-line speed. Rindt believed he could get a quicker lap time with the Lotus 72's rear wing removed, but this rendered the car difficult to control in a corner as there was no downforce. Team-mate John Miles was sufficiently wary of the car's instability to refuse to drive it without the rear wing, but Rindt persevered. He remains the only driver to win the world crown posthumously, having accumulated sufficient points before he perished in practice for the Italian Grand Prix at Monza (the cause of his accident was attributed to a broken brake shaft).

While the Lotus 72 went on to take Brazilian, Emerson Fittipaldi to the world title in 1972 and secured the constructors' prize for Lotus in 1973

with Fittipaldi and Ronnie Peterson driving, the Tyrrell marque was on the rise. Jackie Stewart drove the Derek Gardner-designed Tyrrell 001 to victory in the world championship in 1971 and the 003 to the drivers' title in 1973. One of motor racing's oddballs was the Tyrrell P34 six-wheeler F1 car, raced in 1976 and 1977, the theory being that the four small front wheels presented less wind resistance than the normal-sized pair.

After Tyrrell's blaze of glory it was the Marlboro-McLaren team's turn to shine, and Fittipaldi was champion again in 1974. After setting up his own team in a fruitless venture with brother Wilson, Fittipaldi found further success in the USA and was Indycar champion in 1989. In 1976, James Hunt reigned supreme in the Gordon Coppuck-designed McLaren M23, although his chief rival that year, 1975 champion Niki Lauda, had suffered dreadful burns when his Ferrari crashed at the Nürburgring.

Incredibly, Lauda bounced back to take the 1977 title in the Mauro Forghieri-designed Ferrari 312T. Ferrari was now under the wing of corporate giant Fiat, which ensured secure patronage, if not consistent success. Ferrari's last drivers' world title

for twenty years was notched up by Jody Scheckter in 1979, when he was partnered by the mercurial Gilles Villeneuve in the Scuderia's 312T4s. René Arnoux and Patrick Tambay were the works Ferrari drivers in 1983 when Ferrari beat Renault by ten points to take the constructors' trophy, even though both Alain Prost and Nelson Piquet scored more than the Ferrari duo in the drivers' standings that year. For Ferrari, the mid-1980s were characterised by the elegant 126C V6 turbocharged model designed by Harvey Postlethwaite, with Michele Alboreto and Gerhard Berger in the squad, but the major part of the decade belonged to McLaren, with, successively, Lauda, Prost and Ayrton Senna rising to the top.

THE HIGH-TECH ERA

Back in 1977, when Renault appeared with the turbocharged RS01, Formula 1 was pitched into the modern high-pressure zone. It was the era of extremely high-tech racing cars, and eventually it would be the car manufacturers who were attracted to the TV exposure provided by big-time motor sport. The firm that got the most out of sponsorship was Ford, who bankrolled the Cosworth-Ford DFV, the most widely used engine of the period. It has scarcely been out of the picture in Formula 1 since then (nominally as the producer of engines, although in 2000 it bounced back into Formula 1 as the patron of the Jaguar team).

Technological innovations were frequent during the 1980s, and development went ahead in leaps and bounds. Formula 1 cars were changed beyond recognition, although some developments were outlawed by the sport's governing body as being too expensive or just too effective for their own good. An example of this was the ground-effect Lotus 88 twin-chassis Formula 1 car that was introduced in 1977. This was meant to address severe driver discomfort brought about by the 'ground-effect' generation of cars which worked on the principle that the underside of the car was like an

inverted wing, and when in motion the air was drawn through a system of venturi and side-skirts, and the car was sucked to the track surface. By having a chassis within a chassis, the Lotus 88 provided a more comfortable cockpit while retaining the benefits of ground effect. The authorities refused to let it race, however, and an opportunity for genuine conceptual design was lost.

Team principal Colin Chapman died soon afterwards, but Lotus development engineer Peter Wright pursued the 'active-ride' suspension system on computerised aeronautical principles. 'Active ride' meant that the car responded to changes in the surfaces it was passing over through electronic sensors, and these sensors in turn modulated the suspension accordingly.

Up to 1977, the greatest exponent of the turbocharger had been Porsche, whose 917 Spider was most effective in the CanAm series in the hands of Mark Donohue. Renault ushered it into Formula 1, but other teams were slow to follow suit: matching chassis capability with the turbo's sudden, shattering power delivery took time. It was a fantastically exciting epoch, but by 1986 turbo technology was so phenomenally expensive that only the wealthiest teams could hope to compete. In 1988, FISA moved to stem the rising financial tide by announcing

Ayrton Senna watches a TV monitor to check his rivals' progress as his Lotus-Honda 99T V6 turbo is set up during practice. The 99T had an aluminium honeycomb, carbon-fibre/composite, monocoque chassis and computerised active suspension.

a ban on turbo engines.

One factor that helped to produce more power was the specialised fuel developed by the petrol companies, notably Shell, which produced at least another 100bhp. As fuel restrictions were placed on turbo cars, this factor became more important than ever.

PITS EVOLUTION

The pits have always been a key feature of motor racing and have developed along with the circuits and the machines that use them. The original concept of the pits was just that: a convenient place to work on the cars. They were organised in one place – by the start and finish line – for convenience of lap scoring and because it was near the fuel stocks. It quickly became necessary to have storage for spares and fuel, and the pits became a sort of base for the entrant and his or her car. Here they could find a bit of shelter, keep lap charts and carry out timing. There also needed to be a base from which to pass on signals to the drivers about their performance, their position as it stood relative to their nearest rival, and the duration of the race.

In the 1920s, pits were quite rudimentary, but gradually a long, low line of individual rough-and-ready sheds, roofed but open to the elements, developed. Each car was allocated its own pit. By the 1930s, the motor trade saw the pits as a convenient way of advertising their products, and another dimension was added. Flags and banners sprouted forth, and structures became more robust, built in brick or concrete with corrugated-iron roofs. This was how most of them stayed until well into the 1960s. There was a pit counter for sitting on, keeping out of the way of the traffic, or standing on to get a better view of the cars. When a car drove up to its pit, the mechanics jumped over the pit counter to administer whatever was needed. The pits were still very much a part of the circuit, and cars racing by came very close. At purpose-built circuits, a pit lane was defined, but not until the implementation of wholesale safety revisions in the late 1960s and early 1970s did the pit lane become physically separated from the track.

Changes in the rules occasioned by safety considerations meant that pits complexes developed, especially at the international circuits. As pits facilities grew and teams' requirements increased, the buildings themselves got wider and taller. At Silverstone and Snetterton, members of the public could watch the race from atop the pits, while savouring the delights and dramas of pit and paddock activity. The pit counters were the provinces of wives and girlfriends, often seen clutching lap tables and stopwatches. During the 1960s this band of women developed into a very powerful and influential coterie, along with a select band of dedicated journalists and photographers. In the late 1960s they were joined by a new wave of sponsors and PR advisers, with fleets of promotions girls passing through during lulls in the proceedings.

Safety issues also held sway in the 1960s when it came to designing a pits complex. So that cars refuelling or changing tyres were not exposed to race traffic, the pits themselves were separated from the track by a barrier, and with the advent of the separate pit lane it was not long before the pit counter moved out to the barrier separating pit lane from circuit. There still needed to be a vantage point from which to communicate with the drivers, in spite of the car-to-pits intercom, so the pit wall became a concrete bastion, with teams setting up their timekeeping and telemetry equipment behind its parapets. This, too, sprouted shelters against sun and rain.

Nowadays, all circuits hosting world championship events must conform to a standard which gives most teams a pristine garage for each car where the original pit counter used to be. During a race the toolboxes, refuelling rig, fresh tyres and all the computer hardware are to be found here. Above the pits garages at places like the Nürburgring, Monza or Silverstone are lofty corporate entertainment suites, topped by the press office and administration

departments. The days when the ordinary enthusiast doing the rounds of the paddock, or anyone without a serious purpose, could gain access are long gone.

MCLAREN
The most successful car of the late 1980s was the McLaren MP4/4. What was most impressive about the MP4/4 was that it had no elements in particular that could be identified as the single reason for such a huge advantage. While the FW14B would have the benefit of active suspension, traction control and countless other gizmos, the McLaren was simply the ultimate proof that getting the overall package right is ultimately what counts in Formula 1. McLaren also had the unparalleled

Back in action after premature retirement, Niki Lauda's McLaren-Cosworth MP4B leads Alboreto's Tyrrell-Cosworth, De Cesaris' Alfa Romeo V12 and Piquet's Brabham-Cosworth. In 1982, by this time the Ferraris and Renaults were running V6 turbos, by 1984 turbos were almost universal.

advantage of having Senna and Prost as its drivers, but on the other hand it had to cope with the teething problems inherent in a new engine partnership, as well as rule changes.

The year 1988 was the final one in a transition period that was meant to facilitate the switch from the forced-induction turbocharged era to that of normally aspirated engines. The equivalency formula was calculated to cripple the turbos and give the atmospheric cars an advantage in 1988, but McLaren and Honda proved that racing teams can be more canny than the regulators. They won all but one of the 16 races counting towards the world championship, and this success could not just be attributed to the Honda engine because Team Lotus was using the same one, and even with triple world champion Nelson Piquet at the wheel they won nothing at all. Nor could that level of domination be explained by suggesting that the car was reasonably good and that the opposition did a bad job.

The MP4/4 was designed by Steve Nichols, along with chassis designer Matthew Jeffreys, transmission specialist Dave North, aerodynamicist Bob Bell and suspension technician Dave Nielson. The powerplant was Honda's 1.5-litre (91.5-cubic-inch) V6 turbo engine. It had to be as fuel-efficient as possible because the rules required that turbo cars complete each 322km (200-mile) race on just 150 litres (33 gallons) of fuel. Because the Honda engine was much lower than McLaren's previous turbo, the TAG Porsche unit, the MP4/4 could accommodate a radical new gearbox. The low-line powertrain meant that the McLaren was lower than virtually anything that had been seen in Formula 1. This minimised drag, and therefore fuel consumption. Also, the chassis diffuser could be swept up to generate maximum downforce. Driving position was a problem – drivers were never comfortable lying back almost horizontally – but it was fundamentally reliable, vice-free, and good at every circuit. Ayrton Senna liked its slight understeering tendency, and his technique was to turn in, go hard on the throttle, and the car would just go round.

The domination achieved by McLaren that year was less than popular with all but committed Senna and Prost fans, but it was nevertheless a match that perhaps rivalled the Moss–Fangio duels of the 1950s: a race between the two best drivers in the world in cars of equal ability.

A BRAKE ON TECHNOLOGY

The 1989 season saw the end of turbos and the return of naturally aspirated 3.5-litre (214-cubic-inch) engines in Formula 1, designed to re-establish parity of performance between teams. This did not happen. Anyone without a

Ayrton Senna rounds Spa's La Source hairpin en route to 2nd place in the 1986 Belgian GP in the Lotus-Renault 98T. It had a carbon/Kevlar monocoque with pull-rod suspension front and rear, plus a smaller 195-litre (51-gallon) FIA spec fuel tank.

contract with a major engine supplier like Honda, Renault or Ferrari was destined to be an also-ran. Another form of restriction was that of physical proportions. Tubs were being designed with the smaller, lighter driver in mind, so that relatively big guys like Gerhard Berger became the exception.

Notwithstanding the thinking behind the curbing of technological progress, it was widely held that the changes were regressive and took Formula 1 backwards, placing it alongside Indycar. Had regulations been the same as in the early 1980s with the ground-effect cars, it is feasible that lap times would have been 20 seconds quicker than they were in the mid-1990s. Comparing F1 to Champ cars (Indycars) is difficult, because in a Grand Prix there may be 10 different teams participating with 10 different cars, whereas in Champ cars there are probably just two or three different chassis running in a race. Champ car regulations are much more controlled, too, with possibly 50 times more regulations than F1. There is always room for interpretation of the rules in F1.

More sweeping changes to the cars

came in 1994. Starting with the narrowing of tyre widths, a programme of simplification was instituted: reactive suspension and anti-lock brakes were outlawed and the fly-by-wire electronic throttle was banned, as was traction control. The technical people mourned; after all, some road cars were now better equipped than Grand Prix machines. They believed F1 should be the pinnacle of automotive technology and felt manacled by the FIA's decrees. But technicians have always found a way of circumventing the rules. For example, the top teams had the ability to produce complex software for engine management systems that could duplicate the effect of traction control. This would be undetectable, and thus impossible to police.

The most extraordinary piece of restrictive legislation was the introduction of the plank, the skid-block intended to foul airflow underneath the cars and thus slow them down. It is absolutely incongruous that the most exalted and self-regarding technological sport in the world should resort to placing a wooden plank on the bottom of its cars. However, the sport of motor racing is always going to be bigger than the legislators, and the next generation will have doubtless leapfrogged these particular restrictions.

WILLIAMS

When Nigel Mansell declared at a press conference after devastating the rest of the field in the 1992 South African Grand Prix that he did not believe the Williams FW14B provided any great advantage, Ayrton Senna disagreed. Well, he would, wouldn't he? In fact, the Williams FW14B was a remarkably well-behaved car, displaying no body roll or pitch, capable of being simply pointed into a given corner and retaining an even attitude all the way through it. This imperturbable stance was the result of the first fully developed active suspension system, and Williams was ahead of all but Ferrari by at least a season or more. The active system, developed by Williams' technicians, provided the FW14B's designer Adrian Newey with the scope to capitalise on aerodynamics as never before.

To get the best out of a car in a corner, the ride height needs to provide the most downforce, and on the straight the car should present the least drag; active suspension enabled Williams to achieve the optimum result. Mansell went on to dominate the first five Grands Prix, and after just six more races he took the world title with another victory at the Hungaroring. That this was the earliest stage in the season that the drivers' championship had ever been wrapped up spoke volumes for the FW14B. Mansell ended the season with 14 pole positions, eight fastest laps and nine wins; Williams' number two driver Riccardo Patrese took a single pole, three fastest laps and one win from the 16 rounds.

Nigel Mansell is on record as saying that the FW14B is the best car he ever drove. Part of its brilliance lay in the fact that its only limiting factor was the driver. It would do anything that was required of it, and he was able to utilise to the full the extra downforce the active suspension gave. Equally remarkably, given that a new car is always likely to be prone to teething troubles due to a lack of testing, it not only survived its first race, but won it easily. Newey, creator of Mika Hakkinen's championship-winning McLarens, regards the Williams FW14B as one of his best cars because it was not only very interesting from an engineering point of view, but so dominant in 1992.

SCHUMACHER AND FERRARI

The jubilant arrival of Michael Schumacher on the top of the F1 podium was like a breath of fresh air after the dour rivalry between the top drivers like Senna, Prost and Mansell. Schumacher's beaming face was worth a lot then, even if his tactics in subsequent races against Damon Hill and Jacques Villeneuve when the title was at stake were highly questionable.

Schumacher's winning Benetton of 1994 and 1995 was designed by Ross Brawn, the first F1 car to feature the elevated nose and underslung wing that characterised the single-seaters of the late 1990s. It was no coincidence

Nothing is more terrifying for a racing driver than fire, and all cars have built in extinguisher systems. However, once the car has come to a halt the flames can quickly engulf it, and the driver will try to come to a halt by a marshals' post.

that Brawn transferred to Ferrari along with Michael Schumacher.

For many fans, Ferrari is synonymous with motor racing. After a dearth of tangible success, Ferrari came close to winning a title in 1990 when Alain Prost and Nigel Mansell scored six wins between them with the John Barnard-designed 641, but only in 1999 did Eddie Irvine and Schumacher amass sufficient points to grasp the constructors' title for Ferrari from under the nose of McLaren.

Widely acknowledged to be the best talent in the world, Schumacher vowed to win the drivers' crown for the fourth time, this time driving a Ferrari. The 1999 F1 World Championship came down to a confrontation between the Ferrari and McLaren teams. Both made mistakes that maintained the tension for the drivers' and constructors' championships right up to the last race. After Michael Schumacher's leg-breaking accident at Silverstone, Mika Hakkinen should have had an easy run-in to his second world title, but both he and his team-mate David Coulthard made race-losing mistakes,

and the team made strategic errors that allowed Irvine to move into contention.

In the 1998 and 1999 F1 seasons, Ferrari's main problem with its F399 was the aerodynamics, which were not so good in a straight line. New winglets were tried ahead of the rear wheels, but with no significant improvement. Because McLaren's aerodynamics were apparently the best, on the faster tracks such as Hockenheim and Monza Ferrari tried out a configuration that was similar to the 1998 McLaren. But Ferrari's biggest innovation was in the rear suspension department, and this was a new layout similar to the front. The rear torsion bars were almost horizontal, located on top of the gearbox, while both front and rear suspension incorporated a third horizontal shock absorber. It was a complicated arrangement: shock absorbers inclined along the sides of the gearbox, with horizontal torsion bars. Despite the apparent complexity, it was easy to maintain because adjustments could be made to the suspension at either end in a short time. The ride height could be altered in seconds with a screwdriver.

Ferrari's aerodynamic gains were in part derived from the V-shaped wings fitted to the front and rear of the car, reminiscent of similar structures fitted in the 1970s. When Schumacher returned to the fray at the new Sepang circuit in Malaysia having missed seven races with his leg in plaster, the Ferraris once again gave a commanding performance, but the result was overshadowed by their disqualification for having illegally wide barge-boards. There was no way the infringement constituted a performance advantage though, and the Ferraris were reinstated after appeal. Eventually, Ferrari won its first constructors' world championship since 1983, but McLaren, with

Aerodynamics of single-seater racing cars are extremely sophisticated and are honed to perfection over months of research in the wind tunnel. The front and rear wings have long been fundamental to exerting downforce, while barge boards direct cooling air to the side-mounted radiators. The contemporary coke-bottle shape of the rear bodywork and diffusers are designed to optimise air flow over the back of the car.

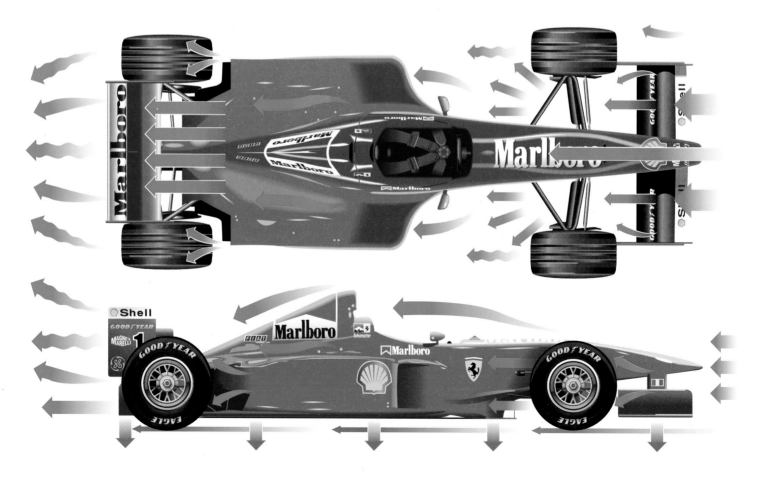

Ford bought the Stewart Team in 2000 and entered a new era with the Jaguar branded cars, with Eddie Irvine and Johnny Herbert driving. The Stewart, on which the Jaguar was based, was a proven winner, and further success was expected.

the better car, lost out through mistakes rather than on performance.

Schumacher's former drive, the Benetton, fared less well, mainly as a result of the introduction of its FTT torque transfer system, which had the adverse effect of shifting 11kg (24lb) in weight to the front of the car. Benetton engineers were forced to configure the car with a wheelbase of 328cm (129 inches), which was about 15cm (six inches) more than any other F1 contender. This meant that it had the longest plank in which to allocate its ballast (a new tendency in 1999 was the extensive use by most teams of ballast to regulate set-ups; this ballast used to be distributed at will, but the FIA dictated that it could only be allocated in small, square 10cm (four-inch) discs incorporated into the wooden anti-skid plank at the bottom of the car) but the aerodynamics and mechanical

effectiveness were not what they might have been. Sixth place in the championship standings was disappointing for a team that had been one of the four big players in the mid-1990s.

JAGUAR
The big news for 2000 was the launch of Ford's Jaguar team, based totally on Jackie Stewart's operation. Stewart's team had learned lessons from McLaren in 1998 and 1999. The SF-3 had a low nose and chassis incorporating McLaren-style fins on top of the bodywork, and the car's aerodynamics were very advanced, helped by the powerful and compact Ford V10 engine, which facilitated better packaging. This included the placement of the oil tank centrally in front of the engine, a solution copied by the Arrows and Prost teams in 1998 and by virtually everyone else in 1999.

For 2000, Eddie Irvine traded places with Rubens Barrichello, while Johnny Herbert stayed put. As to the design of the car, Jaguar's new barge-boards were similar to those that McLaren rejected at the 1999 Japanese GP, and for 2000 it had similar gurney flaps top

and bottom. The Jaguar's Ford V10 engine, built by the company's Cosworth subsidiary, was the lightest on the grid in 1999 at a reputed 99kg (218lb), and the second most powerful on the track, producing an estimated 812bhp. Only McLaren's Mercedes unit was more powerful.

In 1999, the Stewart's fuel tank was found to be inadequate, because the cars could not carry enough fuel to do races with just a single pit stop. Because of the harder tyres, cars often made fewer stops than in 1998, so a larger fuel tank would have been an advantage. Logically, the Jaguar's tank for 2000 was much larger, to allow flexibility for fuel loads and pit-stop strategy.

The Jaguar-Cosworth R1 bore definite similarities to the 1999 McLaren MP4-14, but Jaguar's technical director, Gary Anderson, was confident that once the team was established it would be in a position to innovate.

BAR NONE
Having failed to feature in the results for any Grand Prix in its maiden year, things could only get better for the

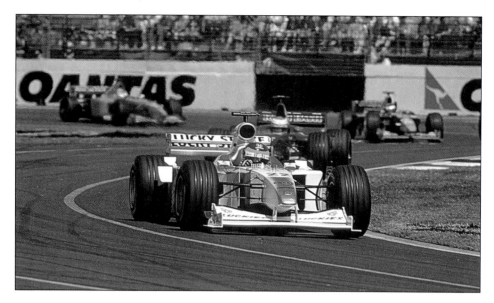

After a miserable debut season in 1999 the BAR team looked good for 2000 with fresh Honda V10 engines. Jacques Villeneuve was 4th at Melbourne, pictured here ahead of a Sauber, Arrows and Benetton. Team-mate Ricardo Zonta was 6th.

BAR (British-American Racing) team in 2000.

Sponsored by the giant British American Tobacco, BAR was headed by a powerful consortium comprising Villeneuve's manager, Craig Pollock, and Rick Gorne and Adrian Reynard of Reynard, with Jock Clear as chief engineer and Robert Synge as team manager. The disappointing 1999 season was not without friction. BAR's technical director, Malcolm Oastler, claimed that the car's aerodynamics were not the problem for the 01, although its drivers, Jacques Villeneuve and Ricardo Zonta, felt there was insufficient grip – witness their terrible crashes in practice for Spa in 1999 at the daunting Eau Rouge curve.

The BAR 02 was a development of the 01, but clearly aimed at achieving reliability. The new car's wheelbase was slightly shorter than the 01, although still fairly long overall. The concept remained similar, with the side-pods, barge-boards and diffuser largely unchanged in size and shape. BAR's second-generation Honda V10 engine was unveiled in Japan in October 1999, and was fundamentally different to the Mugen-Honda powering the 2000

Jordan, being smaller and lighter. That allowed more scope for the placement of ballast to lower the car's centre of gravity, which would help both in terms of finding more grip and allowing a better airflow over the car's rear wing. The exhaust was routed in conventional fashion around the gearbox, which Honda engineers claimed suited their engine better than the short-pipe periscope system employed by Ferrari and Prost, for example. The 02's six-speed transmission was designed and built by BAR and X-Trac specifically for use with the Honda V10 engine, and was mounted longitudinally to enhance the efficiency of the diffuser.

The BAR's front suspension consisted of vertical torsion bars and horizontal dampers inboard; the rear featured an all-new torsion bar arrangement – similar to that popularised by Ferrari two years ago, and widely copied since – replacing the previous model's coil-spring arrangement, which had the added benefit of creating more space for the air to flow over the diffuser.

RENAISSANCE POTENTIAL
The Williams FW22 for 2000 was powered by the new BMW V10 engine, and although similar in size and power to the Supertech unit employed in 1999, it was anticipated that once any teething troubles had been overcome, Williams would enjoy something of a renaissance. Williams introduced its first

seven-speed gearbox for the FW22, mounted longitudinally in the same way as on its 1999 car, and this has become a common feature of Formula 1 cars, in order to maximise the efficiency of the diffuser.

The front suspension consisted of vertical torsion bars operating through horizontal inboard dampers, which was a standard Formula 1 layout. At the rear the torsion bars made for compact dimensions that allowed the rear diffuser to work more effectively. The FW22's wheelbase was seven centimetres (two and three-quarter inches) longer, dictated by its marginally longer engine. The unballasted weight was about the same as the 1999 car, despite an extra skin of Kevlar on the outside of the chassis to strengthen the car. The oil tank was located between the engine and the chassis, as opposed to between engine and gearbox, which was a layout pioneered by Stewart in 1997.

The height of the nose was midway between the low level of the McLaren

and the high position of the Ferrari. The latter configuration provided better airflow to the car's lower body but raised the centre of gravity, so the FW22's positioning was a deliberate compromise. The rear diffuser was similar in shape to its predecessor, while the side-pods were higher than those of the FW21.

OUT WITH THE TRICKY BITS

For a team that was on a high in the mid-1990s, Benetton's results for 1999 were disappointing, with drivers Alex Wurz and Giancarlo Fisichella able to demonstrate only brief flashes of their potential. For the 2000 season, designer Nick Wirth and technical director Pat Symonds went back to basics in the

The high nose of the McLaren MP4 viewed at Melbourne in 1997. Attached to the nosecone by implausibly narrow supports, the carbon-fibre wing incorporates a number of facets that contribute to an efficient airstream over the rest of the car.

quest for a lighter, aerodynamically efficient package. The B200 was a simpler car than its predecessor, with many of the trick components discarded. These included the front torque transfer system, which was designed to improve braking efficiency, and the twin-clutch gearbox that ought to have benefited traction (both proved to be too heavy and not as effective as predicted).

The B200 was much shorter than the B199, which was the longest car on the grid last year. The pushrod suspension layout was the same, though, with torsion bars at the front and coil-springs at the rear, and for the first time Benetton used carbon fibre for the suspension arms. The B200's aerodynamic package was completely revised so that the front wing and its end-plates were reshaped, and the nose was also set lower, while retaining a similar shape. The anhedral curve of the lower element of the rear wing was more pronounced, too. And bucking the

trend slightly, the side-pods were longer for aerodynamic benefit. Most fundamentally, the bodywork in that section of the car was very different: towards the rear, the inward curve of the bodywork was more prominent, while ahead of the side-pods were barge-boards larger than anything seen on a Benetton since 1994. The B200 was also considerably lighter than the B199, and was some 40kg (88lb) under the minimum F1 weight limit, permitting the team to make more use of ballast when setting up the car. This had become a particularly crucial issue for success in Formula 1 by 2000.

PROST HASTE

Having acquired the Ligier team in the mid-1990s, Alain Prost was following the path trodden by several ex-world champions, and success looked assured. By 1999, however, it had still eluded him, and the cars remained mid-field runners. Prost's technical director, Englishman Alan Jenkins, was confi-

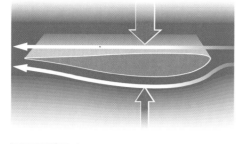

Racing-car wings act in the opposite way to those of aircraft, the faster moving air across the underside of the wing producing an area of lower pressure than that over the top surface with the slower moving air. This pushes the car down onto the track, providing more grip and stability at high speeds.

Cars are also fitted with front wings to exert downforce to the front of the car. High nose allows excellent penetration and the free passage of air to the barge boards at the sides of the car for aerodynamic efficiency.

Weighing in at around 110kg (242lb), it was roughly 15kg (33lb) lighter than the 1999 version, but still 10kg (22lb) heavier than the state-of-the-art engines. Despite the need to be able to do long stints in 1999, the fuel tank was no larger, because the Peugeot engine was considered to be fuel-efficient.

The Prost AP03's aerodynamics marked another significant improvement, and the front of the chassis and the shape and height of the side-pods had something of the look of the Jaguar about them. It also featured McLaren-type fins on the top of the chassis to create a smaller frontal area, at the same time complying with minimum-dimension regulations. The cockpit sides were also designed to be as low as possible, and there was a new diffuser. Like the 1999 car, there were double fins in front of the rear tyres on the AP03, located on top of the bodywork and halfway down it (the majority of F1 cars made do with just the higher one). The rear bodywork had quite a pronounced inward sweep to it, and the engine cover sloped steeply towards the rear in order to improve airflow to the rear wing. At the sides were big McLarenesque barge-boards and relatively small radiator inlet ducts. The torsion bar front suspension was revised by John Barnard and relocated as low down in the chassis as possible to assist weight distribution and lower the centre of gravity. For the first time, the rear suspension was all carbon fibre, and this was possible because the exhaust emissions were redirected.

JORDAN CROSSING

The consistently quick performances of Heinz-Harald Frentzen in the 1999 Jordan (in contrast to his team-mate, Damon Hill, who, mindful of family commitments, declined into retirement from F1) proved conclusively that the team was on the threshold of joining the elite F1 teams. For a while there was a chance that Frentzen would actually steal the title from under the noses of Hakkinen and Irvine. For 2000, it was a case of steady Eddie, as

dent of being able to improve Prost's challenger for 2000, AP03. This vehicle represented a significant advance on its predecessor, pedalled by Panis and Trulli in 1999. In some ways it combined the best elements of Prost coupled with those of Stewart and McLaren, which was not so surprising considering that Jenkins' last Formula 1 car design was Stewart's 1999 SF-3. The shorter engine cover testified to the AP03's reduced overall length. The cockpit and side-pods were shifted

further aft, and the exhaust exited at the top in the same way as the Ferrari.

Peugeot provided a completely new V10 engine – the enshrined number of cylinders for the forthcoming Grand Prix seasons – for Prost to use in 2000, allied to a seven-speed transmission. It represented Peugeot's first attempt at a lightweight new-generation engine similar to those of Ilmor-Mercedes and Ford. Its dimensions were about the same as these two, but at 780bhp it was about 40bhp down on its rivals.

Heinz-Harald Frenzen's Jordan heads Barrichello's Ferrari at Melbourne in 2000. The Mugen-Honda powered Jordan was a stable chassis, albeit heavier than the McLaren and Ferrari, and it was their strongest challenger.

team boss Eddie Jordan opted for an evolved version of his 1999 car rather than make any radical changes.

The Mugen-Honda MF-301 HEV10 engine was not in the same league dimensions-wise as the BAR Honda, Cosworth or Ilmor engines, but it was lighter and lower with more horsepower than its predecessor – about 810bhp. More importantly, Mugen-Honda had a good reputation for reliability. Clearly, Frentzen's ability to win at a power circuit like Monza implied there was no significant power deficit.

As Formula 1 entered the 21st century, the emphasis was, as ever, on weight reduction within the bounds of safety limits. The Jordan EJ10 was considerably lighter than the 1999 car, and all its components were down to their minimum weight. Possibly the biggest evolution to the 2000 season's Jordan was the team's in-house-designed six-speed gearbox, given a longitudinal location in a bid to lower the car's polar moment of inertia. This layout had the advantage of reducing the weight at the back of the car, and offsetting that of the relatively heavy Mugen engine, thus improving the car's handling.

Technical director Mike Gascoyne directed much of the team's efforts into refining the EJ10's aerodynamics, since this remained among the most important areas of development in Formula 1. The EJ10 looked striking: its yellow-and-black livery was far and away the brightest on the grid, and its unusually shaped triangular airbox intake and pyramidal engine cover were unique. The monocoque tub was also slimmer than before, and the overall package was the result of spending twice as much time in the wind-tunnel experimenting with aerodynamics.

The EJ10's rear suspension consisted of composite pushrods that activated gearbox-mounted Penske dampers, which handled well in most situations. The front suspension was given over to a torsion bar layout that produced less friction than the previous coil-springs, operating in conjunction with composite pushrods and Penske dampers. With new technical resources at its disposal, the Jordan team looked to be closer to a status of innovator rather than follower.

REIGNING CONSTRUCTORS' CHAMPS

Ferrari's F1-2000 model was an evolution of the successful F399 with which Irvine and Schumacher won the 1999 constructors' prize. There was a general progression towards improved weight distribution and weight reduction, and technical director Ross Brawn viewed the car as a development of the 1999 car, since that was a good basis from which to start. The F1-2000 had better aerodynamic performance – stemming

The faster a racing car travels the more downforce is exerted by its aerodynamics

Depending on the configuration, the downforce effect on a Formula 1 car will be about equal to its own weight at around 150-200km/h (93-124mph)

The maximum downforce effect at the car's top speed is around double its normal weight

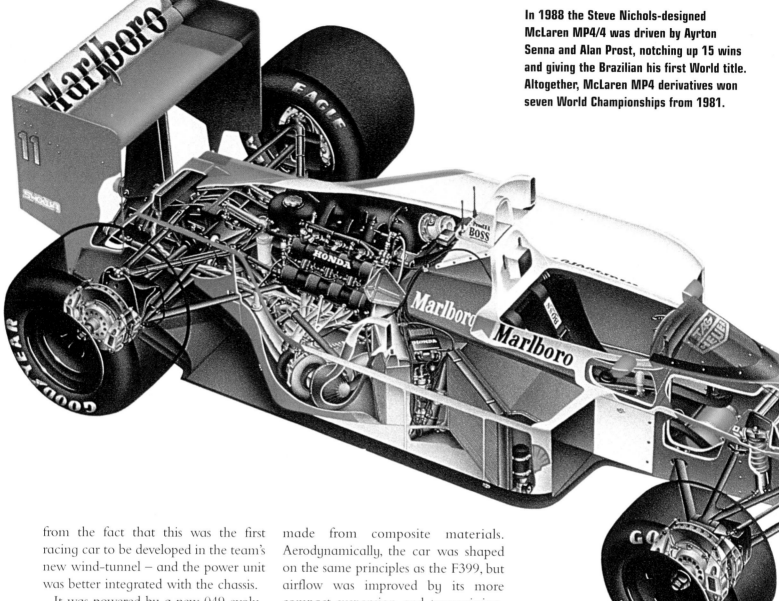

In 1988 the Steve Nichols-designed McLaren MP4/4 was driven by Ayrton Senna and Alan Prost, notching up 15 wins and giving the Brazilian his first World title. Altogether, McLaren MP4 derivatives won seven World Championships from 1981.

from the fact that this was the first racing car to be developed in the team's new wind-tunnel – and the power unit was better integrated with the chassis.

It was powered by a new 049 evolution of the established V10 unit, with the angle of the vee increased from 80 to 90 degrees to lower the overall centre of gravity. A revised lubrication system was installed with a view to improving the car's weight distribution, while new material technology was employed to create smaller, lighter cylinder heads. The on-board Magnetti Marelli data collection systems were also improved. There was an entirely new seven-speed gearbox, now longitudinally mounted, and the transmission was much smaller than before, especially with regard to the differential.

The F1-2000's chassis retained the torsion bar suspension arrangement that it helped popularise, with pushrods at both front and rear. For the first time, key suspension components were

made from composite materials. Aerodynamically, the car was shaped on the same principles as the F399, but airflow was improved by its more compact suspension and transmission, while the nose was higher and more pointed, and the barge-boards were more rounded. The engine cover also displayed a slightly rounded line that the 1999 car did not have.

THE CAR MOST LIKELY TO

The MP4-15 was Adrian Newey's third design for McLaren and it bore a strong resemblance to its predecessors. One reason for that is that McLaren does not alter its paint scheme very much (unless there is a major upset in the sponsor department). In addition, in 2000, the aerodynamic shape of Formula 1 cars had reached something of a plateau. For the last few years, Adrian Newey has generally been regarded as the master of Formula 1 aerodynamics, but with the regulations

remaining unchanged for 2000 he did not suddenly find the scope to produce a radical new look.

The MP4 series has been the most influential design in recent years. While some considered the MP4-14 to have been revolutionary, its designer viewed it as merely evolutionary. It was a highly innovative car, though. Around mid-season, McLaren tried the car with high-rise exhausts in a bid to reduce the heat around the gearbox, and a long-wheelbase set-up was tested in a quest to make the car less

MCLAREN MP4

Make: *McLaren*
Model: *MP4/4*
In production: *1988*
Engine: *1.5-litre (91.5-cubic-inch) Honda V6 turbo*
Power output: *900bhp*
Chassis: *carbon fibre monocoque*

nervous and easier to control, because the MP4-14 was harder to drive than its predecessor. It was also more difficult to set up properly, but one of its crucial advantages was its superior aerodynamics. It was also significantly under the minimum weight limit, which meant that ballast could be dispersed throughout the car to gain the best advantage from weight distribution.

For 1999, McLaren used a torsion bar rear suspension set-up, and this allowed them to ride the kerbs better, which was a significant advantage in chicanes. On

the McLaren MP4-14, the rear torsion bars were in a configuration similar to the 1998 Arrows, with vertical bars on the outside of the chassis. The MP4-14's front suspension was similar to its design for 1998, but incorporating a third horizontal shock absorber at the back. This was first used at the British Grand Prix, which proved to be another turning point for McLaren.

For 2000, a new rear-end set-up was fitted on to the MP4-14 and tested during the winter lay-off. The neater rear end of the MP4-15 McLaren led to an interesting development. The exhaust pipes were mounted close together and blew through the rear diffuser rather than around it, which had the effect of increasing downforce. The inherent problem with this arrangement was that downforce was lost when the exhausts were not blowing, which made the back end nervous. Unlike most F1 cars, where the trend was for short exhausts exiting out of the engine cover ahead of the rear wing (as pioneered by Ferrari in 1998), McLaren's pipes previously exited low down in the diffuser, and although it produced more downforce, the layout was abandoned because it created more aerodynamic instability: the amount of downforce was suddenly reduced if a driver backed off the throttle in mid-corner. Adrian Newey discovered a way to use this layout while maintaining consistent downforce. David Coulthard hated a twitchy rear end, and he was satisfied that the return to the previous exhaust layout would cause him no grief.

The nose of the MP4-15 was shorter than the MP4-14, but the barge-boards were similar. The side-pods were lower, and featured an air outlet on the topside of each one, looking like a ship's funnel, to extract hot air from the radiators so that it did not affect the car's aerodynamics. The general theme for the MP4-15 was to reduce height, and the prominence of the fins on top of the chassis just ahead of the front wheels was a sign that the chassis was lower than before. A deeper Coke-bottle shape towards the rear three-

quarters rendered the back end even narrower, which led to a change in the rear suspension set-up. Whereas the torsion bar had been positioned on the outside of the gearbox casing, it was relocated in the middle of the rocker to give a more conventional layout. Up front, the steering rack was moved inside the top wishbone so that aerodynamics were better. It was not the first time McLaren had used this arrangement, having changed it in 1999 because the steering arm was moving around, but the revised system apparently satisfied the geometry and stiffness requirements.

From 2000, Mercedes-Benz's parent, DaimlerChrysler, owned 40 per cent of the TAG McLaren Group, and it was perhaps fitting that the F1 team got new engines for the 2000 season. The introduction of the all-new engine served as an indicator that McLaren was looking for Mika Hakkinen to clinch his third title in a row (only Fangio has achieved that). The Ilmor-built Mercedes engine was lighter, and was said to be 60 per cent lighter than the 3.5-litre (214-cubic-inch) power-plants used a decade previously. Winter testing had concentrated on better integration of the engine within the chassis. According to Newey, the distinctive high-pitched banshee wail produced by the new engine was caused by sonic resonance from its new exhaust system. The sound of the V10 was likened to a V12, and was simply caused by an acoustic effect set up by the two pipes being set close together. Music indeed.

SWISS ARMY

When Peter Sauber unveiled his challenger for 2000 at the Hallenstadion in Zurich, he also introduced his 200-strong workforce. Most F1 launches have traditionally been lavish affairs involving major theatres – Eddie Jordan's EJ10 was heralded by the cast of Riverdance – but the presence of the entire squad may be unprecedented. Sauber never attained the success in Formula 1 that his cars enjoyed when they carried the Mercedes colours in

While purpose built autodromes have wide run-off areas, there's only Armco and tyre walls lining street circuits like Monaco. Equally, street circuits are notoriously hard on brakes and gearboxes, and Mika Salo stuffed the BAR into the tyres when the brakes failed in the 1999 race.

has less opportunity to refine its balance by using ballast pellets to adjust the weight distribution. This was the case with the Sauber. It was too close to the minimum weight regulations, and rivals had more scope to shift their ballast around to gain an advantage during qualifying. Not terribly

endurance sports car racing, despite some undisputed driver talent at the wheel like Alesi and Frentzen, but the Sauber C19 was significantly lighter than 1999's C18 model, lending support to the possibility that drivers Mika Salo and Pedro Diniz could manage podium finishes in 2000.

As ever, the teams in the 'second division' have always been saddled with using old, although not necessarily obsolete, equipment, and Sauber was no exception. For 2000, the C19 was equipped with Ferrari V10 units from the previous season, in the specification that Mika Salo drove when he stood in at Monza in 1999. Ferrari has always been noted for engine excellence, but the 1999 V10 was heavy by comparison with the incoming generation of power units, on a par weightwise with Jordan's Mugen-Honda, although it was some 20bhp up on Sauber's previous package. The C18's gearbox was the cause of many of the team's problems in 1999, and Sauber also considered employing Ferrari's welded titanium gearbox mated to the later-specification V10 engine, but this proved not to be an economical option

for the Swiss team and the C19's gearbox was a completely new longitudinal seven-speed unit. Being both lighter and narrower, it had the benefit of enhancing the car's aerodynamics, permitting a more defined Coke-bottle shape around the rear of the engine and improving the airflow. It was hoped the car's larger-than-average fuel tank would also confer an advantage, in the light of revised race strategies following the FIA's reduction of pit-lane speeds and consequent lengthening of pit stops.

During the winter off-season, Sauber's aerodynamics expert, Seamus Mullarky, redefined the frontal aspect of the C19 and endowed it with a similar squared-off look to the McLaren MP4-14 and the Stewart SF-3. This included a flatter nose, revised front and rear wings, and side-pods, modifications that were calculated to produce higher downforce with lower drag. Because its late-1999 specification Ferrari engine ran at a higher operating temperature, the C19 also used smaller water radiators, and this was another drag-reducing factor.

If a Formula 1 car is close to the specified minimum weight, the team

FERRARI

Make: *Ferrari*
Model: *F3000*
In production: *1998*
Engine: *3.0-litre (183-cubic-inch) Ferrari V10*
Power output: *812bhp*
Chassis: *carbon-fibre/Kevlar monocoque*

high-tech, but those were the rules, and unless it could offload some weight Sauber was at a disadvantage because poor grid positions place a team on the back foot from the outset. Because its weight was fixed into place, the cars had to qualify in similar configuration to their race trim, with the exception of their fuel load. It was clear, then, that Sauber's technical director, Leo Ress, chief designer Sergio Rinland and their respective teams had to shed some of the car's weight so that significant trim changes could be made to get good qualifying times. They succeeded very well in this, losing as much as 25 to

30kg (55 to 65lb) off the weight of the engine and transmission. The engine was also installed lower, so the car had a lower centre of gravity, and the reduction in rear-end weight also helped even out tyre temperatures and cut down the understeer that afflicted the 018.

SHIFTING SANDS

What does the future hold for Formula 1 (and where F1 leads, Champ cars has tended to follow, or at least take heed)? The ever-shifting sands of regulation changes were once more on the move at the turn of the new millennium. An unprecedented package of changes was discussed by motor sport's think-tank, the Technical Working Group, set up in 1998, and at the time of writing it was likely that the changes would be pushed through in time for the 2001 season.

One of the most interesting changes was the re-emergence of tyre manufacturer Michelin, which had had its heyday in the late 1970s and early 1980s. Its presence in Grand Prix racing for the first time since 1984 would almost certainly trigger a development struggle with the Japanese company Bridgestone, holder of the F1 monopoly in 2000. The sport's governing body, the FIA, were worried. They wanted to peg lap times at 1999 levels, anxious that competition between rival tyre firms would make for faster cornering speeds with a consequent increase in lap speeds, which would render the established safety facilities obsolete. A several-second cut in lap times would hasten the introduction of treaded tyres for dry racing, as opposed to grooved slicks. This was a scheme proposed by Max Mosley, president of the FIA, specifically to curtail lap speeds. A long way down the line it could benefit road car tyres too.

A second tyre company in the paddock would also doubtless tempt

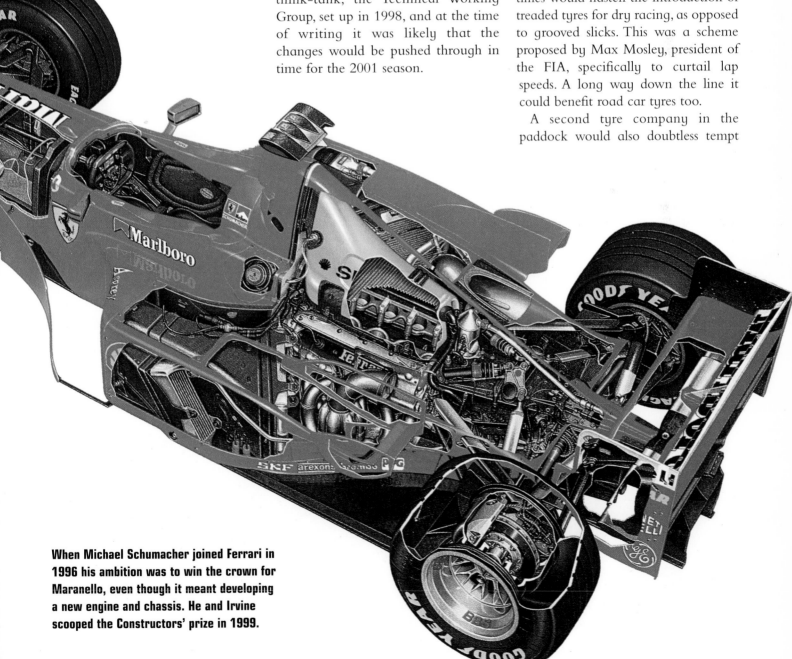

When Michael Schumacher joined Ferrari in 1996 his ambition was to win the crown for Maranello, even though it meant developing a new engine and chassis. He and Irvine scooped the Constructors' prize in 1999.

FORMULA 1 CONSTRUCTORS' CHAMPIONSHIP

1958 *Vanwall*	**1972** *Lotus-Ford*	**1986** *Williams-Honda*
1959 *Cooper-Climax*	**1973** *Lotus-Ford*	**1987** *Williams-Honda*
1960 *Cooper-Climax*	**1974** *McLaren-Ford*	**1988** *McLaren-Honda*
1961 *Ferrari*	**1975** *Ferrari*	**1989** *McLaren-Honda*
1962 *BRM*	**1976** *Ferrari*	**1990** *McLaren-Honda*
1963 *Lotus-Climax*	**1977** *Ferrari*	**1991** *McLaren-Honda*
1964 *Ferrari*	**1978** *Lotus-Ford*	**1992** *Williams-Renault*
1965 *Lotus-Climax*	**1979** *Ferrari*	**1993** *Williams-Renault*
1966 *Brabham-Repco*	**1980** *Williams-Ford*	**1994** *Williams-Renault*
1967 *Brabham-Repco*	**1981** *Williams-Ford*	**1995** *Benetton-Renault*
1968 *Lotus-Ford*	**1982** *Ferrari*	**1996** *Williams-Renault*
1969 *Matra-Ford*	**1983** *Ferrari*	**1997** *Williams-Renault*
1970 *Lotus-Ford*	**1984** *McLaren-TAG*	**1998** *McLaren-Mercedes*
1971 *Tyrrell-Ford*	**1985** *McLaren-TAG*	**1999** *Ferrari*

adversely affected when close up to another car and result in a lack of grip. There could thus be a return to the slipstreaming tactics that have been a major weapon in the racing driver's strategic arsenal in the past.

Cars will also be made less pitch-sensitive, which should reduce the risk of suddenly losing grip when the floor of the car momentarily gets too close to the track – thought to be a key factor in the crash that caused the death of Ayrton Senna. Aerodynamically efficient flat bottoms were to be replaced by a carefully restricted area in which designers could impose their own floor shape to create downforce, and rear downforce was to be reduced by restricting the rear diffusers' side elements. Rear downforce would also be cut by limiting the rear wing to four elements, with three at the top and one at the bottom. Up front, the aerofoil was expected to be raised by 50mm (two inches) in order to make it less effective. The tub and side-pods would also be widened to create higher drag, from a minimum 180cm (71 inches) to 200cm (79 inches).

teams to switch from Bridgestone, because of Michelin's impressive record in F1, which it dominated in its last two seasons up to 1984 (some even consider it to be the best tyre company in the world). Ferrari, linked with Michelin previously, would be a logical candidate for a changeover, bearing in mind it had a three-year contract with Bridgestone. McLaren, on the other hand, would be unlikely to change over, because its engine partner, Mercedes-Benz, has close links with Bridgestone.

But most of the changes being discussed by the Technical Working Group were designed to improve safety, reduce speeds and make overtaking easier. To achieve the latter, F1 racing's technical wizards set out to halve aerodynamic downforce – claimed by drivers to be the major cause of overtaking inability – and increase mechanical grip from tyres by 10 per cent, thus ensuring that grip is compromised less when cars vie with each other for track position. In addition, the tyre's contact patch with the track surface would be limited by cutting an extra groove in it, or even by imposing an FIA-defined tread, while wider rear tyres could be fitted in order to produce more drag. It was also intended that there would be less reliance on front wings, which are

With wins at Melbourne, Interlagos and Imola in 2000 Ferrari were off to a good start. Clearly visible on Barrichello's car are the complex front-wing endplates, side-barge boards and 'coke-bottle' rear bodywork.

FORMULA 1 DRIVERS' CHAMPIONSHIP

1950	Guiseppe Farina (*Alfa Romeo*)	1968	Graham Hill (*Lotus-Ford*)	1987	Nelson Piquet (*Williams-Honda*)
1951	Juan Manuel Fangio (*Alfa Romeo*)	1969	Jackie Stewart (*Matra-Ford*)	1988	Ayrton Senna (*McLaren-Honda*)
1952	Alberto Ascari (*Ferrari*)	1970	Jochen Rindt (*Lotus-Ford*)	1989	Alain Prost (*McLaren-Honda*)
1953	Alberto Ascari (*Ferrari*)	1971	Jackie Stewart (*Tyrrell-Ford*)	1990	Ayrton Senna (*McLaren-Honda*)
1954	Juan Manuel Fangio (*Maserati/Mercedes*)	1972	Emerson Fittipaldi (*Lotus-Ford*)	1991	Ayrton Senna (*McLaren-Honda*)
		1973	Jackie Stewart (*Tyrrell-Ford*)	1992	Nigel Mansell (*Williams-Renault*)
1955	Juan Manuel Fangio (*Mercedes*)	1974	Emerson Fittipaldi (*McLaren-Ford*)	1993	Alain Prost (*Williams-Renault*)
1956	Juan Manuel Fangio (*Ferrari*)	1975	Niki Lauda (*Ferrari*)	1994	Michael Schumacher (*Benetton-Ford*)
1957	Juan Manuel Fangio (*Maserati*)	1976	James Hunt (*McLaren-Ford*)	
1958	Mike Hawthorn (*Ferrari*)	1977	Niki Lauda (*Ferrari*)	1995	Michael Schumacher (*Benetton-Renault*)
1959	Jack Brabham (*Cooper-Climax*)	1978	Mario Andretti (*Lotus-Ford*)	
1960	Jack Brabham (*Cooper-Climax*)	1979	Jody Scheckter (*Ferrari*)	1996	Damon Hill (*Williams-Renault*)
1961	Phil Hill (*Ferrari*)	1980	Alan Jones (*Williams-Ford*)	1997	Jacques Villeneuve (*Williams-Renault*)
1962	Graham Hill (*BRM*)	1981	Nelson Piquet (*Brabham-Ford*)	
1963	Jim Clark (*Lotus-Climax*)	1982	Keke Rosberg (*Williams-Ford*)	1998	Mika Hakkinen (*McLaren-Mercedes*)
1964	John Surtees (*Ferrari*)	1983	Nelson Piquet (*Brabham-BMW*)	
1965	Jim Clark (*Lotus-Climax*)	1984	Niki Lauda (*McLaren-TAG*)	1999	Mika Hakkinen (*McLaren-Mercedes*)
1966	Jack Brabham (*Brabham-Repco*)	1985	Alain Prost (*McLaren-TAG*)	
1967	Denny Hulme (*Brabham-Repco*)	1986	Alain Prost (*McLaren-TAG*)	

Driver safety measures were put forward too. The side-pods would be brought forward, level with the front of the cockpit, and more stringent side-impact tests and better roll-over protec-

Alexander Wurz barrel-rolled his Benetton at Montreal in 1998, demonstrating the amazing resilience of modern F1 cars, particularly the cockpit survival cell, peculiarities such as the wooden plank, visible on the underside of the car, persist.

tion would be instituted. This was prompted by the frightening accident to Pedro Diniz in 1999, from which he was lucky to walk away, when his roll-over hoop collapsed in a multiple roll-over. Also set for revision was the protection for driver's legs, probably by increasing the width of the chassis by 10mm (a third of an inch) in the cockpit area so that 5mm (a sixth of an inch) of foam could be fitted on either side of the driver's legs to absorb impacts.

Predictably, not everyone was happy about the rule changes; for one thing they are always fantastically expensive to implement. McLaren was one of the teams to object to some changes, asserting that they restricted design freedom, damping down on the technical challenge and innovation that Formula 1 should be promoting. It was also felt to be a waste of time in other camps, as the designers would soon regain the lost downforce by other means.

FORMULA 3000

The FIA Formula 3000 International Championship was conceived as a launch pad to project talented young drivers into Formula 1, and includes rounds at Imola, Silverstone, Barcelona, Nurburgring, Monaco, Magny-Cours, A1-Ring (Austria), Hockenheim, Budapest and Spa-Francorchamps. It acts as a supporting event at 10 European Grands Prix, and its importance as a stepping stone for aspiring Grand Prix stars was virtually guaranteed when its 1999 champion, Nick Heidfeld, was confirmed as a Prost-Peugeot driver for the 2000 season.

The forerunner of F3000 was the European Formula 2 Championship, instituted in 1967, and Jacky Ickx was its first champion. He was followed by Frenchmen Jean Pierre Beltoise and Johnny Servoz-Gavin, and the car to have was the Matra-Cosworth. In 1970 it was Clay Regazzoni in a Tecno, then Ronnie Peterson in a March, and Mike Hailwood in a Surtees-Ford in 1972. Jean-Pierre Jarier drove a March-BMW in 1973, as did Patrick Depailler the following year. Jacques Laffite drove a Martini-BMW in 1974, and Jean-Pierre Jabouille's car in 1976 was an Alpine-Renault.

Introduced in 1985 to replace the exhausted Formula 2, F3000 provided a platform for budding Grand Prix drivers to gain experience and prove their worth in cars of F1 stature. Here at Spa in 1996, Apomatox's Christophe Tinseau locks a wheel under braking while keeping ahead of Oliver Tichy.

The Schnitzer-BMW powered March 732 became the dominant Formula 2 car in 1973, and Jean-Pierre Jarier made a name for himself with some spectacular drives in this car, propelling himself eventually into Formula 1.

The next year, René Arnoux was F2 champion in a Martini-Renault, and Bruno Giacomelli drove a March-BMW to victory in 1978, as did Marc Surer in 1979. Brian Henton was in a Toleman-Hart in 1980, Geoff Lees drove a Ralt-Honda in 1981, and Corrado Fabi was in the seat of a March-BMW in 1982. Jonathan Palmer took the crown in 1983, and in its final year Mike Thackwell was champion in a Ralt-Honda. There were plenty of other top-flight drivers in the F2 series, such as Niki Lauda, Carlos Reutemann and Carlos Pace; and makes, including Brabham, Lotus and Chevron. While March and BMW engines were consistently at the top of the podium, most of the best F2 drivers went on to race in F1, with varying degrees of success.

Traditionally, Formula 1 was generally regarded as the zenith of motor sport, and since the inception of the world championship in 1950 there was virtually always a feeder system comprising F3 and, logically, F2. The thing was, the top drivers were not averse to driving in an F2 race even though they

had made it to the top. People like Jim Clark and Graham Hill drove anything, from touring cars to sports prototypes, then skipped over the pond to drive at Indianapolis. As long as a driver is locked into an F1 contract these days he is unlikely to drive much else, although a stint at Le Mans may be permissible, and they certainly get to play the field when the Grand Prix circus pensions them off. Several decades ago, talented young drivers on their way up had the chance of proving their worth against the best in the world, and it was usually clear who was destined for future stardom. Jochen Rindt was a case in point.

LEVEL PLAYING FIELD

In 1985, the F3000 series came in and effectively replaced F2. The idea was to provide a level playing field, with identical chassis, engine, tyres and fuel. It was so-called because the engine capacity limit was 3.0 litres (183 cubic inches), and the logical engine to use was the good old Cosworth-DFV, no longer a force to be reckoned with in Formula 1 in the high-tech turbo era. It did, nevertheless, provide the Formula 3 graduate with a quantum hike in car size and power output. Among those graduates were Johnny Herbert, Mika Hakkinen, Eddie Irvine, Rubens Barrichello, Jean Alesi and Damon Hill, and of course they all

stepped up on to the next rung of the ladder. The only F3000 champions to win Grands Prix have been Alesi and Olivier Panis, although Hill is the only graduate to have become F1 world champion, and his F3000 career was not particularly notable. I witnessed Alesi's mercurial progress in the Tyrrell on his F1 debut at the Paul Ricard circuit in 1990, and he literally tossed the car around, just like an F3000. That, as much as anything, established the credentials of F3000 as a proving ground for young talent.

A decade later, and Nick Heidfeld was poised to give a similar demonstration at Prost, alongside Jean Alesi, by coincidence. The F1 Prost was so radically revised for 2000 that race wins looked unlikely at the start of the season. Heidfeld, then, would be judged against his team-mate's performance as much as against those of the top team's drivers. Occasionally there are exceptions to the rule that you need a stepping stone, and the most recent is Jenson Button, given a Williams F1 drive for 2000 after a promising but not particularly emphatic display in F3. With Williams in a learning year with its new BMW engines, Button would have plenty of time to play himself in without being expected to perform instantly. The F3000 champion in 1998 was Juan Pablo Montoya, and he gave the series a huge boost in the States by immediately winning the Champ car title in 1999. So it can be done.

The parameters that define success and failure involve outright speed and consistency, and the difference between pole position and failing to qualify may be as scant as one-and-a-half seconds – perhaps one or two mistakes a lap. In an entry of maybe 30 drivers – manifestation of a healthy enough interest – more than half the F3000 field scored points in 1999, while the ten qualifying rounds had six different winners. In spite of that broad dispersal of points, Heidfeld was still regarded as the most dominant driver that season, and when a win was not possible he settled for a high points finish. The winning car over the past four seasons has been the Lola chassis powered by the Ford Zytec unit built by John Judd Engine Developments. For 2000, it was decreed that all drivers were to use the Lola B99/50 chassis powered by Ford Zytec V8 engines, shod with Avon tyres and fuelled by Elf.

A number of Formula 1 teams have demonstrated their faith in F3000 as a proving ground for F1, and have developed connections with the formula. This extends to running junior teams: Williams, for example, is involved with David Sears' SuperNova team, Benetton is engaged with Astromega, and Alain Prost and McLaren have their own F3000 operations. Prost F1 recruit Heidfeld had already been signed up on a long-term Mercedes-Benz contract, but was given leave to learn the ropes at Prost, where he would be groomed for a future McLaren drive.

Mercedes-Benz has always been adept at forward planning. Michael Schumacher and Karl Wendlinger were hired to drive the Sauber-Mercedes World Sports Car Championship contenders, and released on the understanding that they would one day answer the call from Stuttgart. After Ricardo Zonta beat Juan Pablo Montoya to the 1997 F3000 title, he was snapped up by Mercedes for its title-winning GT1 sports car, and then dispatched to BAR's débutante F1 team to gain experience the hard way. Other drivers showing well in 1999 included Stéphane Sarrazin, with two victories to his credit, and Bruno Junqueira, and both men had F1 testing contracts for Prost and McLaren's West Competition respectively. In terms of outright pace, Junqueira could rival Heidfeld, but in 1999 a string of race incidents

Business end of the Lola T96/50 F3000 challenger for 1996, showing the John Judd-built Ford Zytec engine, its injection system and manifolding, plus rear suspension and spring-damper set up.

LOLA

Model: *B99/50*
In production: *1999*
Engine: *John Judd-built Ford-Zytec V8*
Gearbox: *six-speed*
Power output: *375bhp*
Chassis: *carbon-fibre/composite monocoque*

The International F3000 Championship provides a supporting attraction to the F1 circus, as Benetton Junior driver Gonzalo Rodriguez – sadly killed in a Champ Car test accident – heads the pack onto the Monaco sea front in 1999.

hampered the Brazilian's performance.

Other British drivers on the pace included Formula Palmer Audi graduate Justin Wilson, who was with Astromega in 1999, and Ulstermen Kevin McGarrity and Dino Morelli. Neither Oliver Gavin nor Jamie Davies have been given the break they deserve, though, and the team-mates were handicapped by poor set-ups in 1999. Certain to be a contender in 2000 was Darren Manning, fresh from winning the Japanese Formula 3 title, and with victories in Macau and Korea. Manning and British F3 champion Marc Hynes took part in F3000 test sessions too.

In these times of ever-safer cars and circuits, it is hard to credit that any driver could perish. But not long before Champ car ace Greg Moore died, the popular F3000 driver Gonzalo Rodriguez was killed at Laguna Seca.

The International F3000 series produces some close racing and more passing moves than F1, sometimes leading to contact, shown here at the A1 ring in Austria in 1998.

Top F1 operations groom future talent in Junior teams with a call on their services in the future. Driving for the Prost Junior Team, Stephane Sarrazin won the International F3000 round at the Hungaroring in August 1999 in a Lola B99 Ford V8.

The Uruguayan had been among the most consistent front runners and had been planning a switch from F3000 to Champ cars in 2000, and his loss was keenly felt. Accidents that happen away from the race circuit, like those of Mike Hawthorn and Mike Hailwood, seem even more futile, so when Jason Watt – runner-up to F3000 champion Nick Heidfeld and winner of the last two F3000 races of the season – was paralysed after a post-season motorcycle accident it was yet another blow for the F3000 circle. Ironically, he had dedicated his final win to his late friend Gonzalo Rodriguez.

The endless round of testing attunes the driver to his car, but that is not sufficient to prepare you for a little-known circuit. Arrive at a track you have only ever been a spectator at with your racing car, and a single practice session is just not enough on which to go out and give a meaningful race performance. So for 2000, qualifying reverted to two practice sessions per driver, which would allow more time for a newcomer to the series to get accustomed to car and circuit.

INTERNATIONAL FORMULA 3000 CHAMPIONSHIP

1985	Christian Danner (March-Ford)	1990	Eric Comas (Reynard-Mugen)	1995	Vincenzo Sospiri (Reynard-Cosworth)
1986	Ivan Capelli (March-Cosworth)	1991	Christian Fittipaldi (Reynard-Mugen)	1996	Jorg Muller (Lola-Zytec-Judd)
1987	Stefano Modena (March-Cosworth)	1992	Luca Badoer (Reynard-Cosworth)	1997	Ricardo Zonta (Lola-Zytec-Judd)
1988	Roberto Moreno (Reynard-Cosworth)	1993	Olivier Panis (Reynard-Cosworth)	1998	Juan Pablo Montoya (Lola-Zytec-Judd)
1989	Jean Alesi (Reynard-Mugen)	1994	Jean-Christophe Boullion (Reynard-Cosworth)	1999	Nick Heidfeld (Lola-Zytec-Judd)

FORMULA 3

Rather conveniently, Formula 3 got going in 1950 when the F1 World Championship was inaugurated. It was a category of racing for drivers of serious intent, although the atmosphere would have borne no relation to the seriousness and self-importance of today's paddocks. The forerunners of F3 were the single-seater 500cc (30.5-cubic-inch) motorcycle-engined cars built and raced just after the Second World War by Charles Cooper and his son John. These diminutive mid-engined Coopers formed the backbone of F3 in its infancy. The success of 500cc racing in the UK led to interest abroad, and other countries followed suit.

In Sweden, speedway tracks were sometimes used, while the Germans used their Autobahns, for which streamlined bodies were ideal. The Italians had some sophisticated multi-cylinder 500cc engines, so the seeds of future competition were already being sown. The sport's governing body, the FIA, declared that the 500cc category would become the International Formula 3 from 1950, and it was the first time there had ever been a Formula 3.

The end-of-season Macau F3 race has the same status as the similar street-circuit event that traditionally supports the Monaco Grand Prix. Here, Jensen Button brings the Promatecme Dallara Renault home in 2nd place in November 1999.

John Cooper built his first F3 car in 1946, sowing the seeds for a whole new Formula. Powered by JAP or Norton motorcycle engines, the Mk III T7 model was dominant by 1950, when Stirling Moss won the support race at the Monaco Grand Prix.

It was also the first international class of racing to originate in Britain.

The rules for F3 called for a minimum weight of 200kg (440lb) and a minimum ground clearance of 10cm (four inches). Success was determined by running a torquey engine, and those that gave most were either Norton or JAP single-cylinder units. These were British motorbike engines, but the Italians set up their own domestic 750 formula based on Fiat engines. In 1950 a Formula 3 race supported the Monaco Grand Prix and it was won by Stirling Moss from Harry Schell, both in Coopers, with Don Parker third in his Parker-CFS. Coopers now dominated Formula 3, and were much imitated by one-off special builders. The only realistic challenger was Kieft, also rear-engined, and the front-engined, front-drive Emeryson. Apart from Moss, another to start his racing career in Cooper F3 cars was Peter Collins, who drove a Cooper-Norton in the support race at the 1950 British Grand Prix meeting.

Formula 3 gave British drivers the opportunity of racing against international opposition on the Continent, and the running costs for an F3 car were low. It was even possible to be a professional racing driver, given the starting money, prize funds and trade bonuses. By 1951, the F3 category had come to be dominated by such drivers, and the amateur status had all but disappeared. The JAP engines that were at first more successful were displaced by Nortons, and soon it was not enough just to have a Norton engine, it had to have been built by a specialist tuner such as Francis Beart or Steve Lancefield. These specialists soon had waiting lists, and costs rose accordingly. One enterprising competitor, Les Leston, even bought a new Norton motorbike just for its engine and sold off everything else, and he went on to become British Formula 3 champion in 1954 in a Cooper.

There were plenty of venues for racing in the UK, some a legacy of the redundant wartime airfields, including Goodwood, Silverstone, Croft and Castle Combe. In 1950, the undulating former motorcycle grass track at Brands Hatch was turned into a tarmac-surfaced race circuit. At first, cars ran anti-clockwise – the opposite of today – and races got off to a rolling start behind a pace vehicle. With just one and a half kilometres (one mile) per lap, Brands Hatch prov
ideal venue for Formula 3 cars, and the

COOPER

Model: *T7*
In production: *1949-1952*
Engine: *998cc JAP V-twin or 500cc Norton single-cylinder*
Power output: *45bhp*
Chassis: *tubular spaceframe*

dedicated Half-Litre Club ran meetings for 500cc (30.5-cubic-inch) cars. Some of these events comprised as many as twelve races, including heats and junior and senior races. At the Daily Telegraph Trophy meeting at Brands Hatch in October 1950, no fewer than 32 of the 45 entries were Coopers.

Cooper was the first British company to build single-seaters in quantity, and over 400 Formula 3 cars were created in their Surbiton premises. Although they evolved multi-tubular spaceframe chassis, and disc brakes were fitted, the cars' suspension and basic mid-engined configuration remained unchanged for some 10 years, as F3 evolved into Formula Junior. By that time Cooper was being seriously challenged by

Lotus, which had also gone rear-engined with the type 18.

FORMULA JUNIOR

Formula 3's temporary replacement proved to be successful at an international and domestic level, in Europe at any rate, and launched a number of young talents, most notably Jim Clark. Forever associated with Colin Chapman's Team Lotus, Jim Clark's mount in F Junior was the Lotus 18, introduced in 1960.

The Mark 18 chassis was so adaptable that it could serve in any of the three significant single-seater formulae of the period. It consisted of a triangulated tubular spaceframe chassis with unequal-length wishbones at the front, plus coil-springs and damper units, and rack-and-pinion steering, and at the back it had reversed lower wishbones, twin radius rods, combined coil-springs, and damper units. There were anti-roll bars both front and rear, and disc brakes front and rear, mounted inboard at the back. The Mark 18 was launched at the 1959 Boxing Day Brands Hatch meeting as a Formula Junior car, driven by Alan Stacey.

Team Lotus generally entered cars for Jim Clark, Trevor Taylor and Peter Arundell, and between them Clark and Taylor cleaned up completely, with Henry Taylor in the Ken Tyrrell Lotus 18 winning the British Empire Trophy. In fact, every Formula Junior event of note in 1960 was won by a Lotus, and that remained the case for most of the Formula Junior era. The succeeding Lotus model for this category was the Mark 20, unveiled at the Racing Car Show at Olympia in January 1961. Its chassis and suspension systems were similar to the outgoing 18, but it had much more rounded bodywork that made the 18 look positively boxy. The Lotus 20 was powered by a 1100cc (67-cubic-inch) engine derived from the 109E Ford Classic unit, allied to a Renault four-speed transmission. The 20 ran with drum brakes all round, and used Lotus's cast magnesium wobbly-web wheels that were 33cm (13 inches)

in diameter at the front and 38cm (15 inches) at the back.

F3 RETURNS

When Formula 3 was reinstated in 1963, one man dominated the scene almost completely, and that was Jackie Stewart in a Cooper-BMC. Then Lotus came out with the type 31. It was a development of the type 22 F Junior car, and that was very much how racing cars evolved. Very often a new type number would only be introduced when development had progressed to the extent that the car being raced bore little relation to how it was when first introduced (Colin Chapman's view was that people would think nothing was happening if he did not introduce a new type number). The Lotus 31 was powered by the 997cc (60.8-cubic-inch) Ford-Cosworth SCA units, and Lotus components produced 12 cars that were sold to private entrants. More prolific was the Lotus 41 launched in 1966. It was still built around a spaceframe chassis with the same 997cc Ford-Cosworth SCA engine, but 61 units were built. These were the days of the 1.0-litre (61-cubic-inch) screamers that flourished in the mid-1960s, and fearsome slipstreaming battles were common on the long straights of power circuits like Reims, Monza and Silverstone.

The formula changed little until 1970, apart from the tyres growing ever wider. The racing was always exciting and closely fought, and there were plenty of drivers out to make a name

Anatomy of the 1972 Alpine-Renault driven by Michel Leclère, revealing the triangulated spaceframe chassis with rollover protection, 1.6-litre (97.5-cubic inch) Gordini-built engine, front-mounted radiator, and streamlined bodywork.

for themselves. Possibly the best year of all was 1969 when there were some fantastic battles between Ronnie Peterson, Reine Wisell and Tim Schenken, while later in the year Howden Ganley and Emerson Fittipaldi joined in.

For 1971 the rules were changed controversially. Engine capacity was raised to 1600cc (98 cubic inches) but with a restrictor on the inlet side of the engine; thus, all the air passing into the engine had to be sucked in through a tiny 20mm (three-quarters of an inch) hole, but rather than keeping costs down, the use of fuel injection and light, reciprocating engine parts boosted engine prices. Power output dropped from 115bhp to 105bhp, despite the increase in capacity. The engine specialists Vegantune, unlike

ALPINE	
Make: *Alpine*	
Model: *A364*	
In production: *1972*	
Engine: *1.6-litre Renault-Gordini*	
Gearbox: *five-speed*	
Power output: *160bhp*	
Chassis: *multi-tubular space-frame*	

their major rivals Holbay and Novamotor, offered a carburettor engine without exotic parts which proved popular, and when the restrictor was opened up a little, power outputs soared to 125bhp.

DESIGN TRENDS

Design trends in Formula 3 have tended to follow those of Formula 1. For much of the 1960s it was the Brabham chassis that was consistently successful in the junior formulae, exemplified in 1971 by the BT35. The most prolific chassis builder of the early 1970s was March Engineering, formed in 1969. March offered cars of both sheet-aluminium monocoque or tubular spaceframe construction, but the monocoque soon became the car to have. The star, though, was Team Lotus driver Dave Walker in a works Gold Leaf Lotus 69, which, like the Brabham, still relied on the spaceframe chassis. Runner-up in terms of race wins was Roger Williamson, who became the protégé of Donington Park circuit owner Tom Wheatcroft, a huge talent who perished in the Dutch Grand Prix at Zandvoort in 1973.

Another make to emerge in 1971 was Ensign, built by former Lotus works Formula 3 driver Mo Nunn,

now a leading figure on the Champ car circuit. The Ensign proved to be a winner almost first time out. It was interesting technically because it was the first non-Formula 1 single-seater to have its radiators mounted at the side of the car rather than in front. Also, its chassis was a cross between monocoque and spaceframe, similar to the contemporary Ferrari F1 car. Works Ensign driver Bev Bond was narrowly beaten into second place by Colin

A round of the British F3 Championship gets under way at Thruxton in 1991, with Rubens Barrichello on pole and Jordi Gené and Steve Robertson making up the front row. The Ron Tauranac-designed Ralt RT35 was the dominant model that year.

Man on the move. Future Prost F1 driver Nick Heidfeld in the Bertram Schaffer Racing Dallara-Opel in a round of the 1996 German F3 Championship. The car has a raised nose similar to its bigger F1 cousins.

Vandervell's Brabham BT35 at the first important International 1600cc Formula 3 meeting, but won his second race in the car.

In France, the established Alpine-Renault company produced some very fast works cars in Formula 3 for Patrick Depailler and Jean-Pierre Jabouille. Naturally, these employed Renault-based engines rather than the Ford twin-cam-based units the British were using. While the Renaults produced as much power as, if not more than, the Ford, BMW and Alfa Romeo units had yet to find reliability. Other F3 chassis manufacturers of the day included Tecno, Merlyn, Royale and GRD.

FORMULA ATLANTIC
The principal British F3 series was sponsored by John Player & Son in 1973, and the following year this major sponsor embraced the Formula Atlantic series. This category was the same as the North American Formula B (Formula A was the US equivalent of the European Formula 5000), and Atlantic cars were basically F2 chassis with the less powerful Ford BDA engine. They were slightly larger than F3 cars and a bit more spectacular – although Tony Brise used an F3 Modus chassis to good effect – and hence stole some of the limelight from F3. The stars of Formula Atlantic were Jim Crawford, who got a works Lotus drive and found fame and fortune in Indycars, Colin Vandervell, John Nicholson, Dave Morgan and the future F1 world champion Alan Jones. A young Tom Walkinshaw was also present. I used to do the rounds of these events as the John Player motor sport press officer, so I got to know some of the teams and personalities quite well.

By far the most bizarre event was the 1974 Dublin Grand Prix, held on the closed roads of Phoenix Park. Crowd

protection comprised nothing more than a rope around the public enclosures, and there was anything from kerbs and park benches to lamp-posts and stray dogs for the cars to hit. So severe was the camber on the 'track' that the racing line had to be dead straight along the crown of the road. At the end of the two-day meeting, not a car was left undamaged. The post-race celebrations were another matter, and probably nobody's liver was left undamaged, judging by the quantities of Guinness consumed.

NEW TALENT
Formula Atlantic attracted a certain amount of foreign talent, like Vern Schuppan, Brett Lunger and Tetsu Ikusawa, but it was really only run at a national level. Formula 3 remained international, which brought a number of Continental and new-world drivers to the fore, such as Jacques Laffite, Larry Perkins, Patrick Tambay, Alain Serpaggi, Alain Cudini and Lionel Friedrich. Top Brits were James Hunt, Ian Taylor, Russell Wood and Tony Brise, and there was a mix of cars including GRD, March, Ensign, Lotus, Martini and Alpine.

For 1974 the rules for F3 were revised by lifting capacity to 2000cc (122

cubic inches), which implied the use of the Ford BDA motor, which gave the drivers another 20bhp to play with. By this time March had extensively revised its F3 chassis, and instead of side radiators there were conventional front radiators under a new wind-cheating nosecone, along with narrower-track front suspension. The previously successful GRD chassis was dropped by racing teams in favour of March, and at first the same thing happened to Ensign, which was too heavily committed to producing an F1 car. Then designer Dave Baldwin revamped the Ensign Formula 3 car and it was back on the pace by the end of the season. The other leading British manufacturer of F3 cars was Brabham, with its monocoque BT41, but, like Ensign, Brabham was committed too much to F1 to concentrate fully on an F3 build and development programme.

In France the Martini and Alpine were profitably developed into the Mark 12 and A364B respectively. What the Martini lacked in the aesthetics department it made up for in effectiveness and strength. In France, Formula 3 enjoyed greater importance and attracted more sponsorship than elsewhere, so leading drivers had to devote themselves to endless testing between

Formula Atlantic bridged the gap between F3 and F2 or F3000. Alan Jones – F1 World Champion in 1980 – drives the Harry Stiller Racing March 732 in a John Player Formula Atlantic round at Brands Hatch in 1974.

races, something that was really exclusive to F1 at the time. Thus, on home ground the French teams were unbeatable. Jacques Laffite emerged as the champion of France and won the all-important Monaco race as well. Another leading Frenchman was Michel Leclère, who drove for the works Alpine team with Alain Serpaggi. The 1972 French champion, Leclère scored a superb win in the wet at Thruxton, and was first at Paul Ricard, Albi and Monza.

Others to shine were the Australian Alan Jones, who came close to taking the F3 title in the works GRD. Russell Wood's March was sponsored by London sports car dealers The Chequered Flag, supporters of the junior formulae since the days of Mike Parkes, but he was let down when it mattered by dud engines.

PROLIFIC OUTPUT

One of the most dynamic racing car manufacturers is Reynard, and its output is as prolific and diverse as Lotus's in its late 1960s heyday. Founder Adrian Reynard started building Formula Fords, progressing to Formula Ford 2000 and thence Formula 3 with his partner Rick

Gorne. They moved into F3 with some trepidation, motivated by a Government grant.

At that time – 1985 – carbon fibre had only been used in the higher formulae and Reynard's intention was to build a simple monocoque shell with just two bulkheads and no inner panels. It could best be described as an egg, with the outer shell taking all the loads. Market forces demanded that they had to make it for £5000, which was relatively tight. Reynard pioneered new moulding techniques and it was constructed in two pieces that were bonded together late in the build process. The shell also incorporated aluminium honeycomb sections, and the floor panel was in aluminium too. The Reynard F3 used in-board pushrod suspension all round. In the event of an accident, it was designed to shear on impact to limit chassis damage. They built 24 units in 1985, and this exceeded the output of all other composite chassis builders.

Initially, however, they found it difficult to convince potential users that carbon fibre was the way to go in Formula 3, because it exceeded their expectations at that level. For some years previously the Ralt RT3 had

been the dominant car in F3 in the UK and elsewhere, and it had many fans. It had the name of senior design personality Ron Tauranac behind it, and the established teams had amassed quantities of data on it, so persuading them to try the Reynard was not easy. The ground-effect chassis was banned in F3 in 1985, though, so to an extent there was a level playing field.

Although Ralt introduced its new RT30 to suit the new regulations, several teams retained their RT3s and updated them with the Intersport kit. It was a testing accident experienced by Tim Davies in a Reynard at Goodwood that swung the balance in Reynard's favour. He struck a bank and landed upside down on a concrete barrier, slicing through a concrete post in the process. In an aluminium tub he would not have walked away, but in the composite tub he emerged unscathed. His survival convinced waverers making the transition from FF 2000 to Formula 3 that the Reynard chassis was worth considering. But still none of the Formula 3 regulars was persuaded; only Swallow Racing, PMC, Dave Price Racing and Madgwick Motorsport signed up for new Reynards.

Madgwick had the benefit of a Saab works engine deal prepared by John Nicholson at McLaren Engines. At a big Silverstone meeting they debuted a sophisticated engine management system, but rain disabled the hot-wire sensors, much to the embarrassment of the manufacturers. Even when that problem was cured, the Reynard-Saabs were rarely competitive.

Reynard fared better than most. Other firms attempting to break into F3 have included Snetterton-based Van Diemen, who took over GRD but soon reverted to Formula Ford. Other experienced and otherwise successful

Formula Ford manufacturers, including Elden, Sparton, MRE, Ray, Vision and Tiga, all tried their hands making F3 cars, but did not succeed. Swallow Racing built its own F3 car in 1987 but Tim Davies failed to win even a single point. The Anson was designed by Gary Anderson, who went on to become chief designer for Jordan Grand Prix, but that too managed no more than a few place finishes. Relatively major players such as Chevron and Lola made no real impression in F3 either, and Lotus did not produce another Formula 3 after the over-complex type 73.

Meanwhile, Reynard won the first six British rounds in 1985, and Spence led the series from Wallace, with Mauricio Gugelmin in a Ralt third and Tim Davies in the other Swallow-Reynard fourth. At mid-season, though, it all started to fall apart, with Madgwick, PMC and Swallow all experiencing problems not necessarily connected with the Reynard cars. The new Ralt RT30 required development, but teams running it had direct support from Ron Tauranac, and it was soon competitive, and won pretty much

Jamie Davies pictured testing at Silverstone in 1997 in the GM-powered TWR Junior Team Dallara. After a promising career in F3, Davies subsequently graduated to F3000 and visualised a switch to Champ Cars for 2000.

everything from mid-season. Andy Wallace had a chance of winning the title right up to the final round, but had to be content with second overall, while Spence ended up third in the series.

Just as the manufacturer–customer relationship is symbiotic in F3000, so it was in F3, and feedback from the teams made the Reynard 863 all the better for it. The Bicester factory incorporated numerous detail improvements over the 853. Rather than using so many bought-in components sourced from outside firms, Reynard made 90 per cent of the car in-house. However, only Madgwick Motorsport and Dave Price Racing bought the cars, and the Reynard banner was carried by Perry McCarthy and Andy Wallace.

The year 1986 was very strong in terms of driver talent, with Damon Hill, Julian Bailey, Johnny Herbert, Gary Brabham and Martin Donnelly in the massed ranks of Ralts. Eddie Jordan Racing was running Maurizio Sandro Sala in a Ralt, and he won three of the first four races. Then Wallace won the second and fifth rounds for Madgwick, and before long he led the series. All the leading runners, including Madgwick, were using Volkswagen engines. Ralts were regarded as being user-friendly and had established a virtual monopoly in British Formula 3, but in 1986 Reynard took the game on to a new

level. Formula 3 cars were becoming very sophisticated as far as aerodynamics were concerned, and the Reynard tub, already noted for its rigidity, was further improved in the wind-tunnel, which was relatively new ground for Formula 3 at the time.

FUEL CRISIS

A controversy broke out regarding the legitimate fuel to be used, and the rules were slightly ambiguous, implying that higher-octane than regular pump fuel could be used. Eddie Jordan Racing's Maurizio Sandro Sala used standard pump fuel, expecting teams that did not to be penalised. It did not happen, and the young Brazilian became demoralised, while Andy Wallace won as he pleased. Since there were points to be had for pole position and fastest lap, and Wallace was never challenged in his bid for the title, he scored all of Reynard's eight victories in the series. It was also the first time since 1979 that a driver had won the British title using a car other than a Ralt, and it was surprising that Wallace was never offered a place in an F1 team.

Reynard flourished on the Continent too, Stefano Modena winning the FIA Formula 3 Nations Cup at Imola, as well as three other races in the Italian series, with a Reynard 863-Alfa Romeo, and Niclas Schonstrom lifted the Swedish Formula 3 title in a Reynard.

In 1987, the Reynard 873 had a longer wheelbase, narrower track and improved aerodynamics derived from a narrower engine bay with a new gearbox and oil tank casing, which also carried the rear suspension linkages and anti-roll bar. The new gearbox had Hewland internals in a Reynard casing, and this was the first step towards Reynard developing its own transmission division. But the choice of engine and engine-builder became a crucial matter for the first time for some years. For a while the consensus was that the John Judd version of the Volkswagen engine was favourite. Then Eddie Jordan Racing went with a new engine-builder, Siegfried Speiss, and with Johnny Herbert at the wheel EJR had a winning combination. Herbert secured the title, winning four of the first five rounds, but eventually rivals Bertrand Gachot, Martin Donnelly, Damon Hill and Gary Brabham, all in Ralts, and Thomas Danielsson in a Reynard all won races, while the TOM's Toyota engine became competitive later on.

The 1990s began with a brief Ralt renaissance, the Finnish pair of Salo and Hakkinen showing most pace, while Michael Schumacher took the German F3 title with his Reynard 903-VW, winning the Macau and Fuji races as well. Reynard's best commercial achievement was to sell its product to the organisers of the Mexican Grand Prix for a one-make F3 series, the first time in history that an FIA-sanctioned formula was run with a single make, an arrangement that continued for several years.

ITALIAN CONNECTION

Dominant makes overlap, and someone will always want to go against the flow by driving an unfashionable marque. But there is a cycle to marque dominance in F3. Broadly speaking, if March reigned in the 1970s and Ralt, followed by Reynard, ruled the 1980s, the top make in the 1990s was Dallara.

From a rapid expansion on the Italian Formula 3 scene, the Italian firm was poised to monopolise Europe. By 1993 Dallara had toppled the declining Reynard, which now pulled out of F3 to concentrate fully on the higher echelons of the sport. The Dallara had control of aerodynamic pitch sensitivity, which had eluded Reynard, and customers were quick to go over to what appeared to be the optimum chassis. Reynard's position altered abruptly as a result.

Founded by Gianpaulo Dallara, the firm went back to 1978, and it had produced and run cars in F2, F3000 and even Formula 1. When it became clear it was not going to happen at the top level, Dallara concentrated on F3, and brought to bear some of its F1 armoury including a wind-tunnel – the first F3 maker to possess one. By mid-season in 1993, British teams were converting to Dallaras. The cars were slimmer and more aerodynamically competent than Ralts and Reynards, quicker in a straight line and more predictable in the corners.

MORE NURSERY SLOPES

Formula Ford was introduced as a category in 1967 to bring competitive single-seater motor sport within reach of the 'man in the street'. Brands Hatch chief executive of the day, John Webb, instigated the formula on the basis that a car should cost £1000. Manufacturers like Lotus, Royale, Palliser and Van Diemen produced chassis tubs and stock Ford 1600cc (98-cubic-inch) engines were specified along with street tyres. Ray Allen won the inaugural

EUROPEAN FORMULA 3 CHAMPIONS

1975	Larry Perkins **(Ralt-Toyota)**	**1981**	Mauro Baldi
1976	Riccardo Patrese		**(March-Alfa Romeo)**
	(Chevron-Toyota)	**1982**	Oscar Larrauri
1977	Piercarlo Ghinzani		**(Euroracing Alfa Romeo)**
	(March-Toyota)	**1983**	Pierluigi Martini
1978	Jan Lammers **(Ralt-Toyota)**		**(Ralt-Alfa Romeo)**
1979	Alain Prost	**1984**	Ivan Capelli
	(Martini-Renault)		**(Martini-Alfa Romeo)**
1980	Michele Alboreto		
	(March-Alfa Romeo)		

The European F3 series ended in 1984, Formula 3 reverting to national championships (although the British championship overlapped by a few years).

1981	Jonathan Palmer **(Ralt-Toyota)**	**1992**	Gil de Ferran
1982	Tommy Byrne **(Ralt-Toyota)**		**(Reynard-Honda)**
1983	Ayrton Senna **(Ralt-Toyota)**	**1993**	Kelvin Burt
1984	Johnny Dumfries		**(Reynard & Dallara-Mugen)**
	(Ralt-Volkswagen)	**1994**	Jan Magnussen
1985	Mauricio Gugelmin		**(Dallara-Mugen)**
	(Ralt-Volkswagen)	**1995**	Oliver Gavin
1986	Andy Wallace		**(Dallara-Vauxhall)**
	(Reynard-Volkswagen)	**1996**	Ralph Firman
1987	Johnny Herbert		**(Dallara-Mugen-Honda)**
	(Reynard-Volkswagen)	**1997**	Jonny Kane
1988	J.J. Lehto **(Reynard-Toyota)**		**(Dallara-Mugen-Honda)**
1989	David Brabham **(Ralt-Honda)**	**1998**	Mario Haberfeld
1990	Mika Hakkinen **(Ralt-Honda)**		**(Dallara-Mugen-Honda)**
1991	Rubens Barrichello	**1999**	Marc Hynes
	(Ralt-Honda)		**(Dallara-Mugen-Honda)**

One of the most successful F3 chassis was the Reynard, dominant in the mid- to late 1980s and early 1990s, pictured with Paul Belmondo in the VW-powered 853. By 1993, with heavy commitments in Champ Cars, and Dallara in the ascendant, Reynard stopped building F3 cars.

race, and Formula Ford went on to become the most popular and wide-spread form of motor racing in the world, which remains the case today. Many F1 world champions have graduated from Formula Ford (in chronological order: Emerson Fittipaldi, James Hunt, Jody Scheckter, Ayrton Senna, Nigel Mansell, Michael Schumacher, Damon Hill and Mika Hakkinen), and while lacking out-and-out speed, it is spectacular, if only because of the desperate tactics of certain competitors.

PROVING GROUND
At the start of the 2000 season, the pundits were questioning the validity of F3 as a proving ground on account of the fact that its 1999 champion appeared to have been overlooked. But

the appointment of Jenson Button to the Williams F1 squad was always going to be controversial, however well he settled into the new surroundings. There was no doubt that the 1999 British F3 champion and Marlboro Blue Riband series winner Marc Hynes deserved an opportunity, and there was no questioning the credibility of his manager, Perry McCarthy, but then the last five winners of the British Formula 3 title have all failed to make it to Formula 1 (thus far). A curious anomaly is that F3's most recent shining graduates – Juan Pablo Montoya, Dario Franchitti and Jenson Button – notched up a mere six Formula 3 race wins between them, and no one can say that Montoya and Franchitti did not make the cut in CART racing in 1999. And then Hynes's thunder was stolen again by Darren Manning's victories in the two events at Macau and Korea. His other rival, Luciano Burti, had been hired as Jaguar's F1 test driver.

It could be that the strength of the F3 series itself conspires against the drivers who win the title. Those that end up

champions have often only made it after a long, hard slog over two seasons, which may mitigate against the status of 'overnight sensation'. Former title winners include Oliver Gavin, Ralph Firman, Jonny Kane and Mario Haberfeld, and the closest any of these F3 champions has come to getting a place on an F1 grid was Oliver Gavin's inauspicious debut with Pacific Racing in Australia in 1994, and that was the year before his championship-winning season in F3. On the other hand, Montoya, Franchitti and Button spent just one year in Formula 3, which begs the question of whether it is worth the effort of hanging around when it is possible to do better by moving on. Budgets do not necessarily come into it when the hands of the gods are extended. Then again, perhaps drivers can jump too soon – or simply into the wrong team with an unsympathetic team-mate.

But what it really boils down to is a superfluity of talent. There is a new F3 champion every year, and it is unrealistic to expect that every one is going to find a place in Formula 1.

CHAMP CARS

At the turn of the new millennium the cars that raced in the **CART** championship were known as Champ cars. They had been referred to as Indycars, so for historical purposes that is how I shall describe them in this section until the name switch. **CART** stands for Championship Automobile Racing Teams, a similar organisation to the Formula One Constructors' Association. Up to 1979 the sanctioning body covering Indycar Racing was the retrospective **USAC** organisation. The dynamic **CART** faction broke away to set up its own flourishing series, which included the Indianapolis 500.

Indycar racing goes back to the earliest days of motor sport, when it evolved on the wooden-board tracks of the county fairs. Its name is derived from the famed Indianapolis 500, an event that occupies the whole of May with qualifying and, ultimately, the race itself. Known as the Brickyard, because of its brick surface dating from 1910, and founded by A.C. Newby, Harry Wheeler, Carl Fisher and James Allison, the track was a four-kilometre (2.5-mile) oval built to outdo the English Brooklands course.

Bryan Herta leads Scott Pruett at Detroit during a round of the PPG CART World Series in June 1997. Driving one of the Team Rahal Reynard-Ford 971s alongside Bobby Rahal, Herta finished the season in 11th place, one ahead of his boss.

Five All-American Racers' Eagles contested the 1968 Indy 500. Bobby Unser's Offenhauser turbo-powered Eagle was the winner, patron Dan Gurney's Weslake-Ford-engined car pictured here came 2nd, and Denny Hulme was 4th in an Eagle-Ford V8.

The USA also had the Vanderbilt Cup races on Long Island, and the 27km (17-mile) Savannah course that hosted the United States Grand Prize in 1908, 1910 and 1911. In 1910, a mixture of European and American drivers completed 24 laps of the Savannah course in Fiats, Benz, Buicks and Marmons. After six hours' close racing, the winner was Bruce Brown's Benz.

INDY ENIGMA

For many years, Indianapolis was something of an enigma to many European enthusiasts. It was a law unto itself with its own set of regula-

The Mustang pace car leads the 33-car field away at the start of the 1964 Indy 500, with Jimmy Clark's Lotus-Ford, Bobby Marshman's Lotus-Ford and Roger Ward's Watson Offy on the front row. After a restart due to a fatal crash (Dave MacDonald and Eddie Sachs), A.J.Foyt was the eventual winner.

tions, and it took a whole month to prepare for just the one 805km (500-mile) race. Only in 2000 was the F1 fraternity fully accommodated with the building of a road section for the US Grand Prix.

Back in the beginning, the Indianapolis track was a business project, unlike Brooklands, which has all but faded from the British memory. Brooklands was a success from the word go, but Indianapolis was in trouble as a result of many accidents. In 1909 the management seriously considered closing the gravel-and-mud circuit. Then in 1910 the brick surface was laid; records for the most bricks to be laid in a day were smashed (some three-quarters of a million of them were used in total). In 1911 the organisers staged a 500-mile international sweepstake on Memorial Day. Prizes totalling $25,000 were offered, which drew enormous interest from the USA

and throughout the world, attracting a large number of foreign entries including Fiat and Mercedes, who took second, third and fourth places respectively in the race. These makes represented the spearhead of a concentrated European onslaught which grew in relation to the prize fund.

It was European interest that kicked off the Indianapolis story. There are roughly five periods: the first was the foreign invasion that took place in the years before and after the First World War; the second belonged to the Miller cars; the third was the reign of the Indianapolis roadster; the fourth was the second European invasion, when the Formula 1 style of racing car replaced the roadster; and in 1996, CART and the Indy Racing League went their separate ways to usher in the fifth era. The introduction of Formula 1 may be the start of a sixth.

The very first Indy 500 was won by Ray Haroun, driving a Marmon made in the nearby town of Indianapolis. He won the event at an average speed of 120.04km/h (74.59mph). Already the Indianapolis cars were brightly painted

120.04km/h (74.59mph). Already the Indianapolis cars were brightly painted and given special names. This Marmon was called the Wasp and was specially built for the event by Haroun from standard Marmon parts. Contemporary Marmon engines were four-cylinder units made up of paired two-cylinder blocks with integral castings. Haroun had a bigger crankcase made and added two extra cylinders, producing a 7817cc (477-cubic-inch) Marmon Six. There were 41 starters for this first event, including Fiat and Mercedes, and Haroun's winning purse was said to have been $14,000.

In 1912 Ralph de Palma led the race in a Mercedes until five laps before the end, when the car threw a con-rod. By 1913 the prize fund had increased to $55,000, and the victorious Jules Goux was alleged to have consumed several pints of champagne during the course of the race. His car was a 1912 Grand Prix Peugeot, with rivals including a Sunbeam that led for the first 50 miles, and there were full teams of Mercedes and Isotta-Fraschini, although none did particularly well.

With Europe embroiled in war, there was little chance of European manufacturers competing, and most US manufacturers were involved with the production of war supplies. So in a bid to keep the ball rolling, the Indy management bought two Peugeots and a pair of Maxwells, and persuaded the Premier Company of America to build three cars similar in design to the Peugeot.

NEW ENGINEERS
Immediately after the First World War a group of engineers appeared on the Indianapolis scene. They were Harry Miller, the Duesenberg brothers and Cornelius Van Ranst, who was a front-wheel-drive transmission and suspen-

sion specialist. In 1920, the Indianapolis formula was reduced to 3.0 litres (183 cubic inches) to conform with the European Grand Prix standard, and the Duesenbergs reduced their engine capacity accordingly. Their Indianapolis engine powered the winning car at Le Mans in 1921, and this coincided with the introduction of Harry Miller's straight-eight engines, based heavily on Peugeot influence.

The Miller Eight was among the most important engines in American racing history, and in 1922 Jimmy

Murphy had one fitted in the French Grand Prix-winning Duesenberg chassis, and it was known as the Murphy Special. The following year four out of 11 Miller-built cars took the first four places at Indianapolis. The Duesenberg brothers responded by supercharging their engines, hiring the General Electric Company to develop the centrifugal supercharger. Their efforts paid off, and in 1924 three of the four Duesenbergs entered for the Indy 500 ran with low-pressure superchargers, and one running a new 16-valve

Lotus boss Colin Chapman supervises as mechanics Jim Endruweit, left, and Dave Lazenby prepare Jimmy Clark's Lotus-Ford 34 for the 1964 Indy 500. Note the four-cam V8's 'snakepit' exhaust system and shorter left-hand drive-shaft and suspension set-up for the all-left turn oval.

This 1954 Pawl Offenhauser Indianapolis Roadster was driven by Roger Ward in the Indianapolis 500 in 1954. He qualified 16th for this race at an average speed of 224km/h (139mph).

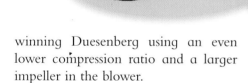

winning Duesenberg using an even lower compression ratio and a larger impeller in the blower.

Miller was by this time matching the Duesenbergs with his own engines and advanced chassis and transmission concepts, which held sway for some 35 years. It was largely Jimmy Murphy who provided the inspiration for the 1925 front-wheel-drive Miller. Having persuaded Harry Miller of its advantages he worked with chief designer Leo Goossen to produce a low, narrow, front-drive car for the 1925 event. Miller used a De Dion front suspension set-up and in-board front brakes. Frank Lockhart took over Murphy's role after he was killed (he was killed at a dirt track race at Syracuse in 1924 – a piece of catch fencing pierced his heart), and for 1926 prepared a rear-drive Miller with the radiator acting as an intercooler for the supercharger. In many respects these technical developments matched those of Lory and Jano in Europe, and it was a glorious period in American racing.

This era drew to a close with the Wall Street crash in 1929, but from 1930 the Indy management encouraged a broader range of entries with less costly cars with an upper capacity limit of 6.0 litres (366 cubic inches) unsupercharged, and this came to be known as the Junk Formula. It was a success from a publicity angle, and there were now 42 starters instead of 33; in fact it was one step short of a free-for-all, and the number of entries vastly exceeded this figure. Racing cars using proletarian stock engines from Chrysler, Ford, Packard, Studebaker and Hupmobile ran at Indianapolis, and even the local Cummins Diesel Engine Company produced a diesel car that finished in

the 1931 race without making a single pit stop.

The Duesenberg brothers had retired

KUZMA

Make: *Kuzma*
Model: *Dean Van Lines Special*
In production: *1954*
Engine: *four-cylinder Offenhauser*
Gearbox: *two-speed*
Power output: *220bhp*
Chassis: *ladder type*

cubic inches), with four valves per cylinder. Here was the origin of the Offenhauser engine that held sway at Indianapolis for over 30 years. A victim of the troubled economic climate, Miller sold his assets and plant and transferred his key personnel, including Goossen, to Fred Offenhauser in 1934. Twelve years later, Offenhauser sold out to Dale Drake and three-time Indy 500 winner Louis Meyer, and the engine was known for a time as a Meyer-Drake. When that partnership changed, the original Offenhauser designation returned.

TRANSATLANTIC RIVALRY

In 1938, the Indianapolis formula reverted to the prevailing European formula of 3.0 litres (183 cubic inches) supercharged and 4.0 litres (244 cubic inches) unsupercharged. Accordingly, some US drivers became interested in the potential of the European machines, and Wilbur Shaw imported a new Maserati. A mistranslation of the order found a 1500cc (91.5-cubic-inch) Voiturette sitting on the dockside, but it was replaced with an eight-

from the racing scene by this stage, but the eight-cylinder Miller engine remained victorious, winning the inaugural race of the new formula. However, the car that finished second was a Miller 4. It was powered by an enlarged version of an old Miller Marine engine design, based on the 16-valve 91. When the two-valve limit was lifted in 1931, this engine reappeared, enlarged by Leo Goossen and Fred Offenhauser to 3.2 litres (195

cylinder CTF just in time for Shaw to win the 1939 Indy 500, a success he repeated the following year.

The Maserati was the inspiration for a new enterprise called the Samson Special, which was powered by the V16 engine created by Frank Lockhart from two 1.5-litre (91.5-cubic-inch) Miller engines, fitted with a separate centrifugal supercharger for each cylinder bank. Another vehicle, the Thorne Engineering Special, used a six-cylinder 3.0-litre (183-cubic-inch) engine with a centrifugal supercharger, while Harry Miller attempted a comeback with a rear-engined four-wheel-drive car with all-round independent suspension and disc brakes. It was way ahead of its time. Then, in 1941, Leo Goossen built a four-cam V8 with central supercharger and fitted it in a 1935 front-wheel-drive Miller chassis. It was called the Novi and it

Driving the 4.2-litre (256-cubic inch) Offenhauser-powered Belond AP Special, Jim Bryan won the Indy 500 in 1957 and '58, and was 2nd in the 1958 Monza 500. The George Salih-designed car was based on a Kurtis spaceframe chassis with two-speed transmission.

KURTIS KRAFT

Make: *Kurtis Kraft*
Model: *Belond Special Roadster*
In production: *1957-8*
Engine: *four-cylinder Meyer & Drake-produced Offenhauser, 4.2 litres (256 cubic inches) or 3.0 litres (183 cubic inches) supercharged*
Gearbox: *two-speed*
Power output: *410bhp*
Chassis: *tubular spaceframe*

The Ilmor-built Mercedes Benz MB500I was used by several top teams from 1994, including Penske, Rahal-Hogan, Bettenhausen, Hall Racing and Galles, and was gradually adopted by more teams as the decade progressed.

scored a fourth place on its first outing. It was the first of a minor dynasty of cars that raced in front- and rear-engine rear-wheel-drive configuration in post-war racing. However, the precedents and precepts laid down by Miller, Offenhauser, Meyer and Drake predominated, and were exemplified by the conventional Blue Crown Spark Plug Special that was victorious for three consecutive years. Its engine used twin carburettors that consumed four and a half litres (one gallon) of fuel every 18km (11 miles), and it needed just one refuelling stop.

The figures that stood out from all the Indianapolis talent were Frank Kurtis and A.J. Watson. Kurtis became the leading chassis builder, and was heavily influenced by the pre-war German Grand Prix cars. In 1953, he

came up with a box-section chassis fitted with an offset engine, and this was the prototype of the roadster generation. Kurtis transformed the Novi with a rear-drive chassis, and it came close to Indy success in 1956. He paved the way for Watson to engineer the Offenhauser engine to perfection, bringing an uninterrupted run of wins for Offy-powered cars between 1959 and 1964.

Transatlantic rivalry came to a head in 1957 and 1958 when the Indycar circus went to Monza for an 805km (500-mile) race involving the banked section that has long since been redundant. The race was effectively boycotted by the European stars in 1957, with the exception of Jack Fairman, John Lawrence and Ninian Sanderson, but the following year there was a real showdown. The US contingent brought over spare Indy-style roadsters for the GP drivers, while Ferrari produced a couple of cars especially for the event for Luigi Musso, Phil Hill and Mike Hawthorn. Stirling Moss drove a 4.2-litre (256-cubic-inch) V8 Maserati

dubbed the 'Eldorado Special', sponsored by the eponymous ice-cream company. Fangio was to drive the Dean Van Lines Special, while Indy stars Jim Bryan and Jim Rathmann were in the Belond AP Special and the John Zink Leader Card Special respectively. The riot of colour and chrome was an eye-opener to the comparatively staid European circus. There were three heats of 63 laps, each won by Rathmann at an average speed of over 270km/h (170mph) average, with cars just inches apart. Moss was consistently the highest-placed GP driver, coming fourth and fifth in two of the heats, while the big 4.1-litre (250-cubic-inch) 12-cylinder Ferrari was a valiant third overall, having been shared by the three nominated drivers. The winner's prize was £11,000 – a fortune in 1958, and a reflection of the purses available in Indycar racing.

Indy roadsters did not look so different to the Formula 1 cars of the 1950s, but standards of preparation and finish were extremely high. The traditional Indy special was based on a Kuzma or Kurtis spaceframe chassis, with the four-cylinder Meyer & Drake-produced Offenhauser engine mounted in front. The mounting depended on the builder, and there were several different configurations. Some engines were canted over at 18 degrees to achieve a low bonnet line, with the driveline to the left side of the driver to produce a low centre of gravity. The standard unit was 4.5 litres (275 cubic inches), and needed either sleeving down or having the stroke shortened to achieve the regulation 4.2 litres (256 cubic inches), or 3.0 litres (183 cubic inches) if supercharged. Offenhauser engines were exceptionally neat-looking, with little in the way of external pipework. The Hilborn injection system was to the left side of the engine and the exhaust on the right, which was achieved by swapping the camshafts over in what was a symmetrical engine design, and in this way the driver was not subjected to the heat of the exhaust. Transmission was by a two-speed gearbox. Front and rear axles were standard one-piece items generally by Halibrand, located by Watts linkages and Panhard rods, while suspension consisted of torsion bars front and rear. The typical Indy roadster had shorter suspension arms on the left of the car because oval circuits have no right-hand bends, so it turned into the banked corners better. They also had disc brakes and massive magnesium alloy wheels. The top designer in 1958 was George Salih, who with Quinn Eperley built the Belond Special that was second in the Monza 500 and won Indianapolis in 1957 and 1958.

CROSSOVER OF TALENT

The Indy 500 has attracted all the sport's top names, and Indycars (meta-morphosing into Champ cars) has grown into one of the world's premier single-seater championships. In the

A supercharger compared with a turbocharger. Forced induction is a way of boosting an engine's performance without increasing the cubic capacity.

1990s, it vied with Formula 1 to be at the cutting edge of technology and driver ability. Since the arrival of Cooper, Lotus and Ford in the early 1960s, there has been a crossover of talent from F1 to Indycars, with world champions like Graham Hill, Jim Clark, Jackie Stewart, Emerson Fittipaldi and Nigel Mansell scoring at Indianapolis and in Indycar racing over the years. Not so many Indycar racers go the other way, though; the discipline of racing on oval tracks is very different from European-style circuit racing, although some CART events are staged on road-type circuits.

These days, Champ cars do not look much different to Formula 1 cars, but for decades the Indycar was an insular breed, refined to a degree, but ending in the blind alley of a big tubular-framed, front-engined roadster, inevitably powered by a four-cylinder Offenhauser engine, the powerplant whose origins lay in a 1920 design by Leo Goossen for Harry Miller. The 4.2-litre (256-cubic-inch) Offy reigned supreme until Colin Chapman and Jim

Clark led the British invasion of 1963. Lotus had a deal with Ford to use stock-block Fairlane V8 power for its mid-engined Mark 29, and in 1965 Clark was victorious in the Indianapolis 500 using a four-cam version of this engine. But that did not stop people using the Offenhauser engine, and in turbo form it was still popular in the 1970s.

Because most teams used the same engine, the cars were very evenly matched: at Indianapolis in 1958, for example, the speed differential between the first and 33rd qualifier was just 6.5km/h (4mph). But the arrival first of Cooper in 1961, then Lotus and Lola, transformed the USAC scene almost overnight. The trade-off was an insight into the highly commercial and profes-sional world of motor racing US-style, and Ford in particular took European racing by storm with its GT40 sports racing cars and support of the Cosworth engine programme – all done in the UK.

Just as the North American teams were inspired by the small British teams in the 1960s, the arrival of carbon-fibre monocoque technology in the 1980s made it logical for US teams to draw on existing expertise in the UK, the heartland of the racing car industry. Thus, the Champ cars arena is serviced by two main manufacturers, Reynard and Lola, although there have been notable exceptions in the last couple of decades, including March, Porsche, Swift, Alfa Romeo, Chaparral, McLaren, Wildcat and the Penske organisation, with a few more obscure makes.

Adrian Reynard began his motor sport career at the age of 18, building drag bikes to run on the former US airfield at Elvington. Reynard began producing Formula Fords in the early 1980s, and it is one of a number of companies that make up the UK's sizeable racing car industry. Many are located within a 160km (100-mile) radius of Oxford because all the resources for designing and building racing cars are in that area; exceptions include Lola at Huntingdon, and there

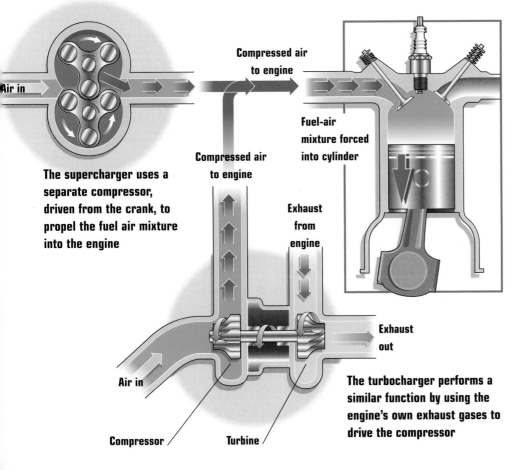

Air in

Compressed air to engine

The supercharger uses a separate compressor, driven from the crank, to propel the fuel air mixture into the engine

Compressed air to engine

Fuel-air mixture forced into cylinder

Exhaust from engine

Exhaust out

Air in

Compressor **Turbine**

The turbocharger performs a similar function by using the engine's own exhaust gases to drive the compressor

Pratt & Whitney gas turbine engines powered the 4WD Lotus 56 'wedges' at Indianapolis in 1968, testing here with Graham Hill and Mike Spence at the Team Lotus factory. Spence perished in practice, Hill crashed, and Art Pollard and Joe Leonard retired, the latter after leading most of the race from pole.

LOTUS

Make: *Lotus-Pratt & Whitney*
Model: *Type 56*
In production: *1968-69*
Engine: *Pratt & Whitney STN6B-74 gas turbine*
Gearbox: *front, rear prop shafts, chain-driven Ferguson 4x4, ZF final drive*
Power output: *430bhp on kerosene fuel*
Chassis: *twin-tube ladderframe*

has always been a small nucleus of operations near Lotus in Norfolk. Reynard has supplied a number of championship-winning chassis, and services teams such as Packard, Walker Racing, Chip Ganassi and Miller, who use a variety of Ford, Honda and Mercedes engines. The latter are also developed and produced in Britain by Ilmor Engineering at Northampton, and the Ford-owned Cosworth Engineering is near by. At least half the drivers in the Indy pit lane today have driven a Reynard of one sort or another.

Logically, Reynard has a distribution base in Indianapolis called Reynard North America, with 10 dedicated staff who supply parts and technical support to Reynard's Indycar customers. Reynard carries out a research and development programme all year round, and its wind-tunnel operates over 200 days a year solely on the Indycar programmes. Most teams running Reynards have UK factory-based liaison engineers who commute regularly during the season to work with the team. Inevitably, there is feedback from the team to the manufacturer, and in this way problems are solved and the product is steadily improved.

The other big manufacturer supplying cars to the CART Championship is Lola, whose cars are run by teams like Newman-Haas, Galles, and Patrick Racing, among others. Like Reynard, Lola builds cars for different teams that have different requirements, such as differing engines and tyres, which have to be incorporated within the design. In a way they are not designing just one Indycar but perhaps three or four variations of it at a time, with further parameters built in for road courses, short oval tracks and superspeedway circuits like Michigan. There is an argument for building two types of car to suit each environment, one for the short superspeedways and ovals and another for the twisting road circuits. But this is not the case, and Champ cars have to compromise between set-ups during the 16-race season. They are often steeply polarised in terms of design requirements and engineering.

Of necessity, Lola's approach to Champ cars is similar to that of Reynard. While the bulk of the operation, from design to manufacture, is essentially factory-based, they maintain a season-long presence in the pit lane, with an engineer working with each client team at most races and during testing. Some of these engineers are involved in the design of the cars, so they have to spend time at Lola's technical centre working on next year's car. Having experienced many of the problems first-hand, they are well placed to provide input into the new models. They need to leave the design of new cars as late as possible in order to get the maximum information from existing cars into the equation.

In practice it appears that the teams that work the closest with the manufacturer derive the greatest benefit, but invariably it is the manufacturer who makes the final decision on engineering matters.

RULES AND REGULATIONS

For a formula which supposedly uses its regulatory system as a means of restricting the cost of racing and keeping the entry-level price down, Champ cars is an expensive business, even by Formula 1 standards. The start-up cost for a new team is astronomical. Each chassis will probably cost half a million dollars, before it has an engine fitted, although that would include the full aerodynamic package. However, a two-car race team would have a minimum of four cars (with a pair as back-up), and on top of that they will probably have the makings of three or four more in spare parts.

What Champ car teams can at least rely on is a more stable environment than Formula 1, with less of the unpredictability of specification-wrecking rule changes that have rendered Formula 1 so expensive over the last couple of decades. In Champ cars, regulations in the mid-1990s placed the emphasis on aerodynamics and safety enhancement. The two were linked, by the reduction of downforce through the lowering of the tunnel height that creates the underbody venturis; this diminished the exit area somewhat, which reduced the efficiency of the downforce from the underside of the car. The underside of the car produces much more efficient downforce than the wings, for example, so it was effectively a way of increasing the drag for the amount of downforce the cars were generating. The aerodynamic package made modern Champ cars different to drive in any given situation, and the G-forces were still prodigious. They were doing things in a different way in F1, but the objective was the same: to slow the cars down a bit, if only temporarily. In Champ cars, the new 1996 regulations cut downforce by as much as 30 per cent, but with time spent in the wind-tunnel it was not long before the engineers had clawed back 15 per cent of that lost downforce, which is typical of the see-saw conflict between the rule-makers and the engineers. Three or four races later, the lap times were on a par with the previous year's.

While a damper was placed on car technology, that of computerised telemetry grew in leaps and bounds. Computers were an obvious innovation that had benefits in all forms of motor sport. They began to appear in the pit lane in the 1980s, taking over the supervision of some engine functions like fuel feed and ignition timing, which had previously been mechanically controlled. Now the computer is omnipresent, and a Champ car contains on-board logging systems that monitor and control over 100 channels of data. Some of that is simultaneously transmitted back to the pits for the engineers, who maintain a constant watch on the minutiae of the car's performance.

Formula 1 World Champions Mario Andretti and Emerson Fittipaldi sandwich Robbie Gordon at New Hampshire in 1993. Mario is in the Newman Haas Lola-Ford T93, Robby drives the Foyt Team's Lola, and Emerson handles the Penske-Chevrolet PC22.

WINGS AND THINGS

Racing car aerodynamics began tentatively in 1967, as designers tried to eliminate lift and drag with a low spoiler which also induced downforce. Porsche had tried a tall aerofoil above the cockpit of its 550 Spyder in 1956 (although this was rejected out of hand by race scrutineers), and Jim Hall's Chaparral sports prototype of 1967 paved the way for the influx of high-mounted wings that proliferated in Formula 1 in 1968. When wings arrived in Indycar racing, aerodynamic efficiency boosted the top speeds of Dan Gurney's Eagles from 290 km/h (180mph) to 320km/h (200mph) in the space of one season. Accidents in F1 as over-ambitious wing struts collapsed predictably led to a rationalisation of wing sizes.

Wings and aerofoils always have a drag penalty associated with the downforce they provide, so they require additional horsepower to drive them forward, but despite their remarkable efficiency, they are not as efficient as downforce derived from the car's underbody. This was virtually a totally neglected section of the racing car for years, and it was only in the late 1970s that it was discovered to be a potential for generating downforce from a venturi effect within the monocoque. Lotus was the main pioneer of what became known as 'ground effect' in Formula 1 with its type 78 and 79 models in 1977 and 1978. Even a flat plate running close to the road would generate downforce. At the turn of the millennium, engineers are still discovering fresh ways to harness more downforce.

DAMPING EFFECT

In the mid-1980s, the European teams began to pre-load their front suspension, which involved having the shock absorbers at full extension and winding pre-load into the spring. This meant that it required quite a lot of force to effect any suspension rhythm in the dampers. Racing cars use mono-tube dampers, which are basically lighter and can be mounted anywhere in the suspension set-up.

The mono-tube was invented in the late 1950s and it has several advantages over the twin-tube damper. Because the piston runs in the outer tube, it allows a very good damping capacity. The oil is in a sealed chamber, but if it were just a sealed chamber of oil, the damper would not work, because if you tried to push the piston in and out it would just be solid. The mono-tube has a floating piston beneath the gas which pushes the floating piston against the oil. When you pressurise the piston it compresses the oil, and if there is any gas there it just pushes it into the oil and makes it one solution. It is basically a gas-free column of oil, although the gas has to be there under the floating piston to accommodate the change in volume. The mono-tube is very consistent, and fade-free because there is no air inside. Basically, a mono-tube damper has only got one valve on the piston, and one leak path – that is, a low-speed leakage that allows the car to have just that bit of motion so it is not completely locked solid. That leak path is common to both compression and rebound damping.

Pre-loading dampers meant a huge leap in performance terms, and it was accompanied by lower ride heights, but achieving the optimum set-up is not necessarily straightforward, and even the most accomplished and best-sponsored teams with theoretically the best drivers can struggle some seasons, especially as sometimes the data that emerges during testing can mislead the engineers.

SLIPSTREAM TECHNIQUES

The design and engineering input, the intensive development, incessant testing and data analyses that create a car that can run on an oval is one thing, but driving it at 320km/h (200mph) for 805km (500 miles) is a different matter. Just as in Formula 1, the aerodynamics of modern Indycars have an adverse effect on the following car or cars. Get too close to the guy in front, and you enter turbulence known as 'dirty air' and your own car starts to lose downforce and grip. This makes overtaking much harder in a sport

INDIANAPOLIS 500 WINNERS

1911 Ray Haroun **(Marmon Wasp)**
    @ 74.59mph (120.04km/h)
1912 J. Dawson **(National)**
    @ 78.72mph (126.68km/h)
1913 Jules Goux **(Peugeot)**
    @ 75.93mph (122.19km/h)
1914 R. Thomas **(Delage)**
    @ 52.47mph (84.44km/h)
1915 Ralph de Palma **(Mercedes)**
    @ 89.84mph (144.58km/h)
1916 Dario Resta **(Peugeot)**
    @ 84.00mph (135.18km/h)
1919 H. Wilcox **(Peugeot)**
    @ 88.05mph (141.70km/h)
1920 Gaston Chevrolet **(Monroe)**
    @ 88.62mph (142.62km/h)
1921 T. Milton **(Frontenac)**
    @ 89.62mph (144.23km/h)
1922 Jimmy Murphy **(Murphy Special)**
    @ 94.48mph (152.05km/h)
1923 T. Milton **(HCS Special)**
    @ 90.95mph (146.37km/h)
1924 L. Corum/J. Boyer **(Duesenberg Special)**
    @ 98.23mph (158.08km/h)
1925 P. de Paolo **(Duesenberg Special)**
    @ 101.13mph (162.75km/h)
1926 Frank Lockhart **(Miller Special)**
    @ 95.90mph (154.33km/h)
1927 F. Souders **(Duesenberg)**
    @ 97.95mph (157.63km/h)
1928 Louis Meyer **(Miller Special)**
    @ 99.48mph (160.09km/h)
1929 R. Keech **(Simplex Piston Ring Special)**
    @ 97.59mph (157.05km/h)
1930 W. Arnold **(Miller Hartz Special)**
    @ 100.45mph (161.65km/h)
1931 L. Schneider **(Bowes Seal Fast Special)**
    @ 93.63mph (150.68km/h)
1932 F. Frame **(Miller Hertz Special)**
    @ 104.14mph (167.59km/h)
1933 Louis Meyer **(Tydol Special)**
    @ 104.16mph (167.62km/h)
1934 W. Cummings **(Boyle Special)**
    @ 104.86mph (168.75km/h)
1935 L. Petillo **(Gilmore Special)**
    @ 106.20mph (170.91km/h)
1936 Louis Meyer **(Ring Free Special)**
    @ 109.06mph (175.51km/h)
1937 W. Shaw **(Gilmore Special)**
    @ 113.58mph (182.78km/h)
1938 F. Roberts **(Burd Piston Ring Special)**
    @ 117.20mph (188.61km/h)
1939 Wilbur Shaw **(Boyle Special)**
    @ 115.04mph (185.13km/h)
1940 Wilbur Shaw **(Boyle Special)**
    @ 114.28mph (183.91km/h)
1941 M. Rose/F. Davis **(Hose Clamp Special)**
    @ 115.12mph (185.26km/h)
1946 G. Robson **(Thorne Special)**
    @ 114.82mph (184.78km/h)
1947 M. Rose **(Blue Crown Spark Plug Special)**
    @ 116.34mph (187.26km/h)
1948 M. Rose **(Blue Crown Spark Plug Special)**
    @ 119.81mph (192.81km/h)
1949 W. Holland **(Blue Crown Spark Plug Special)**
    @ 121.33mph (195.26km/h)
1950 J. Parsons **(Kurtis-Kraft)**
    @ 124.00mph (199.55km/h)
1951 L. Wallard **(Belanger Special)**
    @ 126.24mph (203.16km/h)
1952 T. Ruttman **(Agajanian Special)**
    @ 128.92mph (207.47km/h)
1953 Bill Vukovich **(Fuel Injection Special)**
    @ 128.74mph (207.18km/h)
1954 Bill Vukovich **(Fuel Injection Special)**
    @ 130.84mph (210.56km/h)
1955 R. Sweikert **(John Zink Special)**
    @ 128.21mph (206.33km/h)
1956 P. Flaherty **(John Zink Special)**
    @ 128.49mph (206.78km/h)
1957 Sam Hanks **(Belond Exhaust Special)**
    @ 135.60mph (218.22km/h)
1958 Jim Bryan **(Belond Special)**
    @ 133.79mph (215.31km/h)

where slipstreaming or 'drafting' – using the car in front to cleave the air on your behalf, almost being sucked forward in the process – was crucial to gain a power advantage over a rival's virtually identical engine. Modern

aerodynamics meant that less downforce was available than used to be the case in these situations.

Drivers can use the airflow to their advantage when overtaking another car: they can get underneath his rear

1959 Roger Ward *(Leader Card Special)*
@ 135.86mph (218.64km/h)

1960 Jim Rathman *(Ken Paul Special)*
@ 138.77mph (223.32km/h)

1961 A.J. Foyt *(Bowes Seal Fast Special)*
@ 139.13mph (223.90km/h)

1962 Roger Ward *(Leader Card 500
Roadster Special)*
@ 140.29mph (225.77km/h)

1963 R. Parnelli Jones *(Agajanian Willard
Battery Special)*
@ 145.13mph (233.56km/h)

1964 A.J. Foyt *(Sheraton Thompson
Special)*
@ 147.35mph (237.13km/h)

1965 Jim Clark *(Lotus-Ford)*
@ 150.68mph (242.49km/h)

1966 Graham Hill *(American Red Ball
Special)*
@ 144.31mph (232.24km/h)

1967 A.J. Foyt *(Coyote Ford)*
@ 151.21mph (243.34km/h)

1968 Bobby Unser *(Eagle Offenhauser)*
@ 152.88mph (246.03km/h)

1969 Mario Andretti *(Hawk Ford)*
@ 156.87mph (252.45km/h)

1970 Al Unser Sr *(Colt Ford)*
@ 156.75mph (252.26km/h)

1971 Al Unser Sr *(Colt Ford)*
@ 157.73mph (253.83km/h)

1972 M. Donohue *(McLaren Offenhauser)*
@ 163.46mph (263.06km/h)

1973 Gordon Johncock *(Eagle
Offenhauser)*
@ 159.02mph (255.91km/h)

1974 Jim Rutherford *(McLaren
Offenhauser)*
@ 158.59mph (255.22km/h)

1975 Bobby Unser *(Eagle Offenhauser)*
@ 148.21mph (238.51km/h)

1976 Jim Rutherford *(McLaren
Offenhauser)*
@ 148.73mph (239.35km/h)

1977 A.J. Foyt *(Coyote Ford)*
@ 161.33mph (259.63km/h)

1978 Al Unser Sr *(Lola-Cosworth)*
@ 161.36mph (259.68km/h)

1979 Rick Mears *(Penske-Cosworth)*
@ 158.90mph (255.72km/h)

1980 Jim Rutherford, *(Chaparral-
Cosworth)*
@ 142.88mph (229.94km/h)

1981 Bobby Unser *(Penske-Cosworth)*
@ 139.08mph (223.82km/h)

1982 Gordon Johncock *(Wildcat-
Cosworth)*
@ 162.03mph (260.75km/h)

1983 Tom Sneva *(March-Cosworth)*
@ 162.12mph (260.90km/h)

1984 Rick Mears *(March-Cosworth)*
@ 163.61mph (263.30km/h)

1985 Danny Sullivan *(March-Cosworth)*
@ 182.98mph (294.47km/h)

1986 Bobby Rahal *(March-Cosworth)*
@ 170.72mph (274.74km/h)

1987 Al Unser Sr *(March-Cosworth)*
@ 162.175mph (260.980km/h)

1988 Rick Mears *(Penske-Chevrolet)*
@ 144.809mph (233.041km/h)

1989 Emerson Fittipaldi *(Penske-Chevrolet)*
@ 167.581mph (269.688km/h)

1990 Arie Luyendyk *(Lola-Chevrolet)*
@ 185.981mph (299.299km/h)

1991 Rick Mears *(Penske-Chevrolet)*
@ 176.457mph (283.972km/h)

1992 Al Unser Jr *(Galmer-Chevrolet)*
@ 136.479mph (219.636km/h)

1993 Emerson Fittipaldi *(Penske-Chevrolet)*
@ 157.207mph (252.993km/h)

1994 Al Unser Jr *(Penske-Mercedes)*
@ 157.207mph (252.993km/h)

1995 Jacques Villeneuve *(Reynard-
Cosworth)*
@ 153.616mph (247.214km/h)

1996 Buddy Lazier *(Reynard-Ford)*
@ 147.956mph (238.106km/h)

1997 Arie Luyendyk *(G-Force-Aurora)*
@ 145.827mph (234.679km/h)

1998 Eddie Cheever *(Dallara-Aurora)*
@ 145.160mph (233.606km/h)

1999 Kenny Brack *(Dallara-Aurora)*
@ 163.178mph (262.602km/h)

wing and create a degree of oversteer on a long oval so that his car becomes destabilised. As it moves out of the slipstream, the overtaking car has a tendency to draw out the rear end of the car being overtaken. Just by arriving under the rear wing can induce some understeer in the car in front, and all this is happening at 320 km/h (200mph) in the turbulence of complex airstrips. It makes the sideways thrust you get when passing a truck at speed on the motorway seem like child's play.

The techniques and strategies are intriguing. For example, on a short oval the opportunities for slipstreaming are limited because the straights are short. So if a rival attempts to outbrake you on the inside of a corner, you move higher on the banking, and as he starts to drift away ahead of you into the middle of the corner, you move back down, tuck right behind him and slipstream past him down the straight. On big ovals like Michigan or Indianapolis slipstreaming or drafting is going on all the time, and it is possible to gain a 16km/h (10mph) advantage on the straight just by slipstreaming another car. It is important, though, to have clean air on the car's wings as you go into a turn otherwise the car lacks downforce and it will be difficult to control, so ideally you do not want another car directly in front of you because its presence compromises your own aerodynamics.

TOUGH TUBS

The nature of oval circuits is that the outer edge of the track is defined by an uncompromising wall, which if struck at 250km/h (155mph) causes a wreck, if not a multiple pile-up – Champ cars are designed to cope with such impacts. Drivers have been unlucky, such as Greg Moore who died in 1999, but on the whole the cars are far stronger than they were even 10 years ago.

As with F1, the basis of the modern Champ car is a carbon-fibre tub whose origins lie in the British aerospace industry more than 30 years ago. It is labour-intensive to create such a chassis – observe a TVR or Lotus body being built to see the care and manpower involved – so it is not something that lends itself to mass production. Around 70 per cent of all components are carbon fibre, including the suspension arms, and firms like Reynard and Lola have to produce relatively high numbers in order to service their customers. Thus, utilisation of moulds, curing of tubs and ease of component manufacture are very

LOLA

Make: *Lola*
Model: *T900*
In production: *1985*
Engine: *2.65-litre (161-cubic-inch) Ford-Cosworth DFX turbo*
Power output: *750bhp*
Chassis: *carbon-fibre/composite monocoque*

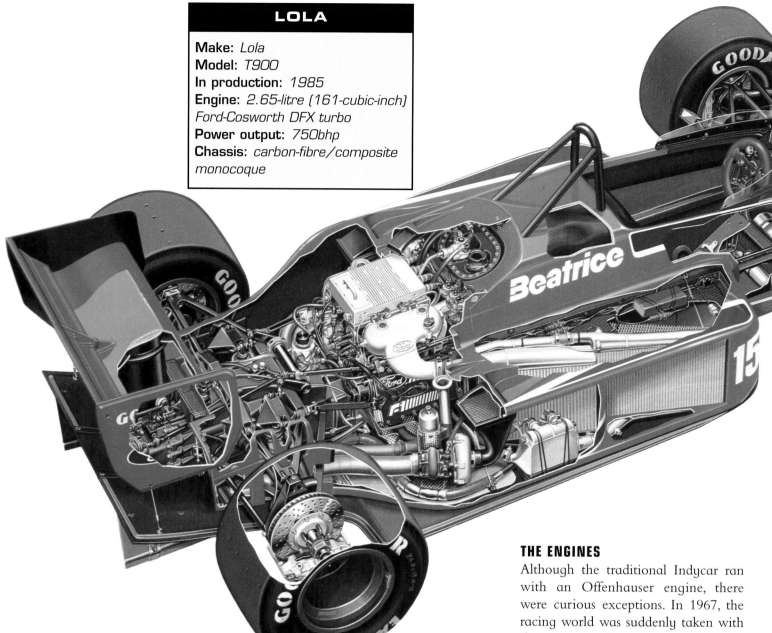

The Newman-Haas Lola-Ford-Cosworth T900 in Beatrice livery was raced by Mario Andretti and just once by Alan Jones in 1985. Mario had three wins and ended the season 5th in the CART Championship.

important, matched by the need to maintain regulation safety standards. Laying up the moulds with the matting that forms the core of the body material is critical, as is placing the material in the load paths where extra strength is needed, to counteract chassis stresses and provide impact protection.

The cost of the materials requires a high degree of skill and accuracy on the part of the operators at the construction stage, and the chassis undergo stringent checks during the manufacturing process. Once a carbon-fibre chassis is compromised by an accident, or being drilled for the addition of an extraneous part, it requires inspection by the manufacturers to ensure delamination has not occurred. A damaged chassis usually goes back to the factory to be repaired, unless it has been totalled.

THE ENGINES

Although the traditional Indycar ran with an Offenhauser engine, there were curious exceptions. In 1967, the racing world was suddenly taken with the notion that aircraft-style gas turbine engines would be the way forward. They were relatively simple, compact and not much more expensive than an Offy. The STP oil company sponsored the 'Silent Sam' gas turbine car that appeared in 1967, and for 1968 struck a deal with Team Lotus boss Colin Chapman for him to build a batch of dramatically wedge-shaped cars, designated the type 56, powered by the Pratt & Whitney turbine and built up on a twin-tube, ladder-frame, stressed-skin chassis with wishbone-type suspension.

The car was tested at Indianapolis by Jim Clark before his death, and he was replaced by Mike Spence, who perished in qualifying. In the 1968 Indy 500, the

engines, while fewer still used Chevrolet power. Cosworth was founded by Keith Duckworth and Mike Costin, both former associates of Colin Chapman, and they grew famous by tuning and modifying stock Ford engines. By 1967, and with Ford backing, Cosworth had launched its DFV engine which became omnipresent in Formula 1 throughout the 1970s and was the mainstay of the emergent F3000 of the mid-1980s. Like Chevrolet's small-block V8, the Cosworth-DFV (double-four valve) engine was a strong, lightweight and resilient powerplant, and it was undoubtedly one of the most successful racing engines of all time.

The DFV gave way to the DFY, and then came the turbocharged DFX, which started to make an impression in the late 1970s. The turbocharged version was dominant for several seasons and ran on into the 1980s. When the regulations cut the maximum-permitted boost by 50 per cent the engine designers responded by increasing rpm to maintain the

320km/h (200mph) speeds on the banked ovals. The chassis designers sought improved aerodynamics, and as the Cosworth XB was several inches lower and narrower than its predecessor it made for a car with less drag, and the consequent gain was about 20bhp. The Cosworth engine used in Champ cars is the 900bhp SD, favoured by teams such as Newman-Haas and Truesports Budweiser.

The engine is an integral stressed member of a modern racing car, its size, shape, weight and power critical to the overall package. Again, it is always in the interests of a team to form a close, symbiotic relationship with an engine manufacturer, in order to gain an advantage over another team using the same chassis, and teams using Ford engines receive support from Ford Electronics, a division of Ford in the USA that provides engine management systems for the Cosworth engine. The Ilmor engine is most frequently associated with Penske, although there are several other teams whose drivers, such as Mauricio Gugelmin and Mark

56s were raced by Graham Hill, Joe Leonard (both of whom started on the front row) and Art Pollard, Hill retiring when his suspension broke and a wheel came off, while the Americans were classified 12th and 13th. The cars were later driven by Parnelli Jones and Vince Granatelli, but the concept died out, only to be revived briefly in Formula 1 in 1970. The type 64 that superseded the 56 turbine was based on the same chassis design but powered by a 2.65-litre (162-cubic-inch) Ford quad-cam V8 fitted with a Garrett AiResearch turbocharger, and it was around this time that turbos became the way forward. They produced grenade-like power surges, and remained a crucial part of the Indycar battery.

The next evolution in the power stakes was the Cosworth-Ford engine, which had become the most ubiquitous motor by 1979. By this time only the Indycar tail-enders were using Offy

CART INDYCAR/CHAMP CAR WORLD SERIES			
1979	Rick Mears (USA), **Penske Penske-Cosworth**	1990	Al Unser Jr (USA), **Galles Lola-Chevrolet**
1980	Johnny Rutherford (USA), **Chaparral Chaparral-Cosworth**	1991	Michael Andretti (USA), **Newman-Haas Lola-Ford**
1981	Rick Mears (USA), **Penske Penske-Cosworth**	1992	Bobby Rahal (USA), **Rahal-Hogan Lola-Chevrolet**
1982	Rick Mears (USA), **Penske Penske-Cosworth**	1993	Nigel Mansell (GB), **Newman-Haas Lola-Ford**
1983	Al Unser (USA), **Penske Penske-Cosworth**	1994	Al Unser Jr (USA), **Penske Penske-Ilmor**
1984	Mario Andretti (USA), **Newman-Haas Lola-Cosworth**	1995	Jacques Villeneuve (CDN), **Green Reynard-Ford**
1985	Al Unser (USA), **Penske March-Cosworth**	1996	Jimmy Vasser (USA), **Ganassi Reynard-Honda**
1986	Bobby Rahal (USA), **Truesports March-Cosworth**	1997	Alex Zanardi (I), **Ganassi Reynard-Honda**
1987	Bobby Rahal (USA), **Truesports Lola-Cosworth**	1998	Alex Zanardi (I), **Ganassi Reynard-Honda**
1988	Danny Sullivan (USA), **Penske Penske-Chevrolet**	1999	Juan Pablo Montoya (COL), **Ganassi Reynard-Honda**
1989	Emerson Fittipaldi (BR), **Patrick Penske-Chevrolet**		

Blundell, also use Ilmor's Mercedes-badged units. Ilmor's first Indycar engine ran in 1986, and won its first race the following season. By the end of 1993 Ilmor engines had entered 122 races and won 86 of them, including six consecutive races at Indianapolis, and in 1994 Ilmor's first Mercedes-badged engine appeared at the Brickyard for the first time and duly topped the podium. Both Penske and Mercedes-Benz own shares in Ilmor, although they continue to operate independently.

In 1996, the engine battle was joined by Toyota. Following success in IMSA with Dan Gurney, the Japanese maker powered the Eagle Mk V of Juan Manuel Fangio II in 1996 and the All American Racers' Reynards in 1997. They have yet to demonstrate real form, and origins in the motor industry are no guarantee of success: neither Porsche nor Alfa Romeo shone, and Buick has never truly hit the high spots.

However, the Eagles–Toyota partnership was successful enough in IMSA sports car racing, Toyota-powered Eagles taking 17 victories in 1995. As the series was cancelled due to escalating costs, Dan Gurney returned to Champ cars (as it already was at that time), bringing along TRV to work together on a new car. Despite its overwhelming success in IMSA, it was anticipated that Toyota would stay the course until success was achieved.

FUTURE CHAMPIONS

Picking a future champion is always fraught with danger, for many reasons; the favourite may experience a string of mechanical failures for one thing. But one of the most likely talents to wager on is Scotsman Dario Franchitti, who finished third in the CART Championship in 1998 and second to Juan Pablo Montoya in 1999. For his third year with Team Green, and his fourth season in CART, the 28-year-old Scot has the benefit of a top team, chassis and engine. His rival Montoya, driving for Chip

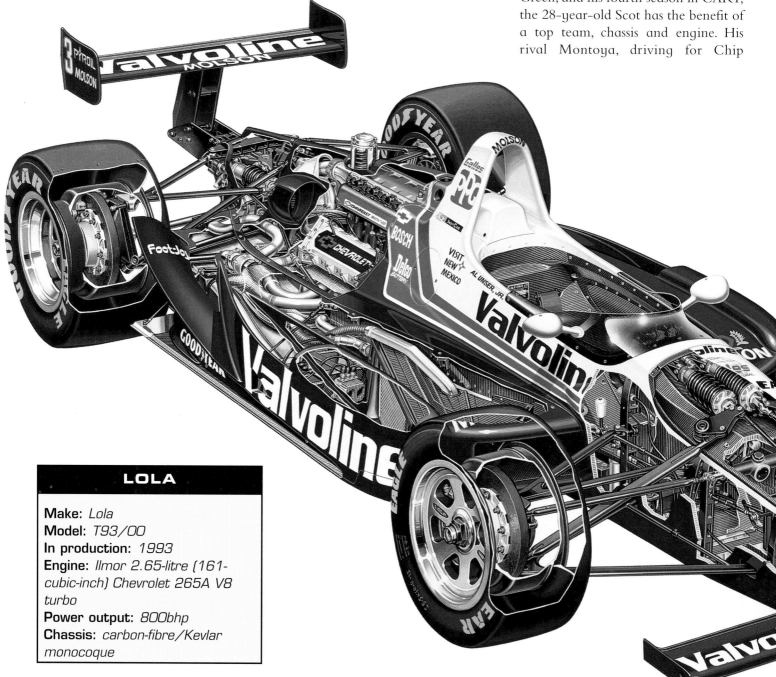

LOLA

Make: *Lola*
Model: *T93/00*
In production: *1993*
Engine: *Ilmor 2.65-litre (161-cubic-inch) Chevrolet 265A V8 turbo*
Power output: *800bhp*
Chassis: *carbon-fibre/Kevlar monocoque*

Refuelling Max Papis' Arciero-Wells Reynard 971 Toyota at Homestead in 1997. The gravity feed system, through the hose visible at the left, means the tank has to be vented by a relief valve, which is via the hose going in at the top of the engine.

Ganassi's four-time championship-winning team, switched from Honda to Toyota engines for 2000, which was a gamble for Ganassi, and indicated that 2000 would be a learning year, even though race wins were a possibility. Andretti and Christian Fittipaldi also won races in 1999, for the Newman-Haas team, but they reverted to Lola cars after a three-year try-out with Swift, so they would probably be faced with a development year. That made the 1999 runner-up Franchitti and Team Green the favourites, with Canadian team-mate Paul Tracy his most likely challenger

The Galles Team ran the Valvoline-sponsored Lola-Chevrolet T93 for Al Unser Jr in 1993. He finished 7th in the CART title stakes with 11 top-ten placings, including a win at Vancouver. Galles also ran similar cars for Danny Sullivan and Adrian Fernandez.

(Tracy beat Michael Andretti to third place in the final championship standings in 1999).

In the engine department, Ford responded to Honda's formidable challenge on power output, driveability and economy, and came out with the new XF engine, which was highly praised after early testing. That augured well for Bobby Rahal's Ford-powered team, which could muster a title challenge for driver Max Papis. His new team-mate for 2000 was Kenny Brack, replacing Bryan Herta who had spent three years in the Indy Racing League, which included victory in the 1999 Indianapolis 500 for A.J. Foyt's team.

With a dearth of success during the last two years of the 20th century, Roger Penske ditched his cars, engines and drivers in a radical bid to regain his winning streak. Abandoning his own Penske chassis and Mercedes engines, he went over to Reynard-Hondas and hired as drivers Gil de Ferran from the Walker team and Brazilian Helio Castro Neves from the defunct Carl Hogan squad (the late Greg Moore would have been Penske's original choice to join de Ferran). Others in with a real chance of success include Montoya's team-mate Jimmy Vasser, and Adrian Fernandez and Roberto Moreno in Patrick Racing's Reynard-Fords. Proven winner Tony Kanaan was down to drive a Swift-

Honda for Jerry Forsythe's second team, the ex-Tasman outfit, which was Swift's only representative in Champ cars. Forsythe's other team was the two-car Player's squad, using Reynard-Fords. For 2000, Patrick Carpentier was team leader with fellow Canadian and rookie driver Alexandre Tagliane. Driving a Toyota/Atlantic car, Carpentier's claim to fame was winning the 1996 Formula Atlantic title, but he had yet to score his first Champ cars win. Driving a Reynard Toyota, Christiano da Matta was team leader at Arciero Wells, which has been Toyota's principal team since it arrived in CART in 1996. Finally, a dark horse was the new team set up by Mo Nunn, whose roots go back to the halcyon days of Formula 3 in the UK. Nunn engineered for the Chip Ganassi team, and was regarded as one of the best in the business. He was set to run Tony Kanaan, and possibly the returning Alex Zanardi, in 2000.

Others to arrive in Champ cars included Johansson Motorsports, run by ex-Formula 1 ace and CART star Stefan Johansson, who had moved up from the Indy Lights Series. The former Prost and Minardi Formula 1 driver Shinji Nakano joined Walker Racing, while those leaving Champ cars were Scott Pruett and Team Gordon's driver Robby Gordon, both of whom relished the challenge of NASCAR's Winston

The Target/Chip Ganassi Racing crew prepares Alex Zanardi's Reynard 971 Honda during qualifying at Laguna Seca in 1997. The Italian went on to finish third in the race, and ended up Champion, having notched up five wins.

lent of European F3 and thus quite a climbdown).

However, the biggest blow to Champ cars as it entered the new century was the absence of the Goodyear tyre company. Mauled by 38 defeats out of 40 races in the past two years, Goodyear decided to retreat to lick its wounds, leaving Firestone as the series' sole supplier.

Indy Racing League

There are two sides to every story, and when the Indianapolis management under Tony George declared independence from CART, the majority of teams stuck with CART and Champ cars (Indycars was dropped as a term of reference at this point). The Indy 500 was bigger than the divided factions, though, and that would survive pretty much no matter what, but with the top players running only on the CART circuit, the so-called Indy Racing League was hard-pressed to attract many well-known names. Veteran F1 driver Eddie Cheever was one notable exception, and UK-based touring car racing supremo Alan Gow formed an IRL team for 2000. The cars were fundamentally the same as those in Champ cars, with Reynards vying with Lolas and a presence from Riley & Scott, G-Force and Dallara. Engine size was limited to 3.5 litres (214 cubic inches), as against 4.0 litres (244 cubic inches) previously, and the new Oldsmobile Aurora V8 was a mere 50bhp down on the bigger lump.

The Indy Racing League concluded

Cup. Al Unser Jr was set to switch to the rival Indy Racing League in his quest for renewed success, and Dan Gurney's All American Racers faced a bleak future with Toyota pulling out, unless new sponsorship or an engine deal came about. It was even possible that All American Racers would run Dan's son Alex in Formula Atlantic (more or less the US equiva-

Pre-season testing at Homestead in 1997 finds Christian Fittipaldi waiting in his Swift 007.i as the Newman/Haas mechanics check the Ford-Cosworth XD turbo engine. This unit was smaller and lighter than previous versions.

Race engines habitually rev to over 16,000rpm, and when they blow up, it's often spectacular. Arnd Meier's Davis/Ban/ Total Lola T97/00 makes the point at Fontana, as its Ford-Cosworth unit cries enough.

its fourth year of competition in mixed mood. On the one hand Kenny Brack won the Indianapolis 500 and Greg Ray won the IRL title in his first year racing for team owner John Menard. However, in view of the animosities surrounding the inception of the IRL series – which viewed Champ cars as the breakaway movement – it was not too surprising that IRL continued to struggle for public acceptance in the USA.

At the heart of the IRL is the Indianapolis 500, which remains the largest one-day sporting event in the world with over 400,000 spectators on the day. But the Indy 500 is like Le Mans: it has always been an institution capable of standing on its own merits. Attendance was so poor at some other Indy Racing League venues that several were dropped from the schedule for 2000. The smallest turnout in 1999 was at Dover Downs in July, when less than 8,000 baked and boiled in the sun to see Ray score an important victory on his way to the IRL title. Dover was promptly dropped from the 2000

calendar, along with one of two sparsely attended races at Colorado Springs.

IRL's rocky road was not improved when tragedy struck at Charlotte, North Carolina, on 1 May 1999. Stan Wattles crashed into the fourth-turn wall; the impact snapped off the car's right rear wheel and sent it spinning across the track, where it collided with John Paul Jr's car. The wheel then hurtled into the grandstand, killing three spectators and injuring several more. That event too was dropped from the calendar because of the bad publicity that would ensue if it was held again. If every cloud has a silver lining, the subsequent tethering of wheels to ensure there could be no repeat of the Charlotte accident at least brought some comfort to the massed ranks at Indianapolis. Like the introduction of beading to retain punctured tyres on the wheel rim in the wake of Jim Clark's fatal Hockenheim crash, it always appears that someone has to get killed before action is taken.

VETERAN TRIUMPH

At Indianapolis, Brack gave his team boss, the veteran driver A.J. Foyt, his first win as a team owner in the Memorial Day 500. Crucially, the Swede stretched his fuel mileage to the end of the race, and it was understandably his best victory since he started

racing. Late in the 1998 season he switched from a Dallara to a G-Force chassis to win the IRL championship, and after his 1999 performance he was well placed to move up to the dominant Champ cars series. Accordingly, he joined Team Rahal to replace Bryan Herta for 2000, a reflection of the relative status of the two championships.

Series winner in 1999, Greg Ray joined Team Menard at the beginning of the year to replace Tony Stewart (who went on to become the greatest rookie in NASCAR Winston Cup history). Ray won three races in a Dallara-Aurora to give Menard his second IRL title, Stewart having won the first in 1997. Inaugural IRL champion in 1996 was Buzz Calkins in a Reynard-Ford, in a tie with Scott Sharp in a Lola-Ford.

INDY RACING LEAGUE	
1996	*Buzz Calkins (USA), Bradley Reynard-Ford & Scott Sharp (USA),* **Foyt Lola-Ford**
1997	*Tony Stewart (USA),* **Menard Lola-Buick/G-Force-Aurora**
1998	*Kenny Brack (S),* **Foyt Dallara-Aurora**
1999	*Greg Ray (USA),* **Menard Dallara-Aurora**

In 1999, IRL series founder Tony George was invited to join forces with CART to unite the two categories, but decided to go his own way and maintain a separate series. However, CART teams need to return to Indianapolis in 2000 in order to satisfy their sponsors, which George was not opposed to, as clearly the big names attract better gates. That could herald a move by more CART teams to partic-ipate in the IRL series. Indeed, one key player on the Champ car scene, former Indy 500 winner Al Unser Jr, moved from CART to the IRL for 2000. Whether he has started a trend remains to be seen.

INDY LIGHTS SERIES

Just as F3000 is a stepping stone to the heady heights of Formula 1, so the Indy Lights Series grooms the future stars of big-time Champ cars and the IRL. As with the two senior series, teams contesting the Indy Lights championship use Reynards and Lolas. In 1999, the top team was Dorricott-Mears Racing, the most consistent performer in the PPG Dayton Indy Lights Championship. It was probably the most hotly con-tested season since the series started in 1986, and the team claimed the top

The Roger Penske Pennzoil Team ran the Chevrolet-powered PC-18 for Rick Mears in 1989, and he came a close second to Emerson Fittipaldi in the CART Championship title race, with three wins, two seconds and a third, as well as several top ten finishes.

PENSKE

Make: *Penske*
Model: *PC18*
In production: *1989*
Engine: *2.65-litre (161-cubic-inch) Indy V8 turbo*
Power output: *790bhp*
Chassis: *carbon-fibre/composite*

three positions as the Spaniard Oriol Servia headed Casey Mears and Phillip Peter. The team's only non-finish was at Long Beach, when Servia hit a tyre wall while running third in the closing stages.

Oriol Servia's title-winning tally of 130 points represented the lowest in the series' history; astonishingly, neither he nor team-mate Mears won any of the 12 races. This, however, demonstrated the openness of the 1999 series rather than any inability on the part of the champion. There were eight different winners and eight different pole-sitters. The 25-year-old Servia picked up his points by finishing second on five occasions, having established the best qualifying record with three pole positions. Mears demonstrated his prowess best on the ovals, although his qualifying form was less impressive. The Austrian Phillip Peter handled the third Dorricott-Mears

INDY LIGHTS CHAMPIONSHIP			
1986	Fabrizio Barbazza (I), **Wildcat-Buick**	1994	Steve Robertson (GB), **Tasman Lola-Buick**
1987	Didier Theys (B), **Wildcat-Buick**	1995	Greg Moore (CDN), **Forsythe Lola-Buick**
1988	Jon Beekhuis (USA), **Wildcat-Buick**	1996	David Empringham (CDN), **Forsythe Lola-Buick**
1989	Mike Groff (USA), **Wildcat-Buick**		
1990	Paul Tracy (CDN), **Tasman Wildcat-Buick**	1997	Tony Kanaan (BR), **Tasman Lola-Buick**
1991	Eric Bachelart (B), **Leading Edge Wildcat-Buick**	1998	Cristiano da Matta (BR), **Tasman Lola-Buick**
1992	Robbie Buhl (USA), **Leading Edge Wildcat-Buick**	1999	Oriol Servia (E), **Dorricott Lola-Buick**
1993	Bryan Herta (USA), **Tasman Lola-Buick**		

Lola, winning at Long Beach, Portland and Michigan; his only other top-six finish was fourth place at Cleveland.

Ulsterman Johnny Kane's fine win at the California Speedway was sufficient

to keep him clear of New Zealand teenager Scott Dixon in the Rookie of the Year stakes. The former British Formula 3 champion was a regular front runner for Team Kool Green, and he accumulated more points than anyone in the second half of the 1999 season. Having graduated from Formula Ford and Formula Holden in Australia, Dixon was impressive in the Indy Lights Series driving for Johansson Motorsports. He qualified and finished third on his debut at Homestead, added a second place at Long Beach, and a fourth at Nazareth to take the championship lead. Retirements followed in four out of the next five races, but Dixon came back to take an excellent victory in Chicago, where he was never headed. For 2000, Dixon moved to the PacWest team alongside Tony Renna.

Two drivers that might have done better but for bad luck were the Brazilian Felipe Giattone, who ended the 1999 season fifth, and Englishman Guy Smith, who drove for Forsythe Championship Racing. Derek Higgins' three wins included a thrilling race at Detroit from seventh place on the grid, and Frenchman Didier André's season improved markedly. Mario Dominguez, Anton Dare and Geoff Boss shone at Homestead, Nazareth and Toronto respectively, although they failed to sparkle anywhere else.

EUROPEAN SUPER TOURING

Saloons, sedans or touring cars – hotted-up family saloon cars to you and me –come in several forms, all peculiar to their native country and all impressive in their own way. In the USA there's **NASCAR** and **TransAm**, while Australia has its own Ford- and Holden-based tourers. In Europe there are plenty of national championships and one-make series for cars as humble as the ubiquitous Ford Fiesta, with Super Touring generally recognised as being the cream of the crop.

S uper Touring' is a relatively new name for what used to be touring car racing, or saloon car racing, whose origins are post-Second World War. Saloon cars were always more prominent in post–war rallying, but they made their mark on the race circuit with the launch of the 160km/h (100mph) Mk VII Jaguar saloon in 1950. Largely thanks to its sports car successes at Le Mans in the 1950s, Jaguar soon became the most prominent touring car manufacturer in the world.

In Britain, touring car racing has been around since the early 1950s, when it was known simply as saloon car racing. Enthusiastic club racers took to the circuits in their Mk VII Jaguars, Jowett Jupiters, Morris Minors, Rileys,

They may look like the repmobiles that ply the motorway fastlanes. But there's a more purposeful stance about them, and beneath the skin, super touring cars are proper racing machines.

The Lotus-Cortina of John Whitmore/Jack Sears dead-heating with the Ford Mustang of Roy Pierpoint/Jochen Neerpasch at the Nürburgring in 1965. The Lotus-Cortina racing operation was split between Team Lotus, the Alan Mann team and the English Ford Line banner in the USA.

Ford Populars and Austin A30s. Members of the 750 Motor Club even raced their pre-war Austin 7s. They were quite frequently pitted against sports cars of the time like Lotuses, Healeys, MGs and XK-120s, which were usually quicker and handled far better, so it became necessary to segregate them. The resulting categories were further broken down into classes defined by engine size, and eventually according to degrees of modification. Other national championships were running elsewhere around Europe with the same makes taking part, so the UK was as good a barometer as any other country in terms of the highs and lows of the various works teams.

The first national all-saloon race in the UK was in May 1952, when the *Daily Express* newspaper sponsored the 'Production Touring Car Race' as a curtain-raiser for its annual Formula 1 and 500cc (30.5-cubic-inch) F3 event at Silverstone. It was won by Stirling Moss in the works-entered Jaguar Mk VII, which had also been campaigned in the RAC and Monte Carlo rallies. Moss repeated his Silverstone win the following year in the same car, and before long saloon car races were suffi-

ciently popular for the national clubs and promoters to stage more serious events. At the 1954 Daily Express inter national meeting, the Jaguar drivers Tony Rolt, Ian Appleyard and Stirling Moss jumped into their Mk VII saloons for an entertaining race, sparring with Daimler Conquest Centuries and vying with Lancia Aurelia and Riley 2.5s in the up-to-3.0-litre (183-cubic-inch) class. In the up-to-2.0-litre (122-cubic-inch) class it was Ford Consuls against Borgwards, while Morris Minors battled it out with Standard Eight, DKW, Renault 4CV and Dyna Panhard at the back of the field.

PERFORMANCE TUNING

Clearly, standard cars' performance could be improved on without too much trouble, although the practice of tuning-up that spawned a whole industry and sub-culture was still in its infancy. By 1955 most competitors were modifying engines and suspension systems. For instance, Ken Wharton's Ford Zephyr was fitted with a light alloy cylinder head, twin exhaust pipes and twin carburettors, stiffer springs, and a racing-style bucket seat. The traditionalists were less impressed, believing that production cars should remain just that. The thing is, a road car on a race track is a very dangerous beast, and modifying just the suspension renders a standard car safer in that context. As a concession to the pundits regulations were tightened up in 1957, with fewer modifications permitted.

Jaguar still ruled the saloon car roost, with Mike Hawthorn giving the new 3.4-litre (207.5-cubic-inch) car a win on its debut at Silverstone. This continued to be Britain's most prestigious saloon car race. The first British Saloon Car Championship was held in 1958, with four classes defined by engine capacity. Round one was the 1957 Brands Hatch Boxing Day meeting, and this was to be the first of a string of victories for a private Jaguar team. The Equipe Endeavour drivers Tommy Sopwith and Sir Gawaine Baillie were the victors. The series also took in the UK's top circuits, Goodwood and Aintree, and Silverstone twice, where it was the support race for the Grand Prix. The traditional Le Mans-type start where drivers sprinted across the track for their cars was ended, partly because seatbelts were coming into use. This event was won by American race legend Walt Hansgen in one of John Coombs's Jaguars. But the first British saloon car champion was Jack Sears in an Austin A105 Westminster, clinching the title from Tommy Sopwith by winning a tie-break race in a pair of identical Riley 1.5s.

A new generation was creeping in, and in 1961, the Peter Berry team ran Jaguars for Bruce McLaren, John Surtees and Dennis Taylor. However, they failed to match Salvadori or Mike Parkes and Graham Hill in the Sopwith team cars. The first real challenge to the Jags came at the 1961 Daily Express Silverstone meeting,

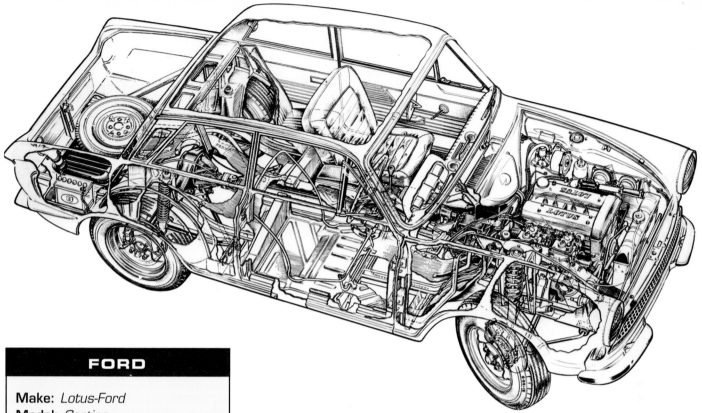

FORD

Make: *Lotus-Ford*
Model: *Cortina*
In production: *1963-7*
Engine: *1558cc (95.1-cubic-inch) four-cylinder Lotus-Ford twin-cam*
Gearbox: *Lotus-Ford*
Power output: *110-150bhp*
Chassis: *unit-construction two-door saloon*

In Europe, Ford was the first company to specify a family saloon as a touring car racer, and it was necessary for Lotus to build 1000 units of the 1558cc twin-cam engined Lotus-Cortina to be homologated for competition use. 1894 units of the Mark 1 model were produced between 1963 and 1966.

when Dan Gurney out-gunned Coventry's finest with his leviathan Chevrolet Impala. Although Graham Hill's Mk II closed up to it under braking and in the corners, engine capacity told on the straight, and Gurney might easily have won had he not lost a wheel.

In 1962, Graham Hill was on one of his many rolls, and as well as winning the Formula 1 World Championship he was top points-scorer for Jaguar. The smaller classes were by now dominated by Austin A40s, Ford Anglias, Riley 1.5s, the ubiquitous Minis and, for the first time, Mini-Coopers.

US-style TransAm racing came to Europe in the shape of Mustangs and Camaros, and in the British Saloon Car Championship in 1972, Brian 'Yogi' Muir was uncatchable much of the time in the 5.0-litre (305-cubic-inch) Chevrolet Camaro Z28.

Driving one of John Cooper's cars, John Love was outright British champion in 1962. Sir John Whitmore was runner-up the following year in a works Mini-Cooper, beaten to the title by the gargantuan Ford Galaxie of Gentleman Jack Sears.

MINI SKIRTED

What the race fans really loved to see was the Mini-Coopers hounding the big cars in a true David-versus-Goliath

scenario. There were often so many Minis in action that there was no track space left as they vied with one another for the racing line. In a Mini it seemed anything was possible, and a few experts came to the fore who could really make them do the impossible around corners, drivers like John Rhodes, John Love, John Whitmore and Warwick Banks, to name but a few.

Also to be found at big events like the 1962 Motor 6-Hour at Brands Hatch

were Sunbeam Rapiers, Vauxhall VK4/90s and Alfa Romeo Giulietta TIs, but the front runners were the Mk II Jaguars. As much as anything, this event was the big Jags' swan-song. Although it was won by Parkes and Blumer, the Mini-Cooper of Denny Hulme and John Aley finished third, after six hours' racing. As well as being a manufacturer of roll-over bars, Aley was a key promoter of the European Touring Car Championship, which was set up in 1963. Appropriately, the winner of the inaugural series was Peter Nöcker in a 3.8-litre (232-cubic-inch) Jaguar Mk II – a German driver in a British car.

HEAVY METAL

In the UK in 1963, the Jaguars were still in contention at the head of the field, but now the top drivers like Sears and Baillie were getting into Galaxies and winning as they pleased. In the first of two Brands Hatch six-hour marathons, it was Jim Clark's turn to trounce the Jaguars in a Detroit monster, while at the second meeting the two Grand Prix stars Dan Gurney

The ubiquitous Mini Coopers could always be relied on to provide giant-killing action, and here at Silverstone, Roy Salvadori's Mk II Jaguar is pursued by a broadsiding Mini and a Sunbeam Rapier in 1963. Nearing the end of its career, the big Jag lost its bumpers to reduce weight and sprouted fatter tyres for better grip.

John Rhodes developed a style all his own for getting the Mini Cooper to go round corners, involving armfuls of opposite lock and clouds of tyre smoke. He demonstrates the technique at Brands Hatch in 1968.

and Jack Brabham, plus all-rounder John Sprinzel, were in Galaxies. But the heavens opened, leaving the big American Fords floundering hopelessly on the soaking track.

By the end of 1963, the new Lotus Cortina had been acknowledged as a racing touring car. More than 100 had been built, and this would be the ace in the pack for saloon car racers for much of the decade. The notion of a family saloon as racing car was down to Ford's Walter Hayes, who commissioned Lotus to build the Lotus Cortina using Ford's new 1500cc (91.5-cubic-inch) block with a Lotus twin-cam head. The cars were assembled at

---

BMC

Make: *BMC Austin-Morris*
Model: *Mini-Cooper*
In production: *1961*
Engine: *transverse-mounted 997cc (60.8-cubic-inch) four-cylinder BMC A-series*
Gearbox: *four-speed*
Power output: *55bhp*
Chassis: *unit-construction two-door saloon*

Lotus's Cheshunt factory with coil-spring and A-frame rear suspension instead of leaf springs, and on occasion they were tested by Colin Chapman himself. The works cars' international debut was at Oulton Park in 1963, in the hands of Jack Sears and Trevor Taylor, where they beat all the Jaguars.

The Lotus Cortina racing operation

was financed and directed by Ford Motor Company. There were three separate 'works' teams, as well as private operations like John Willment's team: the Team Lotus cars contested UK events, the Alan Mann squad raced in the European series, and the North American cars were run by the strangely named Team Lotus Racing with English Ford Line (Dearborn). No fewer than 27 top drivers were signed up over the next few years, including Jim Clark, who two-wheeled his way to the British title in 1964.

In 1964, the Mini-Cooper assault on the touring car scene was double-edged. Ken Tyrrell entered two cars for Warwick Banks and Julian Vernaeve in the European series, while John Fitzpatrick drove for John Cooper in British events. Such was the devastating impact of the Mini-Cooper on the Continent that Banks took the European title outright. In the UK, Fitzpatrick came second overall and also took the 1300cc (79-cubic-inch) class win. The Mini's reputation as a giant-killer lasted more than 10 years. In Mini-Seven form it was the first of the one-make championships that mushroomed in the 1980s, and in its heyday it competed in endurance races like the Spa 24-Hour.

In 1965, engine size was what mattered, as Roy Pierpoint won the UK title with a 4.7-litre (287-cubic-inch) Ford Mustang. The Alan Mann-run Lotus Cortinas had always used 'regular' leaf-spring rear suspension, and Sir John Whitmore won the European Touring Car Championship in one of the red-and-gold Alan Mann cars. At Snetterton for one of the qualifying rounds in 1966, Whitmore was relaxed enough to wave to his fans in the heat of the race, a 500km (310-mile) event. He faced stiff opposition too, from the newly formed works-backed Autodelta Alfa Romeo team. Led by Andrea de Adamich driving lightweight Giulia Sprint GTAs, the Alfa squad boasted the services of Jochen Rindt on occasion. Alfa won the European series in 1966, with de Adamich crowned champion.

THE APPEAL BROADENS

Touring car regulations in Britain were tightened up; accordingly, Group 5 superseded Group 2. The UK's national champion in 1966 was John Fitzpatrick, the former Mini and Fiat Abarth racer, winning the title in a 1.0-litre (61-cubic-inch) Broadspeed Ford Anglia.

Paradoxically, in Britain in 1967, the big American V8 was the ideal machine to have in order to be in contention for an outright win. While Mustangs were fashionable, Alan Mann rediscovered the ex-1963 Monte Carlo Rally Ford Falcons and, with his customary high standard of preparation and Frank Gardner at the wheel, swept all before him in the red-and-gold Falcon. His main challenger was fellow Aussie Brian Muir in the John Willment Galaxie. A Mk 2 Lotus Cortina would net an under-2.0-litre-class win very often, with stars like Jacky Ickx, Paul Hawkins, Jackie Oliver, Graham Hill and John Miles at the helm. The 1.0-litre category was consistently won by John Fitzpatrick in the Broadspeed Anglia, with the Mini-Cooper Ss of John Rhodes and John Handley dominant in the next size up.

Other contenders normally associated with the grand touring category and rallying slipped into the European Touring Car frame in 1968. The 2.0-litre Porsche 911S was now a leading challenger in the hands of Vic Elford, with the occasional Jolly Club Lancia Fulvia thrown in against the 1300 Giulia GTA Juniors. BMW 2002s matched the new supercharged Giulia GT SAs, with the odd Mustang in the

It should have been a winner, but the mighty works-backed 5.3-litre Jaguar XJ12 Coupé proved to be quick but unreliable. Andy Rouse drives the monster at the 1977 RAC Tourist Trophy at Silverstone.

leading bunch. It was an exciting time, with new manufacturers popping up and Grand Prix stars still showing off their skills in saloons.

The British Touring Car Championship came under the jurisdiction of the RAC's Motor Sports Authority in 1968, and it was dominated by Frank Gardner. He was closely associated with the Alan Mann team, and drove its Mk 2 Lotus Cortina and then the new Escort. Ford performed much the same exercise with its Escort as it had done with the Lotus Cortina, except that it was carried out in-house rather than in association with Lotus. A twin-cam engine ensured its acceptance as a racing car, and once again there was little the rest could do to stop Gardner in the Alan Mann car. Before long plenty of others would follow suit with Formula 2-spec Cosworth-Ford BDA-engined Escorts.

Alec Poole took the 1969 championship with the Don Arden team Mini, and then for 1970 motor racing's governing body FIA revised the rules, reverting to a clearer specification for Group 2 cars, which excluded cars like the Porsche 911, but not, it has to be said, all coupés, which meant that there was still scope for Alfa's long-lived GTA derivatives.

Meanwhile, Frank Gardner's weapon for the 1970 British and European series was a TransAm Mustang 302. This thundering beast was a revelation to UK race fans, and won almost every time out, apart from when tyre troubles lost it the Tourist Trophy. This was a glitch that cost Frank the British title. Nevertheless, for several seasons he held more British lap records than any other driver. Unfortunately, Gardner's Boss Mustang was written off, not in a racing accident, but by Australian dockers in the winter lay-off when it was being off-loaded from a ship: it dropped from a crane and plummeted on to the dockside. For 1971 Frank drove the SCA Freight Chevrolet Camaro Z28. There were some nail-biting duels with the similar Wiggins Teape-sponsored Camaro of Brian 'Yogi' Muir, when either one could have won. Present-day classic touring car racing pits examples of these great cars against each other once again.

As the Escort developed into a sophisticated racing car powered by the 2.0-litre (122-cubic-inch) Cosworth BDA engines, with widened wheel arches bulging like boxer's biceps, drivers like John Fitzpatrick and Dave Brodie were able to challenge the 5.7-litre (348-cubic-inch) Camaros of Gardner and Muir. But at the 1971 Motor Show 200, a saloon classic at Brands Hatch, Gerry Birrell scored a lucky win in his Ford Capri as Gardner and Fitzpatrick collided and destroyed their cars against a bridge parapet on the last lap. In Britain it was much the same story in 1972, with Gardner's Camaro regularly cleaning up, but the consistency of Bill McGovern paid off, and he scooped the title honours for

the third year running with his 1.0-litre (61-cubic-inch) rear-engined George Bevan Hillman Imp.

Meanwhile, a major scrap was brewing between the big 3.0-litre (183-cubic-inch) BMWs and the Ford Cologne 3.0-litre Capris in the European Touring Car Championship. The action was characterised by the close racing between the stars of the day in the Cologne Capris and privately entered cars trading door-handles with works, Alpina and Schnitzer BMW CSL coupés. Among the Grand Prix drivers were Jackie Stewart and François Cevert in Capris, and Ronnie Peterson and Hans Stuck Jr in BMWs. In the mid-field category, Dave Matthews and Andy Rouse could beat the BMWs in their Broadspeed Escort. At the end of the season, Jochen Mass was champion in a works Capri, but the Alfa GTA Junior was still dominant in the 1300cc (79-cubic-inch) class, taking the manufacturers' title by virtue of most class wins. In the 2.0-litre (122-cubic-inch) category, Alfa Romeo's bulging-wheel-arched GT-Ams swapped paint with BMW 2002Tiis. Bizarrely, the big Capris and BMWs were also eligible for World Sports Car Championship events that year, and were pitched against sports prototypes at the Le Mans 24-Hour.

BMW COME ON STRONG

By 1973, the mainstream championships had become so expensive to

compete in that privateers had virtually disappeared. It was vital to have sponsorship or a factory contract. Even the might of Ford Cologne failed to match the lightweight BMWs that year, as aerofoils sprouted from the boot-lids of the Munich legends, earning them the 'Batmobile' nickname. Indeed, even the V6 Capris could not live with them. Apart from the BMWs' rear wings, all modified touring cars had chin spoilers under their front valances, as well as broadened wheel arches by now, growing larger with each passing season to accommodate ever-widening tyres.

For a brief period the UK was saddled with virtually bog-standard Group 1 cars, and how dull they seemed in comparison with the modified racers. The regulations were changed as a cost-saving exercise, with classes arranged on a cost-of-car basis. Thus, hard-bitten race fans were treated to the unedifying sight of bargain-basement Soviet Moskvitches leaning their ponderous way around the circuits, seemingly at a snail's pace. It was painful to behold.

Meanwhile, BMW was promoting itself heavily in Britain, but their

The BMW 3.0-litre (183-cubic-inch) CSLs sprouted rear wings in 1973 and were nicknamed Batmobiles. Four teams raced them: Schnitzer, Alpina, Luigi and the works squad, and at races like the Spa-Francorchamps 24-Hours they had the measure of the rival Cologne Capris.

BMW

Make: *BMW*
Model: *CSL 'Batmobile'*
In production: *1973*
Engine: *3.0-litre (183-cubic-inch) straight-six*
Gearbox: *five-speed*
Power output: *280bhp*
Chassis: *unit-construction two-door coupé*

JAGUAR

Make: *Jaguar*
Model: *XJ-S*
In production: *1982-4*
Engine: *TWR-built 5.0-litre (305-cubic-inch) Jaguar V12*
Power output: *375bhp*
Gearbox: *five-speed Getrag*
Chassis: *unit-construction two-door coupé*

The V12-powered TWR-Motul-Jaguar XJ-S was one of the most successful Group A Touring Cars in 1984, with Walkinshaw/Heyer/Percy winning the challenging Spa 24-Hours. Its main challenger was the BMW 635CSi.

thunder was stolen when rally star Roger Clark's team of Alfa Romeo GTVs won the BMW Race Day at Brands Hatch. John Handley and Stan Clark also won the Manufacturers' Award for Alfa in the 1973 Tour of Britain. In the Tourist Trophy at Silverstone, Derek Bell and Harald Ertl won for BMW Alpina after a sterling drive by Jochen Mass in a Capri RS. Overall, the Escort BDAs were sufficiently fast and numerous to pip Alfa for the European Touring Car title by one point.

With big BMWs competing against Opel Commodores and a few Capris for race wins, the Alfa Romeo 2000 GTVs continued to dominate Class 2 in Europe during 1974 and 1975, and by 1976, the Alfetta GTV was taking its place with equal success. This model was developed into the Alfa GTV6, forming the bulk of mid-field action well into the mid-1980s and providing Andy Rouse with the means to win the British championship in 1983. It also provided me with the opportunity to go club racing in 1989. Back in 1974, though, another former Hillman Imp racer, Bernard Unett, took the title with the Sunbeam Avenger, while Andy Rouse scored the first of his string of championship victories in 1975 with a Triumph Dolomite Sprint. Motor sport tends to be episodic, with one model or another head and shoulders above the rest for a while, and the Dolomite Sprint was probably the best British touring car of the mid-1970s (BMW fans may disagree, of course).

Big American cars were excluded after the earlier rule changes, but Richard Lloyd and Stuart Graham revived the Camaro's successes in 1974 and 1975. The TransAm cars' European equivalent was the Ford Capri, and nobody put it to better use than Gordon Spice, winning the 3.0-litre (183-cubic-inch) class five times from 1976 to 1980. In 1976, Jaguar was back with the big 5.3-litre (323-cubic-inch) XJ-12 two-door coupé, which proved fast but unreliable, even in the capable hands of Rouse, Fitzpatrick and Derek Bell. The top European Touring Car scorer in 1976 was Pierre Dieudonné with a BMW 3.2 CSL, Dieter Quester winning the European title in 1977 in a similar car.

While the big shots squabbled for race wins, Unett made off with the British championship the next two years running in the Avenger. The Mini was still a force to be reckoned with, albeit in desecrated form with a squared-off nose, and in 1978 and 1979, engine-tuning wizard Richard Longman was top dog with his 1275 Mini GT. One of motor racing's top all-rounders, Win Percy, took two consecutive UK championships with the TWR Mazda RX-7, capturing a third title in 1982 with the Toyota GB Corolla.

Tom Walkinshaw's TWR organisation brought about the Jaguar revival on the European scene in 1982 with the V12 XJ-S, and the TWR team won the Brno GP, Nürburgring and Silverstone Tourist Trophy that year. Walkinshaw himself narrowly missed out on the European Touring Car title in 1983, but made sure of it in 1984 with a string of impressive victories, including the Spa-Francorchamps 24-Hour. His formidable opponents were the big BMWs, notably those of Dieter Quester, Helmut Kelleners and Hans Stuck. Its success assured, Jaguar then withdrew, leaving TWR to concentrate on racing the four-door 3.5-litre (214-cubic-inch) Rover SD1s, which were almost antiques by then in racing terms, although they had been dominant in their class in the early 1980s. Andy Rouse took two UK championship victories in 1984 and 1985 driving a self-prepared Rover SD1 Vitesse and Ford Sierra Turbo.

TURBO CHARGERS

This was the blossoming of the turbo era. Turbocharged cars were active in Formula 1 and the World Sports Car Championship, and it was a concept that even BMW, Saab and Porsche production cars had been using for nearly a decade. On the European Touring Car stage, the Volvo 242T with electronic traction control was surprisingly successful, with Renault 5 Maxi-Turbo and the R21 supreme in France, and the Alfa 75 Turbo in Italy. In Britain, bewinged Ford Sierra Cosworths began their indomitable rise. Despite their amazing 500bhp, a current BTCC car is faster around Brands Hatch circuit with the somewhat lower 300bhp, proving what a handful RS500 Sierras were to drive. Although Rouse was top Cossie driver in 1986, there were eight different winners at the 12 British rounds in 1987, and by virtue of consistent class wins, Chris Hodgetts was champion in 1986 and 1987 in the Toyota GB Corolla.

The RS500 Sierra Cosworth and the BMW M3 were purpose-built for acceptance, road cars that could be adapted for the circuit without much effort. Build a short run of a production model with enough competition kit on it and you have an instant basis for a race car as well as a future classic. Although they ran in different classes, the Cossie and M3 could vie with one another for outright championship honours. Another old hand, Nottingham garage proprietor and Clubmans racer Frank Sytner, showed what the turbocharged M3 could do in 1988 by taking eleven class wins and giving BMW its first British championship. Another driver who would establish a reputation as a tin-top specialist was John Cleland, who scored for Vauxhall Dealer Sport with the 16-valve Astra GTE the following year.

In 1990, the touring car formula was

refined to a two-class structure: up-to-2.0-litres and over-2.0-litres (122 cubic inches). Rob Gravett drove the Sierra Cosworth to nine victories in its last effective season, while Cleland halted Sytner's (and BMW's) winning streak with the new Vauxhall Cavalier. The following year, the new BTCC with its one-class 2.0-litre limit was launched, and that held sway until 2000, when fresh proposals were on the table.

SUPER TOURING

During the 1990s, touring car racing became acknowledged as the most consistently competitive form of saloon car racing. Now known as super touring, its special brand of close racing attracts the major manufacturers as

well as millions of devoted fans. The current era of touring car racing in Britain began with the 1991 British Touring Car Championship. The Group A supercars like the RS500 Sierra Cosworth were no longer eligible, and were replaced by the less extravagant family saloon-based 2.0-litre cars. This tempted many major manufacturers to participate, and they did this through existing racing teams and dedicated dealerships. Intense rivalry ensued.

The turbocharged Ford Sierra RS500 Cosworth was built by Aston Martin Tickford, and was usually ranged against the 2.3-litre BMW M3. This is the Eggenberger Motorsport car of Soper/Ludwig in 1988.

FORD

Make: *Ford*
Model: *Sierra Cosworth RS500*
In production: *1985-91*
Engine: *four-cylinder 2.0-litre (122-cubic-inch) turbo*
Power output: *500bhp*
Chassis: *seam-welded unit-construction two-door saloon*

At first, BMW, Vauxhall, Toyota, Ford, Mitsubishi, Mazda and Nissan were represented in the UK, and it was a huge success in terms of close racing, pitting front-wheel-drive cars against rear-wheel-drive. Also entered (occasionally) were four-wheel-drive cars like Dave Brodie's 4x4 Sapphire. Qualifying now actually meant that the line-up you saw on the grid was what it seemed, as in single-seater formulae, rather than a mixture of cars from different classes struggling for class points as much as overall success.

The inaugural BTCC title went right down to the wire with the rear-drive Vic Lee Motorsport BMW M3 of Will Hoy beating John Cleland's front-drive Vauxhall Cavalier. In 1991, the dominant team was VLM, Vic Lee's private venture. His cars' BMW engines were prepared by Mike Jordan's Eurotech firm in Coventry, and they proved faster in a straight line than rival BMWs. Part of Vic Lee's success was the choice of Yokohama and, latterly, Toyo tyres, which lasted better than Pirelli and Dunlop at the time. This ensured that drivers Hoy and Bellm were regular front runners, and Hoy got off the mark quickly with wins in the first couple of rounds.

The works BMWs were entrusted to Prodrive, with Jonathan Palmer, Steve Soper and Tim Sugden at the wheel. The series was sponsored by Esso, and eight of the 15 rounds in 1991 were won by rear-wheel-drive and seven by front-wheel-drive cars, although a weight penalty prevented the BMWs from being totally dominant. They had to carry some 99kg (218lb) ballast to counter their rear-drive advantage.

The Prodrive BMW M3s were shod with Pirelli tyres, and this proved their Achilles' heel as the tyres 'went off' after a few laps in hot weather. As it was, Tim Sugden scored once at a cool Brands Hatch in June, while Soper won three times. Cleland's Dunlop-shod Cavalier was fast in a straight line, and stable in long, sweeping bends because of its front-drive layout, but was handicapped like all front-drive cars with torque-steer and axle-tramp as it

struggled for traction exiting corners. Things improved when he went over to radial-ply tyres in mid-season.

The Andy Rouse-prepared Kaliber Toyota Carina finished third in the championship, which was a real achievement for a car with no competition pedigree. It did not start winning until the first-ever BTCC double-round, at Donington Park in July. Thereafter, Rouse used Yokohama tyres, and during the latter part of the season he was the most consistent performer, although the Carina was generally not as agile as either the BMW M3 or the Cavalier.

In 1992, the BTCC was under the management of TOCA, and set out to encourage new manufacturers. Having persuaded Peugeot and Mazda to get on board, TOCA added a sparkling package of support races to transform the BTCC into a top-class travelling show. For manufacturers, the stakes were raised. A good showing on the race track was reflected in a direct pay-off in the showroom, and what developed was a win-at-any-cost attitude, which resulted in even more bumping and boring to put the man in front into the gravel trap. Vauxhall began the season strongly with Cleland winning

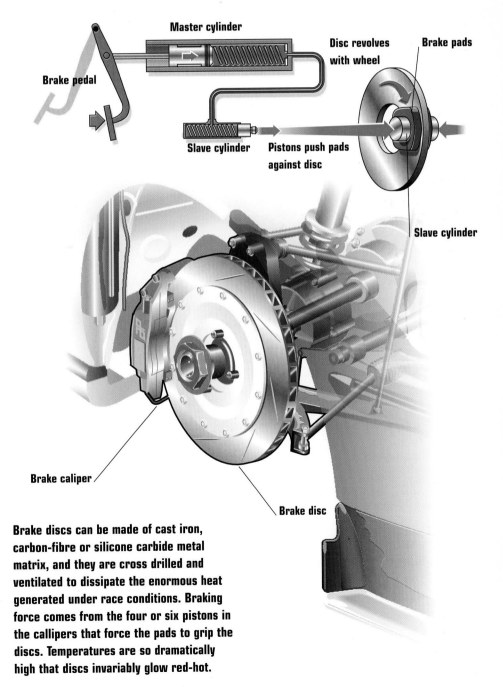

Brake pedal

Master cylinder

Disc revolves with wheel

Brake pads

Slave cylinder

Pistons push pads against disc

Slave cylinder

Brake caliper

Brake disc

Brake discs can be made of cast iron, carbon-fibre or silicone carbide metal matrix, and they are cross drilled and ventilated to dissipate the enormous heat generated under race conditions. Braking force comes from the four or six pistons in the callipers that force the pads to grip the discs. Temperatures are so dramatically high that discs invariably glow red-hot.

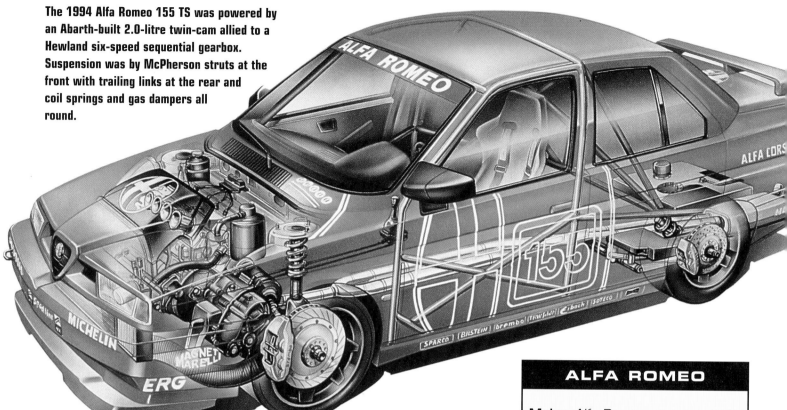

The 1994 Alfa Romeo 155 TS was powered by an Abarth-built 2.0-litre twin-cam allied to a Hewland six-speed sequential gearbox. Suspension was by McPherson struts at the front with trailing links at the rear and coil springs and gas dampers all round.

ALFA ROMEO

Make: *Alfa Romeo*
Model: *155 TS*
In production: *1992-6*
Engine: *Abarth-built 2.0-litre (122-cubic-inch) four-cylinder twin-spark*
Gearbox: *six-speed Hewland sequential*
Power output: *280bhp*
Chassis: *seam-welded unit-construction four-door saloon*

Wheels make a significant difference to the performance of any racing car, and lightweight magnesium alloy units are normally used to reduce the car's unsprung weight. The works-backed Super Touring teams carry large stocks with them to each round.

three of the first five events with the Yokohama-shod Cavalier GSi, but when Cleland was shunted out of the way because of a controversial incident with Steve Soper, Tim Harvey's fourth place at Silverstone in the Listerine-sponsored VLM BMW was enough to give him the title. For his part, Cleland spoke ominously of 'the slippery slope', and the incident caused him to consider what his future tactics should be.

In 1993, the series was sponsored for the first time by *Auto Trader* magazine,

and the season was also notable for Ford's comeback and for the first BTCC challenge from Renault. Both teams gained some race wins. It was also the first year in which FISA adopted the BTCC formula for its international touring car category, which meant that you could see virtually the same cars in action in European national championships, Australasia and even the USA.

BTCC newcomer Jo Winkelhock upset the form books by having the

edge over BMW sparring partner Steve Soper. The Schnitzer BMW squad staked its claim from the outset, running new four-door 318s saloons which were evolutions of the previous year's coupés, and Winkelhock and Soper won seven of the first eight races. While the better-qualifying front-wheel-drive cars squirmed for traction as the lights went green, the Yokohama-shod BMWs sailed sub-limely into the first corner and away from the rest of the field. The late-braking German won at Donington, twice at Oulton, at Pembrey and at Brands Hatch, and established such a lead in the championship that during the latter part of the season he was able to cruise home, the first non-British driver since 1973 to win the BTCC title.

ART FORM

Although the BMWs still ran on Yokohama tyres, Dunlop and Michelin were making up ground. There was also a general trend for super touring cars to have even lower and stiffer suspension, and the slightest tweaks brought about major differences in behaviour. Masses of computerised information was available from the cars' on-board telemetry data-logging equipment, and as cars grew increasingly sophisticated, they handled more and more like single-seaters. So close was the competition between cars that they only had to find half a second to make the difference between being a front runner and an also-ran.

Setting up the car became more of an art form, and team principals like Ray Mallock and Andy Rouse put their varied and extensive race experi-ence to good use to interpret all this data. It accounted for the Ecurie Ecosse Cavaliers' and Ford Mondeos' rapid improvement on the track in 1993. The Mallock-prepared Ecurie Ecosse Cavaliers were putting the works' Dealer Sport cars to shame, and at a fraction of their rival's budget. The RouseSport-prepared V6 Ford Mondeos appeared halfway through the season, and the New Zealander Paul Radisich claimed his maiden BTCC victory, and Ford's 200th win in touring cars, at Brands Hatch. The Mondeo had a wider track than any of its rivals, and was seen to ride the kerbs better than any other front-wheel-drive car.

ALFAS AND ESTATES

The FIA's end-of-season international Touring Car Challenge at Monza pointed the way to increased international competition and to an annual race at a different venue. It took place at Donington in 1994 and at the Paul Ricard circuit in Provence in 1995. In 1996 the race was scheduled for the Salzburgring in Austria, but was cancelled due to an insufficient number of entries. Back at Monza, the scarlet Alfa Romeo 155 TSs mixed it with the visiting BTCC circus, but Paul Radisich's Mondeo was never headed. Alfa Romeo would be one of 10 manufacturers represented in the 1994 British series.

The other major manufacturer to launch an assault on the BTCC in 1994 was Volvo. After the TWR team spent much time testing the 850 saloon and its estate version back-to-back, Volvo elected to go with the estate, as bizarre a vision as you can imagine. But the estate's chassis was apparently more rigid than that of the saloon. As TWR predicted, 1994 was more of a learning year for the team and star drivers Rickard Rydell and Jan Lammers found the estate to be fast but something of a handful in slower corners.

However, it was the Italian team which was to steal the spotlight with a well-planned attack, as the ex-Formula 1 racer Gabriele Tarquini won the first five rounds with the Michelin-

Phillippe Gache's Super Tourisme Alfa Romeo 155 is prepared in the pits garage at Nogaro in 1995. Its 280bhp 2.0-litre engine is canted back at 27 degrees for better weight distribution.

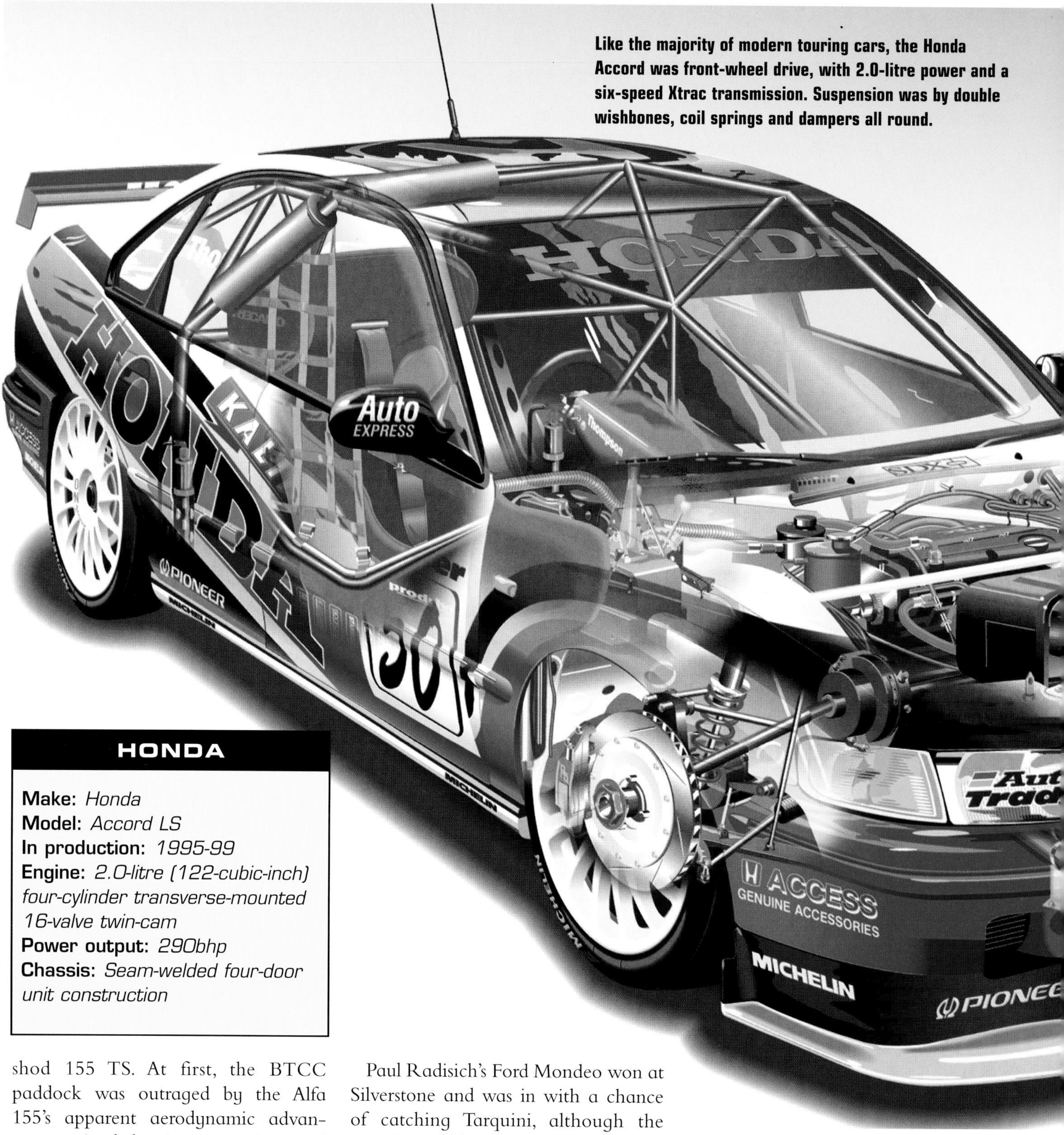

Like the majority of modern touring cars, the Honda Accord was front-wheel drive, with 2.0-litre power and a six-speed Xtrac transmission. Suspension was by double wishbones, coil springs and dampers all round.

HONDA

Make: *Honda*
Model: *Accord LS*
In production: *1995-99*
Engine: *2.0-litre (122-cubic-inch) four-cylinder transverse-mounted 16-valve twin-cam*
Power output: *290bhp*
Chassis: *Seam-welded four-door unit construction*

shod 155 TS. At first, the BTCC paddock was outraged by the Alfa 155's apparent aerodynamic advantage, gained by its rear wing and adjustable front air–dam's splitter, which had been legitimately sanctioned by the FIA, of course. When the Ford team's protest was upheld by the RAC Motor Sports Association, Alfa Romeo withdrew from the May Oulton Park meeting. After a compromise was reached, the Alfas rejoined the fray at Donington. But from then on, the splitters would be pushed back.

Paul Radisich's Ford Mondeo won at Silverstone and was in with a chance of catching Tarquini, although the promise of the previous season had evaporated with a string of engine problems, and he had to settle for third in the title race. Consistency paid off, and Menu ended the season second in the points standings. Cleland's Mallock-prepared Vauxhall entered the reckoning after he had attained a sparkling double victory at Donington, but Allam played a strictly supporting role. Another two wins at Brands

Hatch for Tarquini strengthened his grip on the title. His major setback of the season came at Knockhill, where Harvey flipped him into a spectacular roll. Jo Winkelhock fought back into contention for BMW following a mid-season weight review which resulted in rear-drive cars losing 25kg (55lb), while the rest of the field, being front-drive, gained that amount. Thus, the 1993 champion won four times in the

Engine and brake cooling is more highly evolved in touring cars than in their road-going equivalents, and is also related to aerodynamic considerations. Higher operating temperatures require air to be scooped from the car's lower intakes and ducted to the radiator, while hot air is spilled out through the wheel arches.

1. Air ducted to radiators through lower air intakes

2. Air from radiator ducted out through wheel-arches. Also used to cool brakes

3. Air supply for engine through radiator grille into airbox

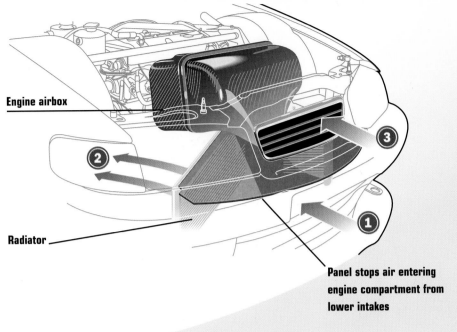

Engine airbox

Radiator

Panel stops air entering engine compartment from lower intakes

dynamically superior 318i. One of these wins was at Silverstone at the British Grand Prix meeting, where he was hounded by the Alfa 155 of Tarquini, sporting its revised front splitter.

Nissan drivers Eric van der Poele and Keith O'dor excelled themselves during this race by depositing their Primeras in front of Nissan's hospitality suite at the first corner. Matt Neal's Silverstone tumble also marked the end of the

Mazda Xedos challenge, which lacked the benefit of sufficient corporate funds to continue, and Neal and David Leslie were left high and dry. Now in the Peugeot team, Patrick Watts did well in the 405, but poor aerodynamics spoiled an otherwise good car. Meanwhile, Tarquini continued to build up the points with high-scoring finishes while Menu emerged as the only possible title contender with a string of good performances. But second place and a win at Silverstone's double-header clinched the titles for Tarquini and Alfa Romeo. The icing on the cake was team-mate Giampiero Simoni's win in the last round of the season at Brands Hatch.

The FIA Touring Car Challenge meeting doubled as the Tourist Trophy race at Donington, and was a decisive win for Radisich and the Mondeo, staving off 38 European Super Touring aces. Frank Biela's third-placed Audi 80 Quattro was punted off by Winkelhock, who claimed the Audi's brake lights were not working. Newly crowned BTCC champion Tarquini managed fourth despite a big first-lap altercation with Cleland and Emanuele Pirro's Audi 80 Quattro.

MORE NEW WHEELS AND FACES

The Schnitzer BMW and Nissan teams pulled out at the end of the season, and Alfa Corsa left its 155TS cars in the hands of Prodrive. The new faces for

1995 were the Williams Grand Prix team's subsidiary running the Renault Lagunas, Honda Accords, and stars such as Derek Warwick, two-wheel champ Johnny Cecotto, Kelvin Burt and David Brabham. For the first time the FIA stopped referring to Class 2 touring cars in favour of the term 'super touring', and there were 25 rounds for the nine manufacturers to contest.

Alfa Romeo promptly suffered a reversal of fortune as Derek Warwick and Simoni struggled with their under-developed new wide-track 155s running outclassed engines. Even when they drafted Tarquini back in at mid-season, there was no recovery, and the star cars for 1995 were the Laguna newcomers and the Volvos, with Cleland's Cavalier soldiering on. There was intense pressure from the 20-valve Volvo 850s, which were saloons now instead of estates, but as a result of a skirmish at Snetterton – Harvey punted out Alain Menu's Laguna in two successive races – TWR was fined a hefty £10,000.

Rickard Rydell started from pole position 13 times, but managed just four wins and third place in the championship, which seemed scant reward. Harvey won rounds three and four at Brands Hatch, and was second to Rydell at Knockhill, and to Hoy at Snetterton. But as Volvo's star waned, so that of the Laguna proved to be in the

Although the Audi A4 Quattros suffered a weight penalty because of their four-wheel drive traction advantage, Frank Biela knotched up enough wins and points finishes to take the 1996 BTCC title.

ascendant, and Renault's success turned out to be positively dramatic towards the end of the year. Menu excelled at the Oulton Park meeting, winning three out of four races there. He and Will Hoy filled the first two places in September, too, to give the Lagunas their first one–two result. The triumph was repeated at the last meeting of the season at Silverstone, Menu winning and Hoy coming second in round 24, and the places were reversed in round 25. Menu's tally of seven wins, one more than champion Cleland, made him runner-up in the championship; Hoy won three times.

The reliability of the Cavalier, now in its last season, made the difference though, and John Cleland claimed his second drivers' title almost at a canter, winning six races and scoring well in almost all the remaining rounds.

In the modern era, serious accidents are thankfully rare in touring car racing, but there was tragedy in the BTCC ranks when Keith O'dor was killed at Berlin's Avus race track. He was competing for Nissan in the German Superturenwagen series and

AUDI

Make: *Audi*
Model: *A4 Quattro*
In production: *1996-8*
Engine: *2.0-litre (122-cubic-inch) four-cylinder dry-sump Audi Sport*
Gearbox: *permanent 4x4, six-speed Audi sequential*
Power output: *296bhp*
Chassis: *seam-welded unit-construction four-door saloon*

had already won a race that day – ironically Nissan's first German success – and had put the year-old car on pole for the next event. In a mid-race incident, his Primera was T-boned by another competitor while it was stationary in the middle of the track. One of the top Australian touring car racers, Gregg Hansford, had also died in a similar incident in his Mondeo at Phillip Island earlier in the year.

FOUR-WHEEL-DRIVE

The FIA's Touring Car Challenge race was held in October at the Paul Ricard circuit. There were 40 of the world's best tin-top exponents present, but most of the BTCC aces qualified well down the rankings. The four-wheel-drive Audi 80 Quattros of German aces Frank Biela, Hans Stuck and Italian

champion Emanuele Pirro set the pace, while the BMW 318is were the Audi's closest challengers, driven by Steve Soper, Johnny Cecotto, Yvan Muller and Roberto Ravaglia. They had been unable to demonstrate much form in the BTCC, and the reason for their renaissance was that the higher-down-force wing settings of the majority of BTCC cars were fine for British circuits, but they simply did not work for the front-drive cars on the ultra-fast Paul Ricard circuit.

The entry of the four-wheel-drive Audi A4s of German star Frank Biela and BTCC rookie John Bintcliffe was the big news for the BTCC in 1996. Ranged against this untried pairing were the Schnitzer BMWs of Roberto Ravaglia and Jo Winkelhock, plus the other front runners of 1995. At the Donington opening rounds, Biela was on his way, and it was the same at Brands Hatch for round three, although Winkelhock came through to win round four. The Audi pairing of Biela and Bintcliffe managed fourth and fifth here, but on the fast, sweeping expanses of Thruxton where at every bend your heart is in your mouth, the Audis once more looked supreme. They cleaned up in round five, but round six was a different matter with Winkelhock and Ravaglia making it a BMW one–two. Someone else had to get a look in at some stage, and Kelvin Burt demonstrated the Volvo's speed at Silverstone, winning round seven. But the BMWs were not far behind. Meanwhile, the Vauxhalls slid further back, the Hondas and Peugeots trod water in the mid-field, and the Mondeos were well out of the picture.

At Oulton Park, round nine went to Winkelhock, and round 10 to Rydell in the Volvo. By the time the circus arrived at sunny Snetterton in June, the Audis were no longer the threat they had appeared to be at the beginning of the year, partly due to the imposition of a 30kg (66lb) weight penalty, administered by the controlling body TOCA in a bid to maintain some sort of parity between the different runners. One consequence was that Jo Winkelhock started both Snetterton races from pole, coming fifth in the first race and winning the second.

Rounds 13 and 14 on the Brands Hatch Grand Prix circuit were somewhat processional compared with what had become the usual cut and thrust of BTCC races, but they were also a double triumph for Alain Menu's Renault Laguna, with Hoy in contention too. Frank Biela's second place in round 13 took him further ahead in the points table, but Menu's pace at Brands made him look like a potential champion. And so it would prove.

The 1997 season was dominated by the Renault Lagunas, with Alain Menu virtually invincible and his new team-mate Jason Plato also a winner. At the late May double-header at Oulton Park, Menu topped the podium twice and was thereafter way ahead in the points table, and Plato lay third in the championship, behind Volvo S40 pilot Rickard Rydell.

The following year it was the turn of Volvo to top the charts, with Rickard Rydell in the S40 taking the drivers' honours. Anthony Reid in a Nissan Primera was the closest challenger, with James Thompson next up. The manufacturers' points positions were reversed, Nissan beating Volvo and Renault taking third. In 1999, Laurent Aiello emerged at the top of the pile, with David Leslie not so far behind. Rydell and Thompson were next up in the points standings, and it was Nissan's year again, ahead of Honda and Volvo.

BTCC IN CRISIS

With many of the same faces in the pack year after year there's a strong element of swings and roundabouts to the results, and maybe just a little bit of complacency creeps in. This manifested itself towards the end of 1999, and in many respects not only the BTCC but super touring in general had reached a crisis point. It was certainly clear that the BTCC had run out of steam. Not only had the manufacturers elected to leave in droves, including 1999 championship winners Nissan, but the continuing jurisdiction of the organising body TOCA was in some doubt. At the time of writing it appeared likely that a consortium which included circuit owners, called British Motorsport Promoters, would take over in 2002. Participating teams felt they had been taken hostage by the organisers, who threatened to import contenders from the national saloon car championships to make up the numbers. The outcome could be a two-tier BTCC with a 'super production' category for the works-backed teams and a second division for privateers. This is not so far removed from the days of the Total Cup independents, and it would also introduce an element of variety, with a number of hatchbacks joining the four-door saloons.

SUPER TOURING IN EUROPE

As the category went into crisis in Europe in 1999, the FIA threw a lifeline to competitors who were still interested, and sanctioned a European Super Touring Cup. There would be six rounds in Italy and four at European tracks not that far away from the Alps: the A1 Ring, Brno, Ljubliana and Magny-Cours. This suggested that the key protagonists would be BMW with its CiBiEmme teams and Alfa Romeo

Touring car racing can be a contact sport, but mud wrestling isn't often on the agenda. But 1999 BTCC Champion Laurent Aiello gives it a go at Silverstone in 1999, indulging in a spot of autocross with his Ray Mallock-prepared Nissan Primera.

The 2.5-litre (152.5-cubic-inch) V6 AMG-prepared Mercedes-Benz C-Class boasted 450bhp and won the German Touring Car Championship (DTM) in 1994 and 1995, as well as the International Touring Car series (ITC) in 1995 and 1996 against equally sophisticated Class 1 opposition from Opel and Alfa Romeo.

under Nordauto, both well versed in super touring practice.

In the wake of the successful 155 touring cars of the early part of the 1990s, Alfa Romeo produced two competition versions of the 156. The milder of the two was the virtually standard Group N car, which ran with the 2.0-litre (122-cubic-inch) Twin Spark engine. Most of the preparation of the Group N model was carried out at the factory, like stripping out the interiors of finished production cars and installing the basic competition accessories like a roll-over cage, racing seat, six-point safety harness and fire extinguisher.

The second was the Group A 156 Superturismo which, like the BTCC-winning 155 of half a decade earlier, complied with a far more liberal set of regulations. The 156 Superturismo power unit was based on the crankcase and cylinder head of the regular engine, but extensively modified with specially made manifolds, pistons, cams and cranks to give square internal dimensions of 86mm x 86mm (3.39 inches x 3.39 inches). A dedicated engine management system controlled the electronic ignition and injection system, with dry-sump lubrication, and it developed 300bhp at 8,200rpm. Like the 155, the whole engine and gearbox unit was set lower and further back in the engine bay to improve weight distribution. Transmission was via a six-speed X-Trac sequential shift allied to a self-locking diff and viscous coupling, while the rose-jointed suspension set-up included driver-adjustable anti-roll bars. High-speed progress of the Group A 156 Superturismo was retarded by mighty 335mm (13.19-inch) Brembo ventilated discs with eight-piston callipers, cooled by way of yellow-coloured

Kevlar ducting that framed the engine bay. The cars ran on white-painted multi-spoke 482mm (19-inch) OZ magnesium alloy wheels shod with Michelin race tyres. Built-in air jacks enabled them to free-stand in the clinical telemetry-dominated surroundings of the pits garages.

Two cars were campaigned by Nordauto under team manager Monica Sims in the Italian national series in 1998 and 1999, driven by Nicola Larini and Fabrizio 'Piedone' ('Big Foot') Giovanardi. Although Giovanardi won at Imola in the car's second outing, they struggled on some circuits to hold their own against the time-served 3-series BMWs.

HIGH-TECH MONSTERS

They are dinosaurs now, in so far as they are extinct. Their reign at the top of the touring car tree lasted but a

couple of years, but in a Jurassic Park scenario, they may come back, albeit with less sophistication. They were the cars of the International Touring Car Championship, introduced by the FIA in 1996 for Class 1 vehicles. The series emerged from the high-tech German DTM touring car series, and in addition to 12 races in Germany and 10 elsewhere in Europe, there were rounds in Japan and Brazil to make a 26-round series. Not international exactly, but getting there.

The Class 1 cars were vastly more modified than the Class 2 super touring machines which contested the BTCC and other national championships, and in 1996 only three manufacturers took part: Mercedes-Benz, Opel and Alfa Romeo. Mercedes raced the big C-class model, Alfa chose the 155 V6, and Opel the V6 Calibra. The Opels and Alfas were four-wheel-

GERMAN TOURING CAR CHAMPIONSHIP (DTM)

1984	Volker Strycek (D), **Gubin BMW**	1990	Hans Stuck (D), **SMS Audi**
1985	Per Stureson (S), **IPS Volvo**	1991	Frank Biela (D), **AZR Audi**
1986	Kurt Thiim (DK), **Nickel Rover**	1992	Klaus Ludwig (D), **AMG Mercedes**
1987	Eric van der Poele (B), **Zakspeed BMW**	1993	Nicola Larini (I), **Alfa Romeo 155 TS**
1988	Klaus Ludwig (D), **Graf Ford**	1994	Klaus Ludwig (D), **AMG Mercedes**
1989	Roberto Ravaglia (I), **Schnitzer BMW**	1995	Bernd Schneider (D), **AMG Mercedes**

drive machines, while the Mercedes was rear-drive only. Their highly sophisticated specifications bordered on Formula 1 territory, and included double-wishbone suspension all round, hydraulically cockpit-adjustable anti-roll bars, ABS brakes, power-assisted steering and, in the Opel's case, magnesium wheel carriers and titanium hubs. The Opel and Alfa had eight-piston calliper front brakes, the Mercedes six, with four at the rear in all cases. The cars were built up on chassis that bore no relation to their super touring cousins, let alone their road-going counterparts. In fact, the way they were put together bore more similarity to NASCAR stock car construction.

The maximum permitted engine capacity was 2.5 litres (153 cubic inches) and six cylinders. No turbos were allowed, but even so, each car produced about 500bhp. The Alfa's engine was developed in-house by Alfa Corse, the Opel's was the result of Cosworth's research, and Mercedes' V6 was derived from their production V8 and developed by the specialist AMG

concern. Transmissions were equally advanced for competition cars: the 4WD Alfa 155 used an automatic computerised six-speed gearbox, the 4WD Opel a semi-automatic computerised Williams six-speed box, and the rear-wheel-drive Mercedes' transmission incorporated a six-speed sequential shift. Both Alfa and Opel had three electronically controlled diff locks, while the Mercedes favoured a mechanical locking diff with ASR traction control.

The Opel, Mercedes-Benz and Alfa Romeo were comparable designs, and highly competitive, but racing success incurred a weight penalty. Anyone finishing in the top five earned ballast of up to 50kg (110lb), which was shed only by coming lower than fifth. The rounds were staged in pairs at each venue, with a gap of 10 minutes between races, and grid positions for the second race were based upon the result of the earlier one. Venues ranged from converted street layouts (like Helsinki) to regular purpose-built circuits (like Hockenheim). At the

tighter street-circuit tracks, physical contact between the contenders was frequent and violent; the second ITC race at Estoril in 1996 had to be stopped because of a completely blocked track.

As in super touring events, the drivers competing in Class 1 ITC came from a variety of racing backgrounds, and it was a popular place for Formula 1 exiles, sports car drivers and all-rounders. The cars were fabulous creations, and it was hard to beat in terms of sheer spectacle, but the championship collapsed in political and financial turmoil at the end of the 1996 season. Plans for a revival of the ITC concept in the revised German DTM in 2000 drew commitments from several manufacturers, including former F1 champion Keke Rosberg managing a team of Mercedes SLKs, a number of Opel teams using V8-engined Astra-based coupés, and a quartet of Audi TT Quattros. Not quite as high-tech as the ITC runners perhaps, but just as formidable-looking.

BRITISH TOURING CAR CHAMPIONSHIP

1958 Jack Sears (GB), **Austin Westminster**
1959 Jeff Uren (GB), **Ford Zephyr**
1960 Doc Shepherd (GB), **Don Moore Austin A40**
1961 Sir John Whitmore (GB), **Mini Cooper**
1962 John Love (ZA), **Vita Mini Cooper**
1963 Jack Sears (GB), **Willment Lotus Cortina**
1964 Jim Clark (GB), **Team Lotus Cortina**
1965 Roy Pierpoint (GB), **Ford Mustang**
1966 John Fitzpatrick (GB), **Broadspeed Ford Anglia**
1967 Frank Gardner (AUS), **Alan Mann Falcon**
1968 Frank Gardner (AUS), **Alan Mann Ford Escort**
1969 Alec Poole (GB), **Arden Mini Cooper**
1970 Bill McGovern (GB), **George Bevan Sunbeam Imp**
1971 Bill McGovern (GB), **George Bevan Sunbeam Imp**
1972 Bill McGovern (GB), **George Bevan Sunbeam Imp**
1973 Frank Gardner (AUS), **SCA Chevrolet Camaro**
1974 Bernard Unett (GB), **CDT Hillman Imp**
1975 Andy Rouse (GB), **Broadspeed Triumph Dolomite Sprint**
1976 Bernard Unett (GB), **CDT Chrysler Avenger**
1977 Bernard Unett (GB), **CDT Chrysler Avenger**
1978 Richard Longman (GB), **Mini Cooper**

1979 Richard Longman (GB), **Mini Cooper**
1980 Win Percy (GB), **TWR Mazda RX7**
1981 Win Percy (GB), **TWR Mazda**
1982 Win Percy (GB), **Toyota GB Toyota Celica**
1983 Andy Rouse (GB), **Rouse Alfa Romeo GTV6**
1984 Andy Rouse (GB), **Rouse Rover Vitesse**
1985 Andy Rouse (GB), **Rouse Ford Sierra Cosworth RS500**
1986 Chris Hodgetts (GB), **Toyota GB Toyota Corolla**
1987 Chris Hodgetts (GB), **Toyota GB Toyota Corolla**
1988 Frank Sytner (GB), **Prodrive BMW M3**
1989 John Cleland (GB), **Dave Cook Vauxhall Astra**
1990 Robb Gravett (GB), **Trakstar Ford Sierra Cosworth**
1991 Will Hoy (GB), **VLM BMW M3**
1992 Tim Harvey (GB), **VLM BMW M3**
1993 Joachim Winkelhock (D), **Schnitzer BMW 318is**
1994 Gabriele Tarquini (I), **Alfa Romeo 155 TS**
1995 John Cleland (GB), **Ecosse Vauxhall Cavalier**
1996 Frank Biela (D), **Audi Sport UK Audi A4 quattro**
1997 Alain Menu (CH), **Williams Renault Laguna**
1998 Rickard Rydell (S), **TWR Volvo S40**
1999 Laurent Aiello (F), **RMR Nissan Primera**

AUSTRALIAN TOURING CARS

In the USA the iconic race is the Indianapolis 500, sports car racing has Le Mans, and the Australians have the Bathurst 1000. Without question it is one of the very best tin-top races in the world, where the racing is fast and furious and goes on for six hours. The series is called V8 Supercars to distinguish from 2.0-litre (122-cubic-inch) Supertourers. The Bathurst Classic is now a 2.0-litre race swiftly followed by the V8 Supercars race which is the one everyone want to see.

The Bathurst Classic is also known as the Tooheys 1000 in deference to its beer sponsor, and is staged on the famously hard, fast, steep circuit called Mount Panorama near Bathurst. It is a real occasion, as much for spectators as competitors. The spot designated the 'Top of the Hill' becomes a virtual no-go area for the police and decent God-fearing types over race weekend, as those with more cubic centimetres than brain cells perform drunken burn-outs and doughnuts on the circuit's campsite back roads.

It has been Australia's most important domestic motor race for over sixty years. The event goes back to Easter 1938, and its history has been episodic according to rule

Waiting for the off at the Bathurst 1000. Although Australia has a flourishing super touring series, it is also home to the V8 supercar saloon category that features indigenous Holden and Ford products. These vehicles are slightly larger than their European counterparts, and smaller than US sedans, but they invariably run 5.0-litre (305-cubic inch) V8 engines.

changes, and the fortunes of the main contenders in Ford and General Motors Holdens have ebbed and flowed accordingly. During the 1950s the Ford Zephyrs were no match for the Holden hordes, which outnumbered the Fords ten to one, even when these had been tuned up. Until the rules were tightened in 1960, Bathurst was a bit of a free-for-all. Then in 1964, the Lotus Cortina turned everything on its

head, and, as in Europe, the lighter Ford could beat the heavier and more powerful Jaguar Mk II. Holden's S4 Bathurst Specials did not get a look in, and before long there were even locally built limited-edition Cortina GT 500s that had been specially tailored for the Bathurst event. Frank Gardner and Kevin Bartlett shared the Alec Mildren team's Alfa Romeo TI Super to win the Six Hours of Sandown Park in 1964

Touring car superstar Craig Lowndes spurs his Holden over the kerbs as he carves his way through the pack, having started at the back of the grid for the April round of the Australian Championship at Adelaide in April 1999.

and 1965, and although subsequently Alfa and other European makes like BMW clawed back some of the ground lost to the Lotus Cortina, it was the dominant car in the mid-1960s. Indeed, Gardner went to Europe to race them with considerable success.

AMERICAN STYLE
Although the Mini-Cooper S was prominent in 1966, the next phase of Bathurst history belonged to the American-style Mustang-derived Falcon GT. This was another comparatively light car, yet it was far more powerful than the Mini-Cooper S, and lap times tumbled accordingly. The big

Holden Special Vehicles hired Tom Walkinshaw's TWR concern to mastermind its touring car racing programme; the result was put to good effect in 1996, 1998 and 1999 by Craig Lowndes who took the Australian title for Holden. At the close of 1999, Lowndes teamed up with Cameron McConville for the Bathurst enduro.

The sound and the fury of the V8 Supercars erupts as the pack charges down John Bowe's backfiring Cat-sponsored Ford Falcon into turn 1 at the start of the Queensland round of the Aussie series in July 1999.

two alternated at the top of the podium as boardroom battles were enacted on the race track. In 1967 it was the turn of the Ford Falcon GT, while in 1968 the Monaro was in the frame as General Motors-Holden smartened up its image. Up to 1972, when Alan Moffat's TransAm Mustang lost out to Pete Geoghegan's Falcon GT, the Aussie Fords reigned supreme. Certain Holdens did win races though, including Bruce McPhee and Barry Mulholland's GTS Monaro 327 V8 which won the Hardie-Ferodo 500 in 1968, and Colin Bond and Tony Roberts who won the event in a similar Holden in 1969.

Both Ford and Holden went in for impenetrable model designations with suffixes that almost defied logic. The Falcon GT Phase I XR was the one to have, followed in succession by the Phase II XW and its ultimate development, the highly desirable XY Phase III GTHO. Australians tend to prefer their saloons to have four doors, and although the late-1960s Falcon,

Monaro and Charger were two-door fastbacks in the popular pony car mould, the next generation were all four-door saloons. These big tourers were involved in breathtaking confrontations on Mount Panorama, and it was usually the Holden Monaro HT and HGs and L34 Torana XU-1 V8s versus the Ford Falcons of one phase or another, and Chrysler was battling in there too with its E49 R/T Charger V8

muscle-car. Of the Europeans, only the Alfa Romeo Giulia GTA coupés of John French and Kevin Bartlett could hold a candle to the mighty V8s. When the power output of these supercars became too scary, the authorities put a stop to the surge, albeit briefly. The low-volume 200-a-year production racers were banned and the rules were changed to allow certain modifications so that different cars came to the fore.

In 1973, when the Bathurst was first run to a 1000km (620-mile) format, falling in with FIA norms at the Nürburgring or Brands Hatch, Moffat and Geoghegan drove a new two-door fastback Ford Falcon XA coupé to victory, and this model remained a potential winner for the rest of the decade. Peter Brock and Brian Sampson won in 1975 in a Torana L34, and Bob Morris and John Fitzpatrick emulated them in 1976. Then Alan Moffat and Colin Bond made it a Ford one–two with Falcon. Superbirds in

Former single-seater ace Larry Perkins cocks a wheel of his be-winged Holden as he negotiates a turn during the Australian touring car series. For 2000, the Perkins Holden team boasted Russell Ingall on the strength, and Perkins started off the season with a 5th at Phillip Island.

Being at the top means giving it ten-tenths, and sometimes it goes horribly wrong. Three-times V8 Supercar Champ Craig Lowndes flipped his Holden in a major way at Calder Park in July 1999. Underside reveals V8 exhaust headers, prop shaft and plumbed-in fire extinguisher.

1977. A Holden A9X Torana and a 308 Commodore in the hands of Peter Brock and Jim Richards bounced back to trounce the Fords in 1978, and it was much the same story in the following years as the two makes see-sawed their way up and down the podium. Peter Brock's Marlboro-Holden Dealer Team

The pits garages at Sandown are as clinical as those at any international circuit. Here, a pair of Holdens are elevated on their built-in pneumatic jacks as pre-race fettling takes place in February 1998.

car set the pace in 1979 and 1980, then Dick Johnson restored Ford's success with the Falcon XD in 1981. The following year, Holden had recovered, and Brock and Larry Perkins's Commodore led a four-car clean sweep in the Bathurst derby.

In 1983 the Australian Touring Car Championship was won by a Wankel-engined Mazda RX7 coupé driven by Alan Moffat, and at Mount Panorama he naturally posed a threat. But it generally takes a big car to stand up to the pounding of 1000km, and it

Being at the top means giving it ten-tenths, and sometimes it goes horribly wrong. Three-times V8 Supercar Champ Craig Lowndes flipped his Holden in a major way at Calder Park in July 1999. Underside reveals V8 exhaust headers, prop shaft and plumbed-in fire extinguisher.

was Peter Brock's Commodore that triumphed again, hitting 270km/h (168mph) along the celebrated Conrod straight. Just to make sure nobody got the wrong idea, Brock and Perkins won the event again with a Commodore in 1984.

RULE CHANGES

Then the rules changed to international Group A specifications in 1985, and Ford was caught on the hop. The victory at Bathurst went to John Goss and Armin Hahne in the TWR Jaguar XJS V12 – the model's final triumph on the international scene. Then Holden put matters to rights, coming back to the fore as Alan Grice and Graeme Bailey won with a Commodore in 1986. Another major change was in the offing, however, and in 1987 Dick Johnson was the first and initially the fastest of the next generation of Ford runners, bringing the new 550bhp turbocharged Sierra Cosworth to

It's Ford versus Holden as the packed V8 Supercar grid roars off towards turn 1 at Eastern Creek during the first round of the ATCC in 1996.

Bathurst. It was an era of comprehensive domination, and in the late 1980s Sierra Cosworths reigned supreme. The Nissan Skyline GT-Rs briefly wore the crown, but the Bathurst winner's circle reverted to its familiar two-make parade with the home-grown 5.0-litre (305-cubic-inch) V8 Ford Falcon and Holden Commodore going for each other.

The 2.0-litre (122-cubic-inch) super touring cars came to Australia in 1990, a reflection of the increasing number of European cars on the streets. British Touring Car Championship regulars Jeff Allam, John Cleland, Win Percy and Steve Soper, plus Kiwi Paul Radisich and German Jo Winkelhock, were honorary Bathurst veterans. Former British saloon car champion Frank Gardner then recruited Soper, Allam and Winkelhock to bolster BMW's four-car assault in 1993. Locals going in for super touring were Geoff Brabham and Jim Richards, both of whom won races at Adelaide with a Mondeo in 1995, while legends like Peter Brock, Mark Skaife, Alan Jones

and Alan Moffat were the big draws at Bathurst's six-hour marathon.

2000

With super touring at a crossroads in 2000, V8 Supercars presented an attractive way to go for some tin-top drivers, including ASTC Champions Brad

Jones in the ex-Tony Longhurst Ford Falcon AU, and Paul 'The Dude' Morris running a Holden Commodore VS. The 2000 season got under way with wins at Phillip Island for Craig Baird and Craig Lowndes, while Garth Tander moved into a series lead with two 2nd places.

AUSTRALIAN TOURING CAR CHAMPIONSHIP

1960	David McKay (AUS), *Jaguar*	1980	Peter Brock (AUS), *Holden*
1961	Bill Pitt (AUS), *Jaguar*	1981	Dick Johnson (AUS), *Ford*
1962	Bob Jane (AUS), *Jaguar*	1982	Dick Johnson (AUS), *Ford*
1963	Bob Jane (AUS), *Jaguar*	1983	Allan Moffat (AUS), *Mazda*
1964	Ian Geoghegan (AUS), *Ford*	1984	Dick Johnson (AUS), *Ford*
1965	Norm Beechey (AUS), *Ford*	1985	Jim Richards (NZ), *BMW*
1966	Ian Geoghegan (AUS), *Ford*	1986	Robbie Francevic (AUS), *Volvo*
1967	Ian Geoghegan (AUS), *Ford*	1987	Jim Richards (NZ), *BMW*
1968	Ian Geoghegan (AUS), *Ford*	1988	Dick Johnson (AUS), *Ford*
1969	Ian Geoghegan (AUS), *Ford*	1989	Dick Johnson (AUS), *Ford*
1970	Norm Beechey (AUS), *Holden*	1990	Jim Richards (NZ), *Nissan*
1971	Bob Jane (AUS), *Chevrolet*	1991	Jim Richards (NZ), *Nissan*
1972	Bob Jane (AUS), *Chevrolet*	1992	Mark Skaife (AUS), *Nissan*
1973	Allan Moffat (AUS), *Ford*	1993	Glenn Seton (AUS), *Ford*
1974	Peter Brock (AUS), *Holden*	1994	Mark Skaife (AUS), *Holden*
1975	Colin Bond (AUS), *Holden*	1995	John Bowe (AUS), *Ford*
1976	Allan Moffat (AUS), *Ford*	1996	Craig Lowndes (AUS), *Holden*
1977	Allan Moffat (AUS), *Ford*	1997	Glenn Seton (AUS), *Ford*
1978	Peter Brock (AUS), *Holden*	1998	Craig Lowndes (AUS), *Holden*
1979	Rob Morris (AUS), *Holden*	1999	Craig Lowndes (AUS), *Holden*

TRANSAM SEDAN SERIES

The TransAm championship has the distinction of being the oldest continuously running road race series in North America. The winners – including Mark Donohue, Dan Gurney, Parnelli Jones and Peter Revson – became household names, noted in other spheres of the sport. The manufacturers involved were the major US players, fielding Ford Mustangs, Chevrolet Camaros, AMC Javelins and Mercury Cougars.

Held on road circuits rather than the purpose-built ovals that were home to stock cars, the series was originally billed as the Trans American Sedan Championship. It was first staged on 25 March 1966, at Sebring International Raceway, Florida, as a warm-up for the 12-Hour Sports Car Race. The regulations were based on the FIA's Groups 1 and 2 saloon car rules, and the sanctioning body and series developer of the TransAm series, the Sports Car Club of America (SCCA), began to develop a professional racing programme. Points in the TransAm Championship were awarded to the car, rather than the driver, and this fostered a manufacturer-based series that eventually brought a huge financial commitment from Ford, Dodge, Chevrolet, Pontiac and AMC. Pontiac was sufficiently bullish to name its road-going pony car the TransAm, and paid the SCCA a five-dollar royalty for every TransAm car it built.

Detroit's Big Three manufacturers hired the 'top guns' to drive their TransAm cars, and their slogan was 'Win on Sunday, sell on Monday.' Thus, Ford Mustangs were piloted by stars like Parnelli Jones, A.J.Foyt, George Follmer and Peter Revson, and they were paid to win.

Bearing the scars of Bussinello's practice crash, Jochen Rindt's Alfa Romeo GTA was first overall and under 2.0-litre (122-cubic-inch) 'U2' class winner in the very first TransAm race at Sebring in 1966. The GTA was powered by a twin-plug head 1600 twin-cam engine.

The original TransAm Championship was divided into two classes: O2 for over-2.0-litre (122-cubic-inch) engines and U2 for under-2.0-litre. The U2 class was the province of primarily European sports saloons such as the Alfa Romeo Sprint 1600 GTA, Ford Lotus Cortina and Austin Mini-Cooper S. Running in the O2 class were the powerful pony cars (an equestrian reference to the Mustang) built by Detroit's big three. There was strong manufacturing support for the independent entrants, and many of the big-name stars were attracted. On pole for the inaugural TransAm Championship race in 1966 was Indy hero A.J. Foyt, with Formula 1 ace Jochen Rindt behind him in an Alfa, alongside Bob Tullius in a Dodge Dart. No fewer than 44 cars started that race, and the winner of the U2 division and the first driver across the line in either class was Rindt, his GTA somewhat battered. Tullius, who finished second overall, was the winner of the O2 class.

Early TransAm races were very long, averaging over five hours in 1966 and three to four hours over the next few years. Seven events were staged during the first year, and there was a remarkable mixture of talent and competition. Stock car greats Richard Petty and David Pearson appeared in 1966, and European touring car champion Sir John Whitmore and Belgian Formula 1 star Jacky Ickx raced Lotus Cortinas several times. In the early days, the U2 class shared much of the limelight with the bigger cars, as they provided more of the action at that stage – the Alfas, Lotus Cortinas and Minis had more race development than the American models – but eventually the O2 cars became the hallmark of the TransAm series. The final race of the inaugural season at Riverside was won by Jerry Titus, who went on to be one of TransAm's biggest stars. Ford won the O2 category in 1966 by just seven points from Plymouth. The U2 class was won by Alfa Romeo, with both Horst Kwetch and Gaston Andrey scoring 58 points.

DETROIT'S BIG THREE

In 1967, the official title of the series was shortened to the TransAm Championship, and the number of events raised to 12. Detroit's big three manufacturers took the opportunity of showcasing their popular muscle cars, financing car preparation and bankrolling drivers. The early TransAm cars were quite literally showroom models fitted with roll-cages, seat harnesses and a few other minor modifications like stiffer suspension. Mercury entered three Cougars for drivers Dan

Gurney, Parnelli Jones and Ed Leslie, prepared by top stock car builder Bud Moore. Chevrolet came in with four Camaro Z28s, a couple of which were entered by Roger Penske for Mark Donohue. Penske built the cars up in his own workshops, and had his own skid-pan facility. Winning the TransAm also became a Ford Motor Sports priority, and its involvement centred on racing legend Carroll Shelby, with Jerry Titus as first driver, backed up by Dick Thompson, with Milt Minter, Ron Bucknum and Jim Adams driving occasionally. Chrysler added tentative support with two cars at the first race of 1967 at Daytona, and Lincoln Mercury hired stock car drivers Cale Yarborough and Lee Roy Yarbrough for one-off appearances.

Bob Tullius won at Daytona in a Chrysler and Jerry Titus won the second race at Sebring. The third event of the year was one of the most closely contested finishes in TransAm history, between team-mates Parnelli Jones and Dan Gurney. The latter won by just three feet, after four hours of racing in temperatures of 110°F (43°C).

Another winner in 1967 was one of the most historically important figures of the series: Mark Donohue, and his team owner Roger Penske. David Pearson also won later in the season in a Cougar. However, the manufacturers' title race for the O2 division went down to the last race of the year at Kent in Washington State between Ford and Lincoln Mercury, and Ron Bucknum's second place was enough to give Ford the title by a scant two points. The U2 title went to the 2.0-litre (122-cubic-inch) Porsche 911S, with driver Bert Everett notching up most points.

Rule changes for the O2 class for 1968 allowed engines up to 5000cc (305 cubic inches). Wheel rim width could not exceed 200mm (eight inches), and flared wings were allowed, along with plastic or aluminium substitute bumpers. Pit stop rules were also changed, to allow repairs and refuelling, and this would have a significant impact on future events with a number of races being won and lost in the pits.

Having just missed the 1967 title, Lincoln Mercury did not return in 1968. The vacancy was quickly plugged by the Pontiac Firebird, but another car appeared that would have an impact on the series: the red, white and blue AMC Javelin, with George Follmer the number one driver. Although it ran well and finished several times, it did not win. Victory was the province of Mark Donohue, who won no fewer than 18 races in the Sunoco-sponsored, Penske-prepared Camaro. The 1968 TransAm season was the one most dominated by a single driver and team in the history of the series, and the 222 points accumulated by Donohue during the year were the most by a single driver until 1984. Donohue's wins carried Chevrolet to the O2 manufacturers' title, with 90 points over Ford with 59 and AMC with 51. Somewhat overshadowed by Donohue was the U2 category, in which Porsche also scored 90 points to win the manufacturers' U2 division, with drivers Everett and Tony Adamowicz.

For 1969, Parnelli Jones drove a Bud Moore Mustang along with George Follmer. The defending champions, the Penske team, had a Z28 entered for Mark Donohue and a second Camaro for Ron Bucknum, while Carroll Shelby prepared two Mustangs for Peter Revson and Horst Kwetch. Jerry Titus ran his own Pontiac Firebird, and AMC was back with a Javelin for drivers John Martin and Ron Grable.

The SCCA's executive director John Bishop left in 1969, and he went on to form the International Motor Sports Association (IMSA), which eventually supplanted the SCCA as the USA's premier professional road racing sanc-

tioning body during the next two decades.

Nonetheless, the 1969 season proved far more exciting than the Donohue procession of the preceding year. Parnelli Jones scored twice for Ford early in the year, Ron Bucknum had two wins for Penske, and George Follmer won at Bridgehampton. Not until mid-season did Mark Donohue manage his first victory of the year, but then he won five in a row, clinching the makers' title again for Chevrolet. The U2 division was totally dominated again by Porsche, with 11 wins and 81 points to Alfa's 28 points.

THE SPLIT

The U2 class ran as a separate series from 1970, and continued to attract many of the top saloon car racers. Inevitably, interest focused on the bigger cars as, once the Mustangs and Camaros were sorted, they were more exciting to watch. When a Mustang or Camaro went by, the ground shook.

Cars were generally becoming more specialised. All teams complied with the spirit of the regulations, but cars were pared down to the paintwork. The builder received the shell as a body-in-white from the manufacturer, with no panels or suspension, and it was not unknown for the shell to be dunked into an acid tank to thin and lighten the metal. The roll-cage was constructed inside it, with strengthening at crucial points. Only then was the suspension installed, and in the meantime the powertrain had been under preparation.

The 1970 TransAm season found Detroit's big three making a huge commitment to the series. The O2 pony cars were racing only among themselves. All the great US drivers were racing in the series: Donohue, Jones, Gurney and his protégè Swede Savage, Follmer, Posey, Revson and Jim Hall. The Penske team switched to the AMC Javelin, and, with Mark Donohue and Peter Revson at the wheel, turned an underdog into a winner. Chevrolet supported Jim Hall with a new model Camaro, while Chrysler came up with two Plymouth Barracudas for Gurney and Savage. A Dodge Challenger was piloted by Sam Posey, while Jerry Titus was still running his own Firebird. Bud Moore fielded a couple of Mustangs for Parnelli Jones and George Follmer, and these two dominated the early part of the 1970 season. The Javelins had teething problems, but by mid-season the renowned Penske preparation had paid off, and only two races were not won by Bud Moore or Penske. There was tragedy too: at Road America, Jerry Titus crashed into the bridge abutment during practice and died later. Although Donohue sustained AMC's title hopes with a second place at Watkins Glen, Parnelli Jones's win and Follmer's fourth at Seattle clinched the manufacturers' title for Ford. In the U2 division, the manufacturers' title went to Alfa Romeo, with eight class wins and 81 points, scored by Horst Kwetch, Bert Everett, Lee Midgely and Gaston Andrey.

TransAm's '02' over 2.0-litre (122-cubic-inch) class was initially the battleground between Ford Mustang and Chevrolet Camaro Pony Cars. Here at Sebring in 2000, Ralph Annis and Alec Hammond relive those early days with 1966 4.7-litre (289-cubic-inch) Mustang and 1968 Camaro.

ABANDONMENT

Despite their success, later that year Ford announced a total withdrawal from motor sports, followed by Chrysler. It was only a matter of time before Dodge and Plymouth dropped their TransAm effort too, and suddenly the series faced a major crisis. What lay behind it was that the Pony Car market – essentially overgrown coupés – which had been expanding since the late 1960s, began to ease back, and the manufacturers just lost interest in bolstering this market segment.

So when Roger Penske entered 1971 with AMC's new Javelin, he was the only fully factory-supported team. Donohue was unquestionably the number one driver, with David Hobbs as back-up. The Ford banner was carried by Bud Moore, now a private entrant using Mustangs built late in 1970 after the last race of the season. Peter Revson and Vic Elford also drove AMC Javelins, but the 1971 series was another runaway year for Mark Donohue, with seven victories. His Michigan win gave AMC the championship, and with 29 wins over five years, Donohue was the most successful TransAm driver in the series' history.

By 1970, the series had matured, with all the big US makes represented. The 1970 Z28 5.0-litre (305-cubic-inch) Camaro of Jim Graham is running in a round of the Anglo American Challenge at Sebring, Florida in 2000.

The U2 class was transformed into a new series in 1971, running as a support race to the TransAm and other SCCA events. The Alfas, BMWs and Datsuns were prominent, Datsun winning the title two years running in the hands of John Morton. Thereafter the U2 class fizzled out.

In the big league, the withdrawal of manufacturers' support, low purses, inconsistency of SCCA sanctioning and personnel, and the state of the US economy and the Pony Car market in particular conspired to threaten the future of TransAm for many years to come. Just seven races were run in 1972. Roy Wood had bought Roger Penske's Javelin programme and hired George Follmer as his driver. Follmer's four wins earned him the drivers' title, and with it came another championship for AMC.

The SCCA responded to the problems facing the series with a major revision to the rules, throwing the door open to FIA Groups 1, 2, 3 and 4 touring and grand touring machines to run alongside SCCA Sedan class A and B cars. What had been the classic American Pony Car road racing series now acquired a totally new look, with Porsche Carreras now lined up against Chevrolet Camaros. Engine displacements up to 7440cc (454 cubic inches) were allowed, and the Chevrolet Corvette sports car suddenly appeared in the TransAm. Liberal Group 4 bodywork revisions were also allowed,

transporting the TransAm series further still from its roots in the showroom. This was just one of many changes to occur between 1973 and 1980, and each change was a reaction to the failure of the previous one.

Only nine rounds were held in 1973 and just three races were run in 1974, when attendance levels fell below break-even. The title, for what it was worth, went twice to Peter Greg in a Porsche 911. For 1975, the series was restructured into a single-class affair, based on SCCA club racing A, B and C production cars and A-class sedans. Race distances were also shortened to 160km (100-mile) sprints. The schedule improved to seven events, from which Corvettes took six wins. John Greenwood won the championship with three of them, and Chevrolet took another manufacturers' title.

A third major rules revision was implemented in 1976, and this time the SCCA returned to a two-class programme comprising categories 1 and 2. Category 1 included the smaller and slower cars prepared to SCCA production and saloon (sedan) specification, and it featured the Javelin, smaller-engined Corvettes, Camaros and the Jaguar XJS. Category 2 represented the bigger, more powerful cars such as Porsche 934s and 935s, Chevrolet Monzas and big Corvettes. There were also exotic FIA Groups 4 and 5 machines, and the two-category system was effective up to 1980.

However, Category 2 ultimately proved too expensive and a shade too esoteric to appeal to many manufacturers and teams. The upshot was that the SCCA's many revisions changed the nature of TransAm racing for good, from a series based on lightly modified stock coupés into a pure racing series, where the cars were built from the ground up as racing machines.

The winner in 1976 was George Follmer, back in TransAm after a sojourn at UOP Shadows in Formula 1, and Porsche easily won the manufacturers' title in Category 2 in 1976 and 1977. The Category 1 drivers' championship for 1977 went to Bob Tullius, with two dominating performances in a Jaguar XJS. In 1978, Chevrolet gained another manufacturers' cup, while 1979 saw a dominant performance in Category 2 by John Paul Sr in a Porsche 935. He won six of the nine races held, taking Porsche to another manufacturers' championship. Bob Tullius won three of the races in Category 1.

RENAISSANCE

New regulations for 1980 made Category 1 cars the focus of the revamped series, based on a weight displacement formula that helped equalise competition. Cars had to comply with rules that included a maximum 250mm (10-inch) wheel width and 2.8m (110-inch) wheelbase, and gradually manufacturers were drawn back to the series.

A fresh crop of young and talented drivers entered the series, providing some of the best racing TransAm had seen for years.

The series was dominated in 1980 by the Porsche 911SC of John Bowers with four wins and three other top five finishes, although Chevrolet were manufacturers' title winners that year. The 1981 series went to Eppie Weitzes in a Corvette with two wins and consistently high placings, Tullius's Group 44 Jaguar coming second. The following year, the average margin of victory for champion Elliot Forbes Robinson in his Pontiac TransAm was a scant 5.5

seconds, which demonstrates how close the racing was. Top actor Paul Newman had a starring role of a different kind in a Datsun 280ZX.

The 18th season of the championship in 1983 comprised 12 events and it was now sponsored by Budweiser, who offered a much-needed boost in prize money. The Budweiser-sponsored team of Camaros driven by David Hobbs and Willy T. Ribbs was ultra-competitive. The Englishman won four of the races, while Ribbs won five. Hobbs took the title by virtue of higher placings in the remaining events, although in most races the pair came first and second. The team collected $155,000 in prize money, and Chevrolet gained its ninth manufacturers' cup.

The 1984 series comprised a record 16 events, and clearly the new formula created a competitive playing field for manufacturers, teams and drivers. It was not so good for the defending champions however, racing the new and unsorted Corvettes. The volatile Ribbs left under a cloud following a pit-lane altercation with another competitor, and went to Ford to drive a Capri (about a year and a half later he left Ford under rather similar circumstances). Lincoln Mercury redoubled its efforts in 1985 with Ribbs and new driver Wally Dallenbach Jr. In one of the most hotly contested championships in TransAm history, Dallenbach and Ribbs traded race win after race win, taking all but three events that year. Although Ribbs had

more wins and more pole positions, his 22-year-old team-mate accrued more points to become the youngest TransAm champion ever.

The quest for the 1986 manufacturers' title was more interesting to observe than the drivers' championship. Although Dallenbach was the first driver to win back-to-back drivers' crowns since Tullius took the Category 1 class in 1977 and 1978, he was at the wheel of the Proto Team's Camaro. As is often the case during the off-season, many of the staff of the Jack Roush organisation had left to form Proto Team, and, with backing from Chevrolet, they lured Dallenbach away from Roush as well. Ironically, in spite of Dallenbach's win in the drivers' championship, Roush's Mercury Capris gained six wins with four different drivers to snatch the makers' title from Chevrolet by nine points, giving Lincoln Mercury its third title in a row.

In the 1987 series the Roush team was the one to beat. Scott Pruett and Pete Holsmer drove XR4 Tis, while Deborah Grey, only the fourth woman ever to compete in the TransAm, ran the Capri. Out of the 12 races, Pruett scored seven wins, nine pole positions and set five fastest laps, and his success at Memphis secured the manufacturers' title for Lincoln Mercury. This was a record fourth straight TransAm Championship for the Ford division, and evidence of the domination of the Roush team. In just 56 races, Lincoln Mercury could claim 37 wins and 75 top-three finishes.

MORE NEW PLAYERS

A new face appeared in 1988 as Audi teamed up with Bob Tullius's Group 44 organisation to form one of the most powerful and controversial race teams to contest the TransAm trail. Another new player was Oldsmobile, entering TransAm for the first time. With typical Teutonic thoroughness, the preparation of the Audi squad paid dividends, with eight wins from 13 events, including five in a row at mid-season. Predictably, other competitors complained about the Audi's apparent advantage with 4x4 traction, and the SCCA imposed weight penalties on the German cars. Despite carrying the extra ballast, the Quattros remained competitive. Hans Stuck's win at Mid-Ohio gave Audi enough points to wrap up the manufacturers' title with three races to go, making Audi the first foreign manufacturer to win the title since 1979. Hurley Haywood also won the drivers' title.

With Audi staying away, the form books predicted Oldsmobile success for the 1989 TransAm, but ultimate victory went to rookie driver Dorsey Schroeder

in a Jack Roush-prepared Mustang, now with official Ford support. It was rewarded with seven wins, culminating in the manufacturers' cup. Six of those victories went to Schroeder, who nearly won a seventh over Darrin Brasfield in the closest recorded finish in TransAm history: Brasfield's official margin of victory was seventeen one-hundredths of a second. Meanwhile, the efforts of Max Jones and Tom Kendall in the Chevrolet Berettas pressured the Ford team for the manufacturers' title. Closing scores reflected one of the tightest battles in the series, with Ford on 89 points, Chevrolet on 77 and Oldsmobile with 75.

The 25th anniversary of the series was celebrated in 1990, with $1.1 million in prize money up for grabs and most of 1989's top contestants after it. Four-wheel-drive and turbocharged cars were banned, and only V8 and V6 engines were eligible. A new points-scoring system and a successful second half of the season saw Tommy Kendall set a new points record for a single season and scoop the drivers' title. The following year, Scott Sharp teamed up with Jack Baldwin in Bud McCall's American Racing Equipment programme, and they proved to be a tough combination to beat, Sharp winning the drivers' title convincingly and helping to take Chevrolet to its second straight manufacturers' title. For the first time since 1970, all three big US manufacturers participated in this 1991 series.

The following year the variety of talent was evident in the fact that eight different drivers – Scott Sharp, Jack Baldwin, Ray Pickett, Tommy Archer, Robbie Gordon, Paul Zinzolozi, Ron Fellows and Darrin Brasfield – topped the podium. The fans were back in a major way too, averaging 85,000 at each event. The final points tally was Baldwin 279 and Sharp 275, the closest margin for a championship since 1970, when Parnelli Jones edged Donohue out by a single point.

Scott Sharp made a comeback in 1993, taking his second championship and making him one of only a handful of drivers to win more than one TransAm drivers' title. Along the way he took nine pole positions and moved ahead of Mark Donohue as the all-time career leader in poles won, with 26 in all. Sharp would also help Chevrolet to its fourth consecutive makers' title.

Five former champions returned in 1994 to battle for drivers' points. Scott Pruett, Dorsey Schroeder, Jack Baldwin, Tommy Kendall and Ray Pickett all had top finishes and

The 1998 TransAm Champion was Paul Gentilozzi, driving a Chevrolet Camaro, giving the marque its 15th title in the category's 34-year history. Gentilozzi, however, switched to Ford Mustang Cobra for 1999. These Camaros are running at Elkhart Lake in August 1998.

In 2000, European models once again changed the TransAm order as Paul Gentilozzi's Jaguar XJR proved a race leader, pictured here at Charlotte, although Brian Simo's Qvale De Tomaso Mangusta was the early BF Goodrich series leader with two thrilling victories.

between them won nine of the 13 races. Scott Pruett emerged the winner in a Chevy Camaro, but Ford at last ended Chevrolet's manufacturers' winning streak in convincing fashion. Roles were soon reversed, however, in 1995, Chevrolet taking its 14th title, but a Ford Mustang Cobra took Tom Kendall to his second drivers' championship. Kendall won through consistency rather than number of victories; in fact, he won only once in the year, edging Ron Fellows into the runner-up spot for the third year in a row. Adverse weather conditions affected a number of events this season in a year dominated by incredibly close racing: the average margin of victory was a mere 3.019 seconds.

FULL CIRCLE

Much has changed throughout the history of the TransAm series, and despite a low point in the 1970s it recovered to offer some of the closest, most competitive road racing in the world. By the end of the decade – the century even – the main man was Paul Gentilozzi, who had switched from his Chevrolet to a Ford Mustang Cobra for the 1999 season.

As the season progressed, it was obvious that Gentilozzi would have to overcome challenges from rivals Brian Simo, Chris Neville and Michael Lewis, all in similar Mustang Cobras, and Johnny Miller in a Corvette, all of whom were in contention throughout the season. By the last race of the season, at Sebring, the title battle had come down to Gentilozzi and Simo, with the defending champion holding

a seven-point lead. Gentilozzi successfully completed his season-long mission with his third flag-to-flag performance of the year, clinching his second TransAm drivers' title. The two drivers easily secured an eighth manufacturers' title for Ford.

For 2000, the cars participating in the B.F.Goodrich Tires TransAm series had their standard rear spoilers replaced by a high-rise rear wing. The 1.83m (72-inch) wing was not compulsory, though, and competitors were at liberty to retain the 1.65m (65-inch) rear boot spoiler.

Along with the new look, significant technical changes were also in the frame for North America's longest-running road racing series, including the return of multi-valve cylinder heads and fuel injection, as well as a wider range of manufacturers and models becoming eligible.

SCCA TRANSAM CHAMPIONSHIP

Year	Driver		Year	Driver
1966	Horst Kwech/Gaston Andrey (AUS/CH), **Alfa Romeo GTA**			**Chevrolet**; C2: John Paul (USA), **Porsche 911**
1967	Jerry Titus (USA), **Ford Mustang**		1980	John Bauer (USA), **Porsche 911**
1968	Mark Donohue (USA), **Chevrolet Camaro**		1981	Eppie Wietzes (CDN), **Chevrolet Corvette**
1969	Mark Donohue (USA), **Chevrolet Camaro**		1982	Elliott Forbes-Robinson (USA), **Pontiac TransAm**
1970	Parnelli Jones (USA), **Ford Mustang**		1983	David Hobbs (GB), **Chevrolet Corvette**
1971	Mark Donohue (USA), **Ford Mustang**		1984	Tom Gloy (USA), **Ford**
1972	George Follmer (USA), **Ford Mustang**		1985	Wally Dallenbach Jr (USA), **Ford**
1973	Peter Gregg (USA), **Porsche 911**		1986	Wally Dallenbach Jr (USA), **Chevrolet**
1974	Peter Gregg (USA), **Porsche 911**		1987	Scott Pruett (USA), **Mercury**
1975	John Greenwood (USA), **Chevrolet Corvette**		1988	Hurley Haywood (USA), **Audi**
1976	C1: George Follmer (USA), **Porsche 934**; C2: Jocko Maggiacomo (USA), **Ford Mustang**		1989	Dorsey Schroeder (USA), **Ford**
			1990	Tom Kendall (USA), **Chevrolet**
			1991	Scott Sharp (USA), **Chevrolet**
			1992	Jack Baldwin (USA), **Chevrolet**
1977	C1: Bob Tullius (USA), **Jaguar XJ-S**; C2: Ludwig Heimrath (CDN), **Porsche 911**		1993	Scott Sharp (USA), **Chevrolet**
			1994	Scott Pruett (USA), **Chevrolet**
			1995	Tom Kendall (USA), **Ford**
1978	C1: Bob Tullius (USA), **Jaguar**; C2: Greg Pickett (USA), **Chevrolet Corvette**		1996	Tom Kendall (USA), **Ford**
			1997	Tom Kendall (USA), **Ford**
			1998	Paul Gentilozzi (USA), **Chevrolet**
1979	C1: Gene Bothello (USA),		1999	Paul Gentilozzi (USA), **Ford**

NASCAR

Outside the USA, there is nothing to match the sheer spectacle and drama of major league stock car racing. The quest for NASCAR's Winston Cup was glamorised in the Tom Cruise movie *Days of Thunder*, and the title is apt, for when the grid takes off at Daytona or Talladega, the ground literally shakes. Always a popular category because of its visual splendour, NASCAR racing quickly developed into one of the most popular forms of motor sport in the USA.

The category was founded in the late 1940s by NASCAR president William H.G. 'Bill' France, who got the ball rolling by organising races on the hard-packed sands and promenade road of Daytona Beach, Florida. He launched the first season of NASCAR racing with a modified stock car event on 15 February 1948, and the inaugural season comprised over 50 races. The participating cars were a mix of saloons (sedans) tuned to give better performance than the standard car. There was everything from Studebakers and Hudsons to Fords and Chevrolets, and even in its first year NASCAR was known for close competition, thrills and spills, and strong allegiances to manufacturers and driving stars.

In these early days, the schedule was similar to today's calendar, in that it began at Daytona in February and ended with a race on 14 November at Columbus, Georgia. One of the first NASCAR heroes was Marshall Teague, who led the first racing lap on the beach and road course, but Robert 'Red' Byron won the 240.7km (149.6-mile) event in a 1939 Ford.

Led by the Chevrolet Monte Carlo of Kenny Wallace, the NASCAR field is strung out along the straightway at Bristol Speedway as cars strive to get into the draft of the one in front in order to find the extra revs to make a passing manoeuvre.

Byron narrowly won the inaugural NASCAR national championship from Fonty Flock, who won 15 races. Completing the top five in the standings after the first NASCAR season were Tim Flock (the youngest of three racing brothers), Curtis Turner and Buddy Shuman. Among the women drivers competing in the first NASCAR season were Ethel Flock Mobley, Sara Christian, Mildred Williams and Ruth Nixon. More than $100,000 in prize funds was at stake throughout the season, which was big money for those days, and Byron collected $1,250 for his championship win.

For 1949, Bill France Sr revitalised the 'Strictly Stock' division, which was one of the most significant events in the history of the sport of stock car racing. At the same time, a number of other clubs began staging events in the southern and eastern states, mostly contested by modified pre-1939 cars with tuned-up engines. In a bid to elevate NASCAR above its rivals, Bill France staged his Strictly Stock race on the Broward Speedway, a 3.2km (two-mile) circular course on an airport perimeter road in southern Florida. He followed this with a 241km (150-mile) Strictly Stock race with a $5,000 purse at the 1.2km (0.75-mile) Charlotte

Daytona Motor Speedway is the notional home of NASCAR. Originally a combined beach and road course, the 2.5-mile (4km) D-shaped banked circuit was opened in 1959, and here, the field forms up for the legendary Daytona 500 in 1997.

Speedway in North Carolina, and 33 late-model stock cars contested the race, which was won by Jim Roper in a Lincoln. The series was won by Red Byron again, from Lee Petty, while the Flock brothers, Bob and Tim, were to the fore. Their brother, Fonty, won the 1949 NASCAR modified championship.

The Strictly Stock division was renamed the NASCAR Grand National Circuit for the 1950 championship season, because Strictly Stock was thought to be too restrictive. 'Grand National' was derived from the UK's premier horse racing event at Aintree, with all its thoroughbred connotations. Possibly the most significant event of the year was the construction by Harold Brasington of Darlington International Raceway in South Carolina. The circuit opened with an 805km (500-mile) race for stock cars on the 2km (1.25-mile) banked oval speedway, with an unbelievable 75 cars taking the start. And if that number is

incredible, the number of events held is equally bewildering these days, when a championship comprises 16 to 20 rounds. No fewer than 41 NASCAR Winston Cup race meetings were held in 1951, for instance, with seven-time race winner Herb Thomas securing the championship.

EXPANSION

NASCAR was quickly becoming very popular. Under the influence of driver Marshall Teague, in 1952 the Hudson Motor Company decided to enter NASCAR racing, providing cars (Hornets) and parts to racing teams. Hudson also introduced a high-performance parts kit, which was listed in its catalogue and therefore made them eligible for Winston Cup competition. The Pure Oil Company, signed up as the circuit's official fuel supplier, based its national advertising campaign on major Winston Cup events. On its first promotion in California, the NASCAR Winston Cup race at Gardena was won by Marshall Teague. Another driver, Frank Mundy, who was unable to secure a drive in a racing car, simply rented a car and finished 11th. At Detroit, no fewer than 16 different makes of car made up the 59-car field on a 1.6km (one-mile) dirt oval at the

Michigan State Fairgrounds. Winner was Tommy Thompson, ahead of Curtis Turner. The first Winston Cup race to be staged under spotlights was run at Columbia, South Carolina, and won by a Studebaker. At Darlington Raceway, 82 cars took the green flag for the annual Southern 500, the largest grid in Winston Cup history. Teague came through from 47th to take the lead on the 13th lap, but Herb Thomas outlasted the competition to take the win.

The field gets the green flag at the Texas raceway for a round of the NASCAR Winston Cup in April 1987, led by the Ford Thunderbirds of Ricky Rudd and Bill Elliott. The stands are brim full of spectators and the cars are liveried so distinctively that even from the back it's possible to identify the stars.

Taking advantage of this leap in the popularity of stock car racing, Bill France Sr launched the NASCAR Short Track Division for circuits smaller than 0.8km (half a mile). Separate points standings were earmarked for the series. Also introduced was a new Sportsman's Division, a series for weekend racers, and this went on to become the NASCAR Busch Series Grand National Division. The Speedway Division was announced the following year, featuring Indianapolis-type single-seater racing cars powered by stock engines, with a view to attracting cost-conscious owners. Buck Baker, driving a Cadillac-powered special, won the inaugural race at Darlington International Raceway. But the Speedway Division was destined never to take off like the Winston Cup series.

RADIOS AND TELEVISION

For the first time in 1952, teams were using two-way car-to-pits radios, which did not come into Formula 1 or European Super Touring until the 1980s. In the 201km (125-mile) Modified Sportsman race on the 6.6km (4.1-mile) Daytona beach and road course, driver Al Stevens communicated with team owner Cotton Bennett and two observers, finishing third in class and 27th overall in the 97-car field.

The NASCAR Winston Cup series comprised 34 rounds in 1952, and Tim Flock won the first of his two NWC national championships to deny defending champion Herb Thomas his second straight title. Flock won eight races in all on his way to a championship win, rolling his Hudson Hornet midway through the final race, which was won by Thomas in another Hudson. Hornets handled reasonably well because their step-down chassis gave them a lower centre of gravity. Thomas also scored eight victories, but Flock gained the title on the basis of more top-five and top-10 finishes. Lee Petty, Fonty Flock and Dick Rathmann completed the top five in the points standings.

Herb Thomas made no mistake in the 1953 Winston Cup series though, winning his second national championship from Lee Petty. Although he dominated the season, 10 different drivers won races, and runner-up Petty scored as many top-10 finishes as Thomas with one less start. Thomas, however, was the only driver to compete in all 37 races, and he racked up 12 victories (more than twice as many as the next-highest winner) to become the first two-time NASCAR Winston Cup champion. He earned $28,909 in purse and points money from the $202,507 tour fund, while Hudson was the dominant manufacturer, scoring 22 wins out of 37 events.

NASCAR staged a unique event at the Langhorne Speedway, Pennsylvania, in June 1953, billed as the inaugural International Stock Car Grand Prix. It was a 321km (200-mile) race open to foreign and domestic

By the mid-1960s, the fastback shape was popular, typified by the 7.0-litre (427-litre) Ford Torino and Mercury Cyclone, pictured here. The cars were still recognisable as production models, despite their welded in roll cages and race modifications.

saloon cars and was intended to settle arguments about the relative merits on an oval course of home-grown cars and imports such as Mercedes-Benz and Jaguar. Seven US makes lined up against four foreign makes including sundry Porsches and a Volkswagen. Lloyd Shaw's Jaguar took pole position, but Dick Rathmann's Hudson led on all 200 laps to claim victory for the USA ahead of four other American makes. Nick Fornoro came eighth in a Porsche.

The forerunner of the modern super-speedway was opened on 30 May

1953, a new 1.6km (one-mile) paved (as opposed to dirt) speedway at Raleigh, North Carolina. The Raleigh track was described as 'super fast', and the bends featured very high banking. The inaugural event was a 482km (300-mile) NASCAR Winston Cup race, won by Fonty Flock, who came through 43rd on the grid.

Tim Flock's season was interrupted when he got run over on the infield at the Piedmont Interstate Fairgrounds track in Spartanburg, but he returned after a lay-off to take pole for a 161km (100-mile) race at Hickory Speedway, North Carolina. Making his debut at this race was Ned Jarrett, father of current stock car driver Dale Jarrett, and twice NASCAR Winston Cup champion. He finished 11th. The family dynasties that would spring up surprisingly often in NASCAR (and

CART) racing were in their gestation period. The 1954 title was won by Lee Petty, the father of 'King' Richard Petty, victorious in seven out of 34 starts and amassing an impressive 32 top-10 finishes. Between them, Petty and Herb Thomas won 19 of the 37 events on the schedule.

Domestic television was hardly new in the States, but in 1954, for the first time, viewers could catch something of the spectacle of stock car racing. A half-hour television programme called Wire Wheels was shown on WABD-TV in New York City with the first show devoted entirely to the Daytona Speed Week. Other car racing pro-grammes followed, with NASCAR driver Mel Larson producing Desert Dust, a half-hour weekly show on KYTL-TV in Phoenix, Arizona, and Autorama on WICC-TV in Bridgeport, Connecticut. In those days, UK viewers were lucky to see a brief highlight of the British Grand Prix or Le Mans.

Meanwhile, Tim Flock and team owner Ernest Woods used two-way radios in the Daytona Beach race, the first time radios had been used in NASCAR's premier event. Flock won, but was disqualified following the dis-covery by post-race scrutineers of a carburettor offence. Lee Petty was declared the winner. Disgruntled,

The aerodynamics might have looked a tad incongruous but together with the Dodge Daytona, the Plymouth Superbird shown here sporting an elevated rear wing, was hugely spectacular between 1969 and 1972.

PLYMOUTH

Make: *Plymouth*
Model: *Roadrunner/Superbird*
In production: *1967-9*
Engine: *6980cc (426-cubic-inch) pushrod Chrysler V8*
Gearbox: *three-speed*
Power output: *350bhp*
Chassis: *unit-construction sedan, welded-in roll-cage*

Flock stopped racing for the rest of the season. His brother, Fonty, also left NASCAR to participate for a rival organiser.

MORE CHANGES

More significantly, Pure Oil introduced the first tyre specifically produced for stock car racing, and General Textile Mills produced a new hard-shell racing helmet that replaced the leather-strapped Cromwell headgear. Flameproof overalls were also made available by Treesdale Laboratories.

There were other innovations. Bill France Sr was still very much at the helm, and he decided to launch the NASCAR Auto Association, a club that provided travel information and hotel, restaurant and garage service recommendations as well as discounts for the 11,000 or so NASCAR members. France also announced plans for a 4km (2.5-mile) high-banked track to be built at Daytona Beach, the headquarters of NASCAR. West Coast

The NASCAR Busch series for modified pickup trucks provides just as much rivalry and excitement as the stock cars. This is 1995 Craftsman Truck champion Ron Hornaday in action at Richmond in 1997.

promoter Bob Barkheimer brought another 10 circuits into the NASCAR fold, so that the organisation moved away from being based predominantly in the south-eastern States. The first road race for NASCAR stock cars was staged at Linden, New Jersey, and the imported cars had their revenge as the event was won by Al Keller in a Jaguar, making it the only NASCAR Winston Cup event to be won by a foreign car.

New on the scene for the new season in 1955 was Mercury outboard engine proprietor Carl Kiekhaefer from Wisconsin, who hired Tim Flock to drive and won his first race as an owner at the Daytona beach and road course. Kiekhaefer's racing Chrysler 300s were carried from race to race in covered transporters, which was an innovation, and they quickly became regarded as the cars to beat. Racing success breeds sales in the showroom, and sales of new Chryslers rocketed in the USA. There is nothing like a bit of competition to stir things up, and Chevrolet and Ford promptly set up factory teams to compete with Kiekhaefer's squad; accordingly, big advertisements began to appear in the media featuring NASCAR racing. Chrysler took a two-page spread in

national US magazines featuring Chrysler driver Lee Petty and his family.

The first superspeedway race run under the lights, the 161km (100-mile) NASCAR Winston Cup event on Raleigh Speedway's high-banked oval, took place this season, and it was won by Herb Thomas, but Tim Flock notched up a record 18 Winston Cup victories to take the 1955 championship, in which Kiekhaefer shared the honours in his first season.

When is a saloon car a sports car? Possibly when it is a convertible. A merger between NASCAR and the Society of Autosports and Fellowship Education (SAFE) led to the formation of a NASCAR Convertible Division for the 1956 season. No fewer than 47 convertible races were held during the course of the year, Bob Welborn beating Curtis Turner in the final points standings.

Team owner Carl Kiekhaefer entered six cars for the beach and road course at Daytona, one of which was driven by Charlie Scott, only the second black driver to compete in a NASCAR Winston Cup event (Joey Ray was the first at Daytona in 1952). Tim Flock headed home the 76 starters, and the

Kiekhaefer team – Buck Baker, Herb Thomas, Speedy Thompson and Flock – reeled off 16 consecutive Winston Cup victories for the season, which was likely to remain a record for some time. The season was notable for including the only NASCAR Winston Cup race to be run in the pouring rain, at the 6.4km (four-mile) Elkhart Lake circuit in Wisconsin. It was won by Tim Flock in a Mercury, but Buck Baker, with 14 wins, captured the 1956 title.

THE REAL BEACH

The final NASCAR Winston Cup race on the sands of Daytona Beach was staged on 23 February 1958, and was won by Paul Goldsmith from Curtis Turner. The next new circuit to host meetings was the twisting road course at Riverside International Raceway in southern California, which opened its gates in June. The Crown America International Stock Car race featured international entries including a Rolls-Royce, and Eddie Gray beat 45 other contenders to the chequered flag.

Richard Petty began his dominant NASCAR career, with sixth place in the 161km (100-mile) Convertible Division race at Columbia on 12 July.

Blasting off the banking comes the Mercury Cyclone followed closely by Ford Torino, going high, and Dodge Daytona, aiming low, to make their passing moves. All three are powered by 7.0-litre (429-cubic-inch) V8 engines.

His first Winston Cup event was not so successful though: he was placed 17th out of 19 at Toronto, Canada. Richard's father, Lee, posted 44 top-10 finishes from 50 starts in 1958 to wrap up his second NASCAR Winston Cup championship. Another to impress was Glenn 'Fireball' Roberts, who won six of his 10 starts during the course of the 51-race season.

The new 4km (2.5-mile) D-shaped Daytona International Speedway opened for practice runs on 1 February 1959. The banked section was slightly dished, and angled at a daunting 31 degrees. The first event, a 161km (100-mile) Convertible Division race, was won by Shorty Rollins, while Bob Welborn took the accompanying Grand National event. Lee Petty and Johnny Beauchamp almost finished in a dead heat, Joe Weatherly's lapped car making the dramatic ending a three-wide affair. The finish was so close that it took 61 hours for NASCAR officials to declare Petty the winner in a 1959 Oldsmobile. Petty went on to wrap up his third NASCAR Winston Cup title, winning 11 races from 42 starts.

ON AIR

The first live network television coverage of Grand National racing went out via CBS Sports in January 1960 from Daytona International Speedway. The opening of the speedway in 1959 launched a new era for stock cars, and it was not long

before the Daytona 500 began to rival in popularity and prestige the long-established Indianapolis 500. New banked and asphalt-surfaced super-speedways also opened in Charlotte, Atlanta, and Hanford, California.

Richard Petty scored his first NASCAR victory on 28 February in a 161km (100-mile) race at the Charlotte Fairgrounds dirt track. Rex White recorded six victories on his way to the 1960 title, scoring 35 top-10 finishes from 40 starts, but a total of 18 different drivers won races during the 44-race season. Runner-up was Richard Petty, and Bobby Johns finished third having started only 19 races.

The first event in the Race of Champions genre, an All-Star event reserved for Grand National race winners during the 1960 season, was staged at Daytona Speedway during the Speed Week. Eleven drivers competed in the 25-mile event, and Joe Weatherly passed Fireball Roberts on the final lap for victory. Roberts, however, led from flag to flag in the 250-mile race at the Marchbanks Speedway at Hanford, and this remains the only superspeedway event in which the same driver led every lap – testimony to the effectiveness and excitement of slipstreaming (drafting), which is the normal practice.

For the 1961 season, David Pearson landed a factory-backed drive with John Masoni and chief mechanic Ray

Jeff Gordon's Chevrolet Monte Carlo is helped on its winning way by the 'Rainbow Warriors' crew during a pit stop at Riverside, California in May 1999. The mechanic at the back of the car indicates the refuelling is complete, while the fresh wheels are torqued up.

Fox. With a lap and a half to go at the Charlotte speedway, Pearson was leading Fireball Roberts by three laps when he blew a tyre. Instead of heading for the pits to change it, Pearson chose to limp on, and he smoked his way around the track at 50km/h (30mph) as the hard-charging Roberts sliced away at his lead. Fireball almost made it, but Pearson just managed to hit the finish line first to claim his first Winston Cup victory. Although the Charlotte track is smaller than Daytona and Talladega, and speeds might not be as high, it still requires the highest driver concentration and car performance to win here. Pearson showed a cool head that day; indeed, a team of doctors once monitored some of the top drivers in

the scorching-hot Southern 500 at Darlington, and they were astounded to discover that Pearson's pulse rate actually decreased in the heat of competition.

Pearson went on to win two more races, at Atlanta and Daytona, but consistency paid off for Ned Jarrett, who took the 1961 title. Jarrett won just the one race, but managed 34 top-10 finishes from 46 starts to end the season comfortably ahead of Rex White.

Fireball Roberts was the star of the 1962 Daytona Speed Week, triumphing in the fourth Daytona 500, and the final NASCAR convertible race took place on 12 May at Darlington International Raceway's Rebel 300, with Nelson Stacy the winner. But more significantly, Ford announced that it would defy the 1957 Automobile Manufacturers Association resolution that banned manufacturer representation in NASCAR Grand National racing, and set up a number of factory-backed teams with Holman & Moody's premises in Charlotte as its

stock car racing headquarters. One of Ford's first customers was 19-year-old Mamie Reynolds, daughter of US Senator Robert R. Reynolds, whose team debuted in the Southern 500 at Darlington International Raceway, with Darrel Derringer at the wheel. The car was destroyed in a crash, so Mr Reynolds bought a Ford from Holman & Moody to win the September round at Augusta, Georgia, with Fred Lorenzen driving. The 53-race series was won by Joe Weatherly for team owner Bud Moore, with nine race wins to his credit.

The Wood Brothers were becoming famous as a crack team, and in 1963 DeWayne 'Tiny' Lund drove their Ford to victory in the Daytona 500, managing to complete the 200-lap race distance without a tyre change. Also at Daytona, Johnny Rutherford, who would go on to achieve fame in Indycars, won the second Twin 100-Mile Qualifying race for the Daytona 500, and between 1959 and 1971 points were awarded for the Twin Qualifying races at Daytona, and they were considered official NASCAR Winston Cup events.

Back in 1963, while actress Jayne Mansfield greeted Junior Johnson in the victory lane following his win at the 239km (148.5-mile) Grand National race at Orange Speedway in Hillsboro, North Carolina, Herman Beam finished ninth. Nothing too remarkable there, but it was the 84th consecutive NASCAR event in which he had been running at the finish, and that record still stands today. Another US racing legend, Roger Penske, drove a Pontiac to victory in the NASCAR Pacific Coast Late Model event at Riverside, while fearless Fred Lorenzen became the first driver to win more than $100,000 in a single Grand National season. Weatherly won his second consecutive championship in an unorthodox manner, having to beg for rides for most of the contests. He drove

No mistaking the chief sponsor of Terry Labonte's Chevrolet Monte Carlo, pictured here at New Hampshire in 1997. Like Jeff Gordon and Ricky Craven, Labonte's car was run by one of Rick Hendrick Motorsports' three teams.

for nine different teams, winning three times to pip Richard Petty to the title.

In 1964, the Goodyear Tire & Rubber Company decided to test its Life-Guard inner liner for stock car racing tyres, designed so that drivers could get their cars back to the pits on the inner liner if they picked up a puncture (the Firestone Tire & Rubber Company came right back at them the next year and introduced the rubber fuel cell, designed to minimise fuel leaks and lessen the likelihood of fire in the event of accidents, and it became mandatory on all NASCAR stock cars). The Chrysler Corporation made a decision too: to revive its 1956 hemi-head hemispherical combustion chamber engine to make an assault on the Grand National season. Richard Petty led a one–two–three sweep for Chrysler's Plymouth teams in the Daytona 500. As a measure of the improvement in Chrysler's performance, Petty's speed at Daytona was 280.690km/h (174.418mph), compared to his previous year's best of 247.486km/h (153.785mph).

Billy Wade, driving Bud Moore's Mercury, became the first driver to win

four Winston Cup Grand National races in succession. Wade, the 1963 Rookie of the Year, took four straight race wins on the annual Northern Tour at Old Bridge, New Jersey, and Bridgehampton, Islip and Watkins Glen, all in New York State. Despite this feat, the 1964 champion was Richard Petty with nine race wins, the first of seven titles. It had been a gruelling season too; of a record 62 Winston Cup events, Petty and his arch rival David Pearson, who finished third in the point standings, competed in all but one.

FORD ON A ROLL

Another successful stock car driver emerged in the early 1960s in a factory-backed Ford, and by the time the decade was over, Lee Roy Yarbrough had qualified for the NASCAR hall of fame. For example, in 1969 he won the Daytona 500, the World 600 at Charlotte and the fabled Southern 500 at Darlington, considered at the time to be the stock car version of the Triple Crown – actually known as the Winston Million. Yarbrough chalked up 14 major victories in a

career that was cut short by illness, but with his help Ford was on a roll, and in 1965 it won 32 consecutive NASCAR Grand National races to establish an all-time record for manufacturers in major league stock car racing.

Ned Jarrett, the eventual champion for 1965 with 13 race wins, won a 161km (100-mile) Winston Cup race at Shelby, North Carolina, by 22 laps from runner-up Bud Moore, and that margin of victory remains the greatest in terms of laps in the history of NASCAR racing. His son Dale won the Southern 500 at Darlington by 19.25 miles (14 laps) and that was the greatest margin of victory in terms of miles in NASCAR history (Darlington was then measured at 2.21km, or 1.375 miles).

THE SPONSORS ARRIVE

In 1969 and 1970, after a period dominated by the race track talents of Richard Petty and, particularly, David Pearson, the big three manufacturers' presence in NASCAR came to an end. The void was filled by the sponsors whose commercial interests were often outside the motor industry.

If there was one factor in the growth of NASCAR through the 1970s and 1980s it was the entry of the R.J. Reynolds tobacco company into the sports marketing field in 1971. Hard on the heels of Marlboro's wide-ranging involvement and John Player & Son's Lotus tie-in, Reynolds came in with its Winston brand to become the first major non-automotive sponsor in stock car racing. Paradoxically, this coincided with the arrival of the most exotic cars to be seen in stock car racing: the Dodge Daytona and Plymouth Superbird. They took the fastback styling popularised by the Mercury Cyclone and Ford Torino and added 'droop snoot' front-end extensions and ultra-high-rise rear wings.

In 1969, Bill France completed what was known as the ultimate superspeedway, the Alabama International motor speedway at Talladega. It had the same general appearance as Daytona, but it was banked a little more steeply at 33 degrees, as well as being longer and a bit faster. In fact, it was the fastest circuit in the States. France was encouraged to construct the track by Governor George Wallace in order to

A mass pit stop — most of the teams make use of a caution period to replenish fuel and fit fresh rubber. NASCAR has strict rules about how many mechanics and tools are allowed to work on the cars.

promote the delights of Alabama. First to crack the 320km/h (200mph) barrier was Buddy Baker in 1970 in a Dodge Daytona, shod with a new compound of Goodyear tyres. At the 805km (500-mile) race at Talladega on 12 April 1970, 40 stock cars vied for a $134,000 purse. Bizarrely, a truck record was also set at Talladega when Johnny Ray's 18-wheel Kenworth rig averaged over 148km/h (92mph). Mark Donohue's record for the speedway, set in 1975, was 355km/h (221mph).

ROLLING START

Stock car races begin with a rolling start. The cars form up in echelon behind the pace car according to how fast each qualified, and they are led around the circuit for one lap. Nowadays green lights signal the off; it used to be a guy with a green flag. As the cars hit the straight, the race is on.

One of the most memorable races of the last few decades was the 1976 Daytona 500, which produced one of the most incredible finishes in racing history. The stars were David Pearson, the Silver Fox, and the King and reigning champion, Richard Petty, the top two all-time winners poised for a classic showdown. In the final lap of this $343,000 event Petty had his Dodge in front, but Pearson began to reel him in. Down the long back-shoot

Pearson regained the lead slipstreaming by Petty, and both cars wound up well over their engines' rev limits in a frenetic run for the chequered flag. At turn four, they hit, and all hell broke loose. Petty's Dodge slithered to a halt just a few feet from the line, coming to rest with a stalled engine; Pearson's crippled Mercury was still running, and he made the line for one of the most spectacular wins in stock car history.

THE PERSONALITIES

Although the manufacturers remained in the background, their official exit from the proceedings launched the cult of the driver personality. There had been 'greats' in the 1950s and 1960s, but it was almost certainly Richard Petty who shifted the emphasis from car to driver. In his 35-season career he changed car brands six times, from Oldsmobile to Plymouth, Ford, Dodge, Chevrolet and Pontiac. When he made the switch from Dodge to Chevrolet mid-season in 1978, the race fans cheered just as loudly – they could not care less what he was driving. Petty amassed 200 wins and seven titles; compare that with veteran owner-driver Dave Marcis, who in 30 years has notched up just five wins and no titles. Back in the 1950s, J.D. McDuffie started 653 races and won not a single one. These guys exemplify the spirit of

the journeyman NASCAR driver; guys like Petty are the geniuses.

Most of the stars are extraordinary people. Cale Yarbrough was an all-state football player who, having been struck by lightning in his living room, fallen out of an aeroplane with a half-open parachute and jumped off an 80-foot-high platform into a swimming hole and on to an alligator, decided racing was what he wanted to do. Yarborough won 83 NASCAR races and was the only man to win three consecutive Winston Cup championships (1976 to 1978).

Champion in 1981, 1982 and 1985, Darrell Waltrip started in Winston Cup racing in the early 1970s as an independent, and joined Junior Johnson in 1981. That year his successful run against veteran Bobby Allison in 1981 carried him centre stage, and he won the championship in the last race of the season at Riverside.

Dale Earnhardt, like Petty, won the NASCAR Winston Cup series seven times between 1980 and 1994, including three doubles, and claimed that cocooned in the roll-bar maze of his Chevrolet he felt more at home than anywhere else. Earnhardt sharpened his skills on the short tracks in the south for five years before moving up to the major league arena. He was 1979 Rookie of the Year and won his first Winston Cup in 1980. Known as the 'Intimidator', Earnhardt's father, Ralph, won NASCAR's 1956 Sportsman Division series.

Title-holder in 1995, 1997 and 1998 was Jeff Gordon – aged just 24 when he won the championship for the first time. In 1999, Gordon, going for a hat-trick, led the Winston Cup with seven victories, but it was the consistency of Dale Jarrett that allowed him to claim the championship, even though Jarrett failed to score a win in the final 14 events. Also in 1999, the engine builder

Robert Yates won his first championship as a team owner, while Tony Stewart won a record three races as a rookie. Stewart's team-mate, Bobby Labonte, also pressured Jarrett after the Hendrick Motorsports driver Gordon fell out of contention, but he failed to finish seven times due to mechanical problems and an accident. The younger Labonte failed to finish once, but scored five victories. He had started from pole five times, while Jarrett had not managed a single one, but finishing 24th or lower seven times ended his championship aspirations.

In 2000, Mark Martin was still looking for his first title at the age of 40; he was sidelined with injuries in 1999. He scored consistently as usual, but broke a knee and a wrist, and aggravated an old back injury in a practice crash at Daytona. He recovered well enough to take a second podium finish at Dover, but he just could not sustain the pressure on Jarrett when it counted.

Chevrolet teams could only muster three winning drivers in 1999, which proved to be the primary cause for its downfall in the manufacturers' challenge. The Intimidator Earnhardt rejuvenated his race career with two wins at Talladega, but also upset the fans when he collided with fellow Chevy driver Terry Labonte on the last lap at Bristol. As a result Labonte, champion

in 1984 and 1996, had only one success in 1999.

The resurgence of the Pontiac marque in 1999 was down to Joe Gibbs Racing. The team became a potent two-car Grand Prix contender by adding Stewart to the line-up alongside Bobby Labonte. It also took advantage of a factory-backed engine programme and the bigger rear spoilers required by NASCAR. The Gibbs team's eight victories reflected the Pontiac's stability on high-speed tracks and greater downforce on the flat ones, and these successes were the best for GM's other marque since Penske Racing South scored ten wins in 1993. Scion of the Andretti family legend, John Andretti, gave Pontiac its ninth win, forcing it away from the field at Martinsville after falling a lap behind. He regained the lead by means of a two-tyre pit stop late in the race.

Owner-driver Ricky Rudd disbanded his team to take a seat alongside Dale Jarrett at Robert Yates Racing in 2000, and of the one-car teams, Pontiac driver Ward Burton fared best in the 1999 standings. The loners always tend to be at a disadvantage because of smaller budgets, reduced testing and lack of chassis information, but then again nobody is truly poor in NASCAR racing: in 1999, each of the 37 drivers earned over $1 million in purse money, even before year-end

bonuses were awarded. The year's top earner was Jeff Gordon, who garnered $5.3 million.

THE STOCK CAR SHELL

Even though they are known as stock cars, the racing machines used in NASCAR Winston Cup racing are not simply stripped-down versions of a production Chevrolet Monte Carlo, Ford Taurus or Pontiac Grand Prix. Like super touring cars, they are purpose-built from the ground up for racing. For example, a production Chevrolet Monte Carlo is a unit-construction car, a monocoque of sorts, with the body panels all robot-welded together on the production line to form the complete car. But a typical NASCAR stock car, such as Terry Labonte's No. 5 Kellogg's Cornflakes Chevy Monte Carlo, has a hand-made chassis frame with a mixture of steel and fibreglass body panels attached to it.

While some teams contesting the Winston Cup series build their own cars, a lot of others buy a rolling chassis (with suspension and steering parts fitted; nowadays, steering components

They may be badged as different marques, but the bodyshells are virtually identical. Battling side by side are Terry Labonte's Chevrolet Monte Carlo and Buckshot Jones's Pontiac Grand Prix, both constructed to similar specifications.

Bobby Labonte on his way to second place in his Pontiac Grand Prix at Charlotte, North Carolina, during a round of the Winston Cup in May 1999. Bobby was taught much of the NASCAR craft by elder brother Terry, and was able to beat him on occasion.

are almost always mounted ahead of the front wheels) from one of several specialist car building operations, then set the car up to their own requirements. One of the leading US stock car chassis builders is Laughlin Racing Products in Simpsonville, South Carolina, and a number of NASCAR teams run cars built up on Laughlin shells. Another top builder is Hendrick Motorsports of Harrisburg, also in North Carolina, the hub of the NASCAR racing world. Once the chassis frame is completed, it can be shelled as either a Ford or General Motors racing car. A set of wheels and tyres enables the car to be pushed around the workshop at this stage, while its powertrain is installed and the colour scheme is sorted out. A major part of the appeal of NASCAR

is the glamour and spectacle of the cars, and their liveries these days are highly finished with the aid of computer graphics.

POWERPLANT

The typical NASCAR stock car is powered by the 5866cc (358-cubic-inch) V8 engine that was once considered at its limit producing 450bhp. By 2000, it was developing 750bhp. Maximum engine capacity is 5866cc, whether it is a Ford or GM engine, and it has to be a pushrod unit with just two valves per cylinder and carburettors, which is really a derivative of the V8 engine from the 1970s muscle cars.

If a certain camshaft works better, it is soon common property as NASCAR teams tend to source their pistons and camshafts from the same suppliers; but if a team comes up with something that it feels could be a technological advancement for the sport, it will approach a manufacturer and request such an upgrade in equipment or components. That was certainly the case with the new General Motors SB2 engine, which was essentially designed

in the race engine shops and proposed to NASCAR by GM and accepted.

Racing operations building their own engines generally have their own specialist tuners, but where a team buys or leases engines from another team or an engine-building firm, a tuner is included as part of the package. The engine builder and assemblers put the units together at the workshop, but the tuner maximises its performance potential for qualifying and the race. A restrictor plate engine has to be fine-tuned for flat-out speed. A restrictor plate is a thin piece of aluminium with four holes bored in it, placed between the carburettor and the intake manifold to limit horsepower, and engine builders compensate for the power loss it causes by fitting different cams and cylinder heads.

Probably more than in any other category, horsepower is a crucial factor in a NASCAR race team's success, because of the relatively unsophisticated engine hardware. Careful attention is paid to everything that goes into a race car's engine in order to generate the maximum amount of horsepower possible. Exhaust pipe diameter is also critical. Smaller diameter pipes will produce low to middle rpm torque, while larger diameters produce middle to high rpm torque, and one may be beneficial at a road circuit, the other on a banked oval course.

SAFETY ISSUES

The make-up of the stock car evolved in response to the NASCAR rule book, and that included safety precautions. One of the first safety devices to evolve was the seat harness. Not only does a full racing harness provide total restraint in an accident, it also holds the driver firmly in place when cornering. The roll-cage, though, is the backbone of a NASCAR stock car, or any saloon racer, and in this case it is made from 45mm (one-and-three-quarter-inch) diameter seamless steel tubing to a specified pattern. More than 40m (130ft) of tubing goes into one car.

Just as tyre technology has made a crucial impact on single-seater racing,

Races can be won or lost in the pits, and the action is frantic amid flailing air lines and cumbersome fuel canisters as Jeff Burton's crew strives to get his Ford Taurus back into the fray at Talladega Speedway in 1999.

so it has on stock cars. Tyres grew in diameter and width, and an inner liner was devised to keep the car steady in the event of a puncture. The inner liner has no function within the tyre unless a puncture occurs, allowing the driver to get back to his pit. Tyre pressures are double-checked before races, including the inner liner, which is important because its air pressure needs to be greater than that of the tyre. If the two are the same, equalisation occurs and the tyre can start vibrating.

In the late 1980s there was a series of incidents at superspeedways in which cars became airborne, and this led to the development of roof flaps. Mounted within the roofline of all NASCAR stock cars, roof flaps are designed to deploy if a car spins backwards or sideways. They are located at the rear of the roofline, and pop up when a car spins round, helping to prevent it from lifting off the ground by creating turbulence and disrupting the airflow over the vehicle. The key innovator in this field was Rousch Industries, and the roof flaps are manufactured by one of its companies.

PIT STOPS

As in other formulae, the pit area at NASCAR tracks has a pit lane separat-

ed from the circuit by a pit wall, and on the other side of the pit road are the garages. At one time, most of the work on racing cars took place in garages with dirt floors or in the paddock, but modern cars are set up with such precision that a level floor is critical to duplicate the alignment settings of the suspension, and to evaluate problems. Prior to a race, all tools, tyres and equipment are laid out in designated positions for swift access. The team also needs to check its car's performance on the race track, so TV monitors are set up in each garage and NASCAR provides a satellite link to the pits camera to record the race, pit stops and lap scoring.

There are many rules in NASCAR that govern what goes on when a car makes a pit stop, including how many crew members are permitted on the pit road, the number of tools they can bring with them and whether or not they can bring them back over the wall when they are finished. Teams are only allowed seven men over the pit wall, and if one of them goes behind the wall, he cannot return. If he does, a 15-second penalty is incurred. Racing teams even go to the lengths of measuring pit walls and duplicating them back at base, in order to do practice pit stops.

Pit stops are such a key to winning in

Jimmy Spencer's Ford Taurus lifts a wheel on the rumble strips at Sears Point road circuit during a round of the Winston Cup series in 1999. This behaviour in cornering is caused by the stiff suspension and taut chassis typical of racing cars.

NASCAR that the authorities instigated a pit stop competition in 1967 at North Carolina motor speedway, and the top teams meet once a year and do battle to lay claim to the title of fastest pit crew in stock car racing.

GIVE US A LIFT

The NASCAR season comprised 34 events in 1999, plus tyre testing with Goodyear, which involved teams clocking up a huge mileage going from track to track. Transporters are vital to the sport, and they have evolved a great deal too. In the 1960s it was common for racing cars to travel on trailers to and from circuits, but a decade later the well-heeled teams used box-wagons with trailers, rising to converted 18-wheeler semi-trucks. By the mid-1980s they were using specially built trailers that could accommodate two racing cars, one behind the other, plus all the team's equipment.

By the 1990s, a variation on this was the tail-lift trailer, taking one car on top of the other, and these two-storey transporters allow a lot more room for parts, spare engines and equipment. The cars are loaded with an electric or hydraulic lift, which raises and lowers the cars about two-and-three-quarter metres (nine feet) to and from the upper deck. Once loaded, the cars are strapped in for transportation. The most favoured rig in NASCAR is a 16m (53ft) long transporter made by Featherlite, and just

The speedway's outer wall is totally unyielding, yet some of the bravest over-taking moves take place inches from it. Here, Dale Jarrett takes seven-times Winston Cup Champion Dale Earnhart – 'The Intimidator' – at Dover Downs in 1999.

as long-haul trucks provide accommodation for the crew, the front part of the racing car transporter doubles as a dining room, reception area or changing room. Some have bunks and are fully appointed with creature comforts, and they are the mother-ships of the track-side operation.

TRADE SECRETS

There are numerous tricks that can be used to gain a hundredth of a second in the ultra-competitive racing environment – some legitimate, some not. The most blatant case I heard of was a car that was built just slightly smaller than the standard size; it looked all right but achieved less drag than the rest of the field. A folk tale, possibly.

But small, simple things – a coat of silicone, or bending out the front wings (fenders) to create slightly better aerodynamics – can make a difference, and no one is above giving another rival a nudge going into a corner. More subtly, a pound of air pressure in one tyre and one less in another can affect turn-in because it can change the spring rate by as much as 50lb. Even something unseen like a lighter-weight oil in the engine or chilling the radiator water with ice is not unheard of. Strategic application of gaffer tape over the grille area increases frontal downforce, reducing the flow of air into the engine compartment, and that is something else done to get a good qualifying lap. Teams spend ages on the dynamometer trying to get the most out of a powertrain, or in the wind-tunnels to get the spoiler settings right. Nothing beats track time, and hours are spent pounding around in search of that elusive split-second's performance gain. Small suspension adjustments can mean everything.

But whichever configuration they race in, there is no denying that the 320km/h (200mph) NASCAR monsters are about the most spectacular racing cars in the world.

NASCAR WINSTON CUP CHAMPIONS

Year	Champion	Year	Champion	Year	Champion
1949	Red Byron (USA), Parks Novelty Oldsmobile		Pontiac/Worth McMillion Pontiac/Major Melton	1981	Darrell Waltrip (USA), **Junior Johnson Buick**
1950	Bill Reufard (USA), **Buesink Oldsmobile**		Chrysler/Petty Plymouth/Wade Younts Dodge	1982	Darrell Waltrip (USA), **Junior Johnson Buick**
1951	Herb Thomas (USA), **Thomas Plymouth/Sandford Oldsmobile/Fabulous Hudson**	1964	Richard Petty (USA), **Petty Plymouth**	1983	Bobby Allison (USA), **Di Gard Buick**
		1965	Ned Jarrett (USA), **Bondy Long Ford**	1984	Terry Labonte (USA), **Billy Hagan Chevrolet**
1952	Tim Flock (USA), **Chester Hudson Hornet**	1966	David Pearson (USA), **Cotton Owens Dodge**	1985	Darrell Waltrip (USA), **Junior Johnson Chevrolet**
1953	Herb Thomas (USA), **Fabulous Hudson Hornet**	1967	Richard Petty (USA), **Petty Plymouth**	1986	Dale Earnhardt (USA), **Childress Chevrolet**
1954	Lee Petty (USA), **Petty Dodge/Chrysler**	1968	David Pearson (USA), **Holman-Moody Ford**	1987	Dale Earnhardt (USA), **Childress Chevrolet**
1955	Tim Flock (USA), **Mercury Chrysler/Westmoreland Chevrolet**	1969	David Pearson (USA), **Holman-Moody Ford**	1988	Bill Elliott (USA), **Elliott Ford**
		1970	Bobby Isaac (USA), **K&K Dodge**	1989	Rusty Wallace (USA), **Beadle Pontiac**
1956	Buck Baker (USA), **Satcher Kiekhaefer Ford/Chrsyler/ Dodge**	1971	Richard Petty (USA), **Petty Plymouth**	1990	Dale Earnhardt (USA), **Childress Chevrolet**
		1972	Richard Petty (USA), **Petty Plymouth/Dodge**	1991	Dale Earnhardt (USA), **Childress Chevrolet**
1957	Buck Baker (USA), **Babb/Baker Chevrolet**	1973	Benny Parsons (USA), **LG de Witt Chevrolet**	1992	Alan Kulwicki (USA), **Kulwicki Ford**
1958	Lee Petty (USA), **Petty Oldsmobile**	1974	Richard Petty (USA), **Petty Dodge**	1993	Dale Earnhardt (USA), **Childress Chevrolet**
1959	Lee Petty (USA), **Petty Oldsmobile/Plymouth**	1975	Richard Petty (USA), **Petty Dodge**		
		1976	Cale Yarborough (USA), **Junior Johnson Chevrolet**	1994	Dale Earnhardt (USA), **Childress Chevrolet**
1960	Rex White (USA), **Piedmont Ford/Friendly Chevrolet**	1977	Cale Yarborough (USA), **Junior Johnson Chevrolet**	1995	Jeff Gordon (USA), **Hendrick Chevrolet**
1961	Ned Jarrett (USA), **Courtesy Ford/BG Holloway Chevrolet**	1978	Cale Yarborough (USA), unior Johnson Oldsmobile	1996	Terry Labonte (USA), **Hendrick Chevrolet**
1962	Joe Weatherly (USA), **Bud Moore Pontiac**	1979	Richard Petty (USA), **Petty Chevrolet**	1997	Jeff Gordon (USA), **Hendrick Chevrolet**
1963	Joe Weatherly (USA), **Bud Moore** Pontiac/Bud Moore Mercury/Fred Harb Pontiac/Pete Stewart Pontiac/Cliff Stewart	1980	Dale Earnhardt (USA), **Osterlund Chevrolet**	1998	Jeff Gordon (USA), **Hendrick Chevrolet**
				1999	Dale Jarrett (USA), **Robert Yates Ford**

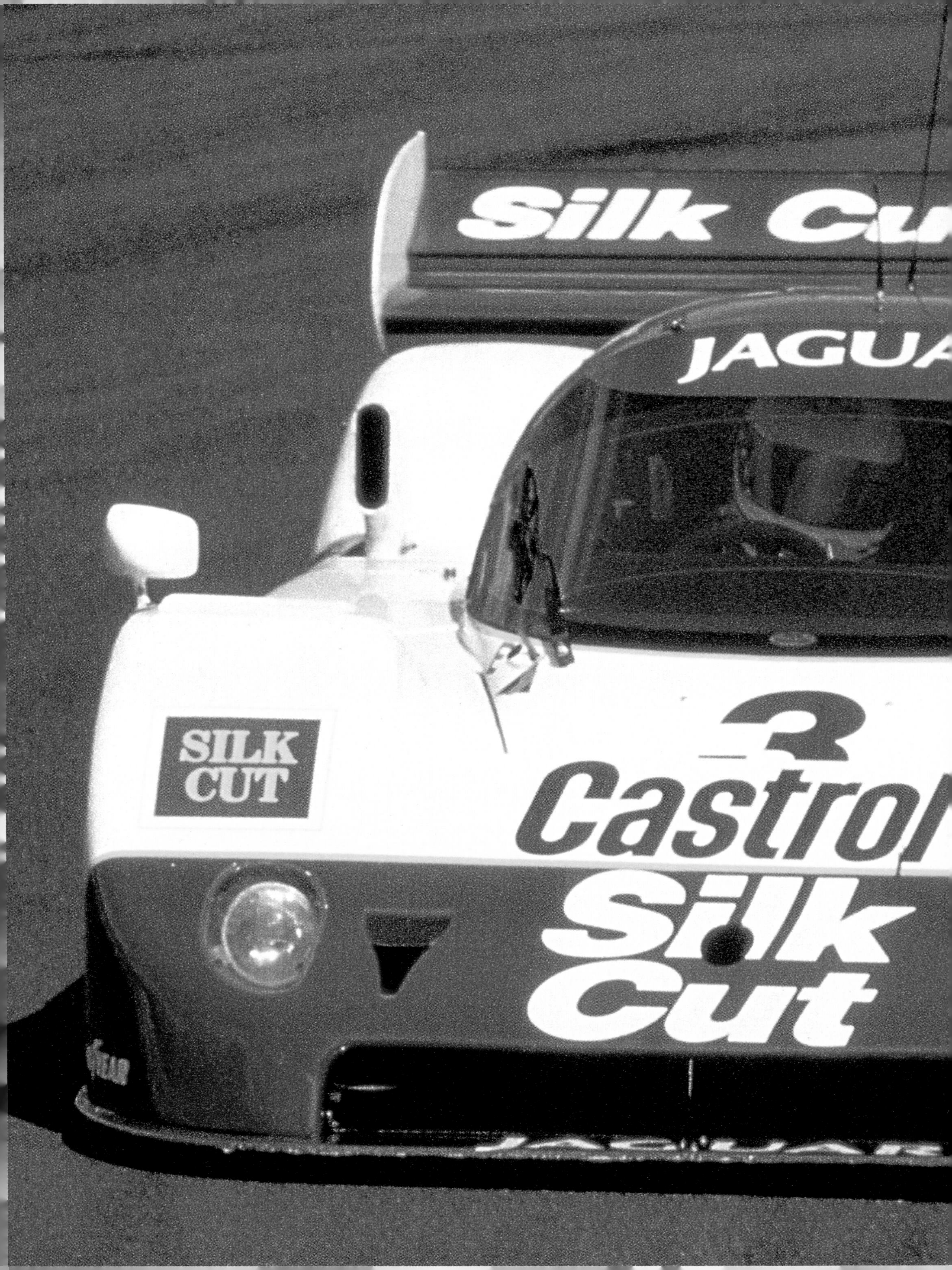
Silk Cu
JAGUA
SILK CUT
Castrol
Silk Cut

SPORTS RACING CARS

The sports and GTs arena of the sport is populated by a diverse mix of categories and championships, most of which feature several different makes of cars. There have been races for production sports cars, modified sports cars, factory prototypes competing in the World Championship for Makes, and, coming more up to date, grand touring cars in GT1, GT2 and GT3 format, plus the American Le Mans Series (ALMS) that replaced the IMSA (International Motor Sport Association) championship, and the International Sports Racing series.

The best barometer of the state of sports GT racing (the twin disciplines of sports car and GT racing often overlap) is the Le Mans 24-Hour race, which has the best and most extensive continuity for these categories. The same manufacturers return to the Sarthe circuit – not necessarily every year, but they are, inexorably, drawn back to pit their machinery against the state-of-the-art vehicles. The Le Mans classic falls mid-season, usually in mid-June, and it has more often than not been the centrepiece of the predominant sports racing

This Jaguar XJR-11 driven by Martin Brundle/Jan Lammers ran with a 3.5-litre twin turbo V6 power for most World Sports Prototype events in 1990, but the XJRs were fitted with 7.0-litre V12s for their successful assault on Le Mans that year.

championship of the day. Other events, such as the Sebring 12-Hour and the Nürburgring 1,000km (620 miles), have also achieved legendary status, but Le Mans goes back further. Therefore, one way of chronicling the development of sports racing cars is to look at Le Mans highlights, and feature the cars that were winning.

LE MANS
In the 1920s the British and Americans tackled the Le Mans endurance race with considerable success. One of the first Englishmen to grasp the significance of a Le Mans win in terms of marketing potential was Bentley's London agent John Duff, and he and Frank Clement finished fourth in the inaugural 1923 race in Duff's 3.0-litre (183-cubic-inch) model. Generally seen as wonderful old cars, the supercharged Bentleys were certainly stoutly engineered, so much so that Ettore Bugatti labelled them 'racing lorries'.

The 'lorries' returned the following year and gave Bentley the first of its five victories there. Bentley's two-car attempt in 1925 and the three-car assault in 1926 failed, but under the ownership of South African millionaire Woolf Barnato, the Bentley boys returned to win in 1927. This was the year of the celebrated White House

crash, in which Callingham's 4.5-litre (275-cubic-inch) Bentley, trying to avoid a stalled Schneider, went into a ditch, only to be hit by the two following 3.0-litre Bentleys of George Duller and Sammy Davis (despite a lengthy pit stop to repair his car, Davis managed to recover and win the race). The following year, Barnato himself, partnered by Bernard Rubin, won in a 4.4-litre (268.5-cubic-inch) car against stern opposition from Chrysler and Stutz. The golden year for Bentley, though, was 1929, when the Cricklewood marque occupied the first four places, Barnato and Tim Birkin taking the laurels. The gathering gloom of world depression meant that Bentley's last fling was in 1930, when they came first and second following the retirement of a Mercedes SSK.

THE ALFA 8C
The next car to enjoy a run of success at Le Mans was the Alfa Romeo 8C-2300. This handsome machine brought Alfa Romeo its first major successes in sports car racing, having been a prominent force in Grand Prix racing since 1924 with the famous P2. Surprisingly, for a manufacturer that had been involved in racing since its formation back in 1910, Alfa Romeo was not represented at Le Mans until 1930, when

This supercharged 4.5-litre Bentley is similar to the Le Mans winners of the late-1920s. Barnato/Rubin shared a 4.5-litre (275-cubic-inch) car in 1928, while 6.6-litre (403-cubic-inch) speed Six Bentleys carried off the honours in 1929 and 1930.

Earl Howe and L.G. Callingham finished fifth in a privately owned 6C 1750. At the same time, the firm's accomplished designer, Vittorio Jano, was working on the 8C-2300. It was powered by a supercharged 2336cc (142.5-cubic-inch) straight-eight engine, producing almost 180bhp, and was capable of running along the Mulsanne Straight at 193km/h (120mph).

Earl Howe immediately acquired one for 1931 and, racing with Tim Birkin in the absence of Bentley, became the first Le Mans winner to exceed 3,000km (1,864 miles). In 1932, six 8C-2300 Alfa Romeos were entered, two of which fought a long duel for the lead. When the privately entered Howe/Birkin car blew its head gasket, Raymond Sommer and Luigi Chinetti were unchallenged in the works car. Sommer had to drive for more than 18 hours because exhaust fumes had made Chinetti ill. The latter would go on to become the Ferrari concessionaire in the USA.

In 1933, Nicola Romeo's company passed into Italian state ownership and the competition department came under the control of Scuderia Ferrari. Enzo Ferrari hired Tazio Nuvolari for what would be his only Le Mans, co-driving with Sommer. A leaking fuel tank cost them precious time, but Nuvolari made a stunning comeback after his mechanics staunched the leak with chewing gum. He caught up with one of the other Alfa Romeos, driven by Chinetti, as they went into the final lap, and swapped places twice before Chinetti missed a gearshift. Nuvolari swept past once more to win by just 400 metres (just over 1300 feet). A British-entered 8C completed Alfa Romeo's top three placings.

The 8C's fourth and final Le Mans victory went to a French-entered car driven by Chinetti and Philippe 'Phi-Phi' Etancelin. It was one of four Alfas entered in 1934, but the only one to finish. Four privateer cars were entered in 1935, but just one came home, this time in second place behind the winning Lagonda.

BRIEFLY BUGATTI

If Ettore Bugatti felt that the Bentleys were like lorries (or trucks, if you prefer), his sports racing cars of the late 1930s were known as 'tanks' because of their streamlined, albeit rather slab-sided appearance. Outright victory at Le Mans had eluded Bugatti's racing

team ever since the inaugural event in 1923. In 1936, the race engineers at Bugatti's Molsheim factory adapted their latest Type 57 road-going sports car, fitted with a 3.3-litre (201-cubic-inch) DOHC straight-eight engine, and the first car was based on the short-chassis 57S, clad in streamlined all-enveloping bodywork.

Several French manufacturers had opted to run in sports car racing around 1936 because they were unable to match the awesome German Silver Arrows Grand Prix machines. So, as a snub to the Silver Arrows, the French Grand Prix, held on the banked Montlhéry road course south of Paris, was run as a sports cars event in 1936. There were no truly exciting cars present, and Raymond Sommer won it in the Bugatti. Next year, two Bugattis were prepared for Le Mans, but a double fatality in a six-car accident at the White House S-bend early in the race marred the proceedings. One of the Bugattis failed to finish when its fuel tank developed a leak, but the other one, driven by Jean-Pierre Wimille and Robert Benoist, took an easy victory. It had covered more than 3,200km (2000 miles).

The team missed the 1938 race because it was involved with the development of a new car that could take on the new 4.5-litre (275-cubic-inch) Delahayes and Talbots, but returned in 1939 with a single car entry, based on

the 200bhp Roots-supercharged Type 57C. It was driven to victory by Wimille and Pierre Veyron, and established another new distance record. However, Ettore Bugatti's triumph was marred by the death of his eldest son, Jean, who was killed testing this particular car on a public road near the factory.

JAGUARS POUNCE

In the post-war era, two new makes came to the fore: Ferrari (of which more later) and Jaguar. Two victories scored by the XK120's 'Competition' or C-Type model brought the Jaguar marque into the public eye and established a permanent association with Le Mans.

The Coventry marque first came to Le Mans in 1950 with three alumini-um-bodied XK120s, and two of them finished well up the field, behind a couple of Aston Martin DB2s. The potential of spaceframe-chassis racing cars was clear, and Jaguar built the XK120C, designed by the former aircraft aerodynamicist Malcolm Sayer. It was powered by Jaguar's 210bhp 3.4-litre (207.5-cubic-inch) straight-six twin-cam, and four cars

The 240bhp 3.0-litre (183-cubic-inch) Aston Martin DBR1 of Tony Brooks on its way to victory in the wet at Spa-Francorchamps in 1957, averaging 103.74mph. Astons were 1st and 2nd, ahead of four D-type Jaguars.

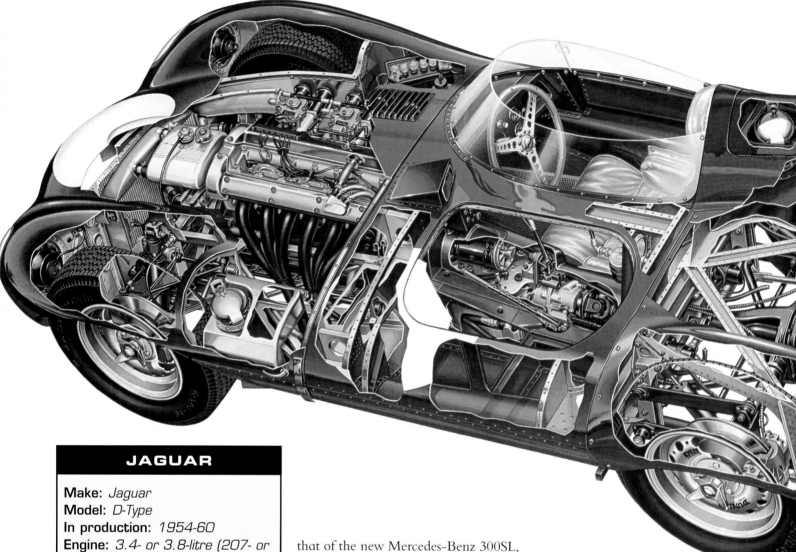

JAGUAR

Make: *Jaguar*
Model: *D-Type*
In production: *1954-60*
Engine: *3.4- or 3.8-litre (207- or 232-cubic-inch) straight-six*
Power output: *285bhp*
Chassis: *central aluminium mono-coque with tubular sub-frames front and rear*

were entered for Le Mans in 1951. The strategy often used in endurance racing is to send out one expendable car, driven by the fastest driver, to act as a hare in order to tempt the opposition into pursuit and potential mechanical failure. Jaguar's hare at Le Mans that year was Stirling Moss, partnered by fearless Jack Fairman, in a bid to break the Talbots that formed the principal opposition. The tactic worked, at the cost of a blown head gasket, and their team-mates Peter Whitehead and Peter Walker won by almost 10 laps.

The following year the nose of the car was redesigned to increase its 258km/h (160mph) top speed to match

that of the new Mercedes–Benz 300SL, but it had a smaller cooling aperture, which caused all three cars to overheat into retirement. For 1953, Jaguar entered three 220bhp C-Types equipped with disc brakes. The winning crew, Tony Rolt and Duncan Hamilton, were originally listed as reserves, and they had left the circuit before they were told they could race. Jaguar team manager Lofty England discovered them sitting on a pavement in Le Mans somewhat the worse for wear, and although they began the race with hangovers, they came through to win. The Moss/Walker C-Type finished second.

Jaguar's unmistakable D-Type of 1954, with its distinctive fin behind the driver's head, carried on where the C-Type left off. It was somewhat unusual in construction in that it had a mono-coque centre section with tubular sub-frames front and rear to carry the suspension and powertrain. The D-Type

The D-type Jaguar had a long career by racing car standards, from 1954 to 1960. The 1957 Le Mans winning D-type of Flockhart/Bueb ran a fuel injected 285bhp 3.8-litre straight-six twin-cam, while the Ecurie Ecosse cars had 3.4-litre engines.

was also styled by Malcolm Sayer, and was powered by the 3.4-litre (207.5-cubic-inch) Jaguar straight-six twin-cam, producing 250bhp, and was capable of over 270km/h (170mph). At Le Mans, the D-Type driven by 1953 winners Rolt and Hamilton finished second behind a Ferrari, after an unscheduled pit stop to replace Rolt's goggles, which had steamed up.

The 1955 race produced a thrilling duel between Mike Hawthorn's Jaguar D-Type and Juan Manuel Fangio's Mercedes 300SLR. Mercedes had fitted its cars with a flip-up air brake to

gency services' access to and from the circuit. Hawthorn continued his battle with Fangio, but the Mercedes team later withdrew, leaving Hawthorn and Ivor Bueb to take a rather hollow victory.

After that accident there were strong international pressures to end motor racing altogether, and it was summarily banned in Switzerland. But, inevitably, life went on. Having pioneered disc brakes with the C-Type, Jaguar introduced fuel injection on the D-Type in 1956, increasing power output to over 265bhp. The works team returned to Le Mans with three cars, and lost two of them in an accident in the first hour; the third was delayed by a misfire. However, the Ecurie Ecosse team D-Type of Ron Flockhart and Ninian Sanderson saved the day for Jaguar, overcoming the Aston Martin DB3S of Stirling Moss and Peter Collins to win by over a lap.

Having decided that it had done enough, and still somewhat sensitive over the Le Mans tragedy, Jaguar then withdrew from competition. The mantle was carried by Ecurie Ecosse, who entered three cars for the 1957 race, two of them having new 300bhp 3.8-litre (232-cubic-inch) engines. The Aston Martins, Ferraris and Maseratis proved fast but fragile, and the reliable Ecurie Ecosse D-Types finished first and second, with Flockhart and Bueb in the winning car. Privately entered D-Types came third and fourth, and the other Ecurie Ecosse 3.8-litre car was sixth. That turned out to be the zenith of the D-Type's career, as although it continued to be raced until 1960, it produced little in the way of results.

LOTUS BLOSSOMS
Of all the small teams that left their mark on Le Mans, indeed motor sport in general, Lotus was one of the most determined. Colin Chapman evolved a series of sports racing cars of unsurpassed beauty in the 1950s, styled originally by Frank Costin and best exemplified by the Eleven of 1956. Chapman's philosophy was based on

light weight, good handling and small, efficient engines, which in the 1950s meant Coventry-Climax units. He had always harboured the desire to race and win at Le Mans, and in 1955 Team Lotus entered the 1100cc (67-cubic-inch) Climax-engined Mark 9 for himself and the experienced Ron Flockhart. Other British manufacturers running in this class were Cooper, Kieft and Arnott. Chapman was disqualified in this instance (the year of the tragedy) for reversing back on to the circuit without permission from a marshall.

Undaunted, Team Lotus was back at Le Mans in 1956 with a trio of Elevens, bent on achieving a result. Two were 1100cc cars for Reg Bicknell/Peter Jopp and Cliff Allison/Keith Hall, and the other, for Chapman/Mac Fraser, ran with the 1500cc (91.5-cubic-inch) Climax unit. In order to comply with new Le Mans regulations, their tubular spaceframes were wider at the centre to permit mandatory full-width open cockpits and full-width aerodynamic screens to be fitted. As the race progressed, Cliff Allison hit a stray dog, and while running second in class the Chapman/Fraser car was eliminated by the failure of a big-end bolt. But the Bicknell/Jopp 1100 carried on to finish seventh overall and first in the 750 to 1100cc (46- to 67-cubic-inch) category, placing fourth in the Index of Performance considered so important by the French. Its average speed for the 24 hours was 141.54km/h (87.97mph), and it had been timed at 192.18km/h (119.44mph) over the flying kilometre on the Mulsanne Straight, which spoke volumes for the Eleven's aerodynamics.

Team Lotus built five new Elevens especially for their assault on Le Mans in 1957. There were three 1500s, an 1100 and a 750. All ran with wire wheels, except for the 750, which was fitted with magnesium alloys. Changes in the regulations called for a full-width screen, two regular seats and a flexible tonneau cover. To improve the aerodynamic potential, the windscreen's top lip was flipped over in line with the rear bodywork. This was now

create more wind resistance to slow them in corners, a rather primitive response to Jaguar's disc brakes but nonetheless quite effective. The Jaguar could manage 282km/h (175mph) down the Mulsanne Straight to the Mercedes' 270km/h (168mph), but the German car handled better. The battle was to end with the worst accident in the history of motor racing. As he moved towards the pits for a routine stop, Hawthorn caused Lance Macklin to swerve his Austin-Healey 100S into the path of Pierre Levegh's Mercedes, which launched it into the trackside abutment where it disintegrated and cut a swathe through the spectators in the enclosure. As the titanium burned, Levegh and over 80 spectators perished. Despite the horror, the race continued. Even people in the Lotus pit further up the track were not aware of the enormity of the incident, and the authorities probably decided that to stop the race would impede the emer-

Probably the most beautiful sports racing car of all time, the Ferrari 330P3/4, powered by the 450bhp 4.0-litre (244-cubic inch) V12 unit, the P4 won the title in 1967. This is Jackie Stewart at Brands Hatch during the '67 BOAC 500.

elevated to correspond with the height of the rear wings, and the flexible tonneau covered the void of the passenger seat. In a bid to push the aerodynamic envelope a bit further, Team Lotus intended to use inflatable tonneau covers (like miniature li-los) to streamline the entire passenger compartment, but there was no time to make these. They were required to produce the hoods for each car for the scrutineers, however, and whether they would have worked or not is a moot point.

Americans Mac Fraser and Jay Chamberlain took over the 1100 of Le Mans novices Ashdown and Stacey and finished the race ninth overall, winning the 1100cc (67-cubic-inch) class and coming second in the Index of Performance. The privately entered Elevens of Dalton/Walshaw and Hèchard/Masson finished 13th and 16th overall, classified second and fourth in the 1100cc class. More remarkably, the 744cc (45.4-cubic-inch) Climax-FWC-engined car of Allison/Hall was 14th overall, winning its class and the Index of Performance. All four Elevens contrived to cross the finishing line together at 1600 hours having trounced the class favourites, the DB Panhards, the Stanguellinis, even the Coopers and Porsches in the Index of Performance. That was the high spot of Team Lotus's Le Mans appearances. When his Type 23 was excluded by scrutineers on a technicality concerning wheel nuts, Chapman swore he would never return to the Sarthe.

MARANELLO'S FINEST
It is inevitably the bigger cars that get the lion's share of the glory though, and Ferrari has always had more than its fair share. The gorgeous Testa Rossa dominated its era at Le Mans, and it will probably best be associated with Phil Hill and Olivier Gendebien's extraordinary run of victories.

It was developed during 1957 for the World Sports Car Championship's 3.0-litre (183-cubic-inch) regulations, and christened Testa Rossa, or 'Red Head', because its engine's camshaft covers were painted the same colour as the bodywork. While a TR250 prototype showed potential at Le Mans in 1957 using a 3117cc (190.2-cubic-inch) engine, the chassis was modified and fitted with a 300bhp 2953cc (180.2-cubic-inch) V12 unit designed by Gioacchino Colombo. The tubular spaceframe chassis was clad in aluminium bodywork fabricated in Modena by Sergio Scaglietti. The 250TR was raced by privateers as well as the works team, and there were no fewer than ten Testa Rossas on the grid at Le Mans in 1958.

Throughout the year, Ferrari fought with Aston Martin's gorgeous straight-six-engined DB3Ss, but clinched the title when Phil Hill and Gendebien won Le Mans. The same pair were leading in 1959 when their Ferrari's head gasket failed late on the Sunday morning. It was the last of seven 250TRs that had started, and four of them were sidelined by failures of their new and unproven five-speed transmissions. That left the way clear for Aston Martin to win the World Sports Car title, an achievement that was long overdue.

The Ferrari Testa Rossa of 1960 had a dry-sump engine mounted lower in the chassis, coupled with a new four-speed gearbox, and new suspension. Five TR60s ran at Le Mans, and, amazingly, two of them ran out of fuel in the third hour. Despite this oversight, the team went on to take the first two places, with Olivier Gendebien and Paul Frère in the winning car. It was to be the first of six consecutive Ferrari victories.

In 1962, Gendebien and Phil Hill took the win with a Testa Rossa built for the new prototype class. The open-cockpit 330TR1/LM was built on a lengthened TR61 chassis powered by a 360bhp 4.0-litre (244-cubic-inch) V12 Superamerica engine. This was the last time a front-engined car won at Le Mans.

Ferrari's winning 250 P V12 prototype of 1963 was a well-balanced, technically advanced and sophisticated car that the minimal opposition, with one exception, could not oppose. That exception was Porsche, which by 1963 had accumulated more class wins in post-war days than any other manufacturer, threatening Ferrari on slower circuits like the Nürburgring and the Targa Florio.

A GIANT ENTERS

When Ford entered the arena, it was touch and go whether the muscle flexing of the American giant would prevail or appear ridiculous. The Ford GT40, so called because it was just 40 inches (just over a metre) off the ground, evolved from a decision made by Henry Ford II in 1962 to increase the company's international status by winning Le Mans. The car was based

on the Lola GT, which was created independently of Ford in 1962, and after initial race successes Ford was attracted by its specification. Lola chief Eric Broadley was hired by Ford, and his design adapted for the GT40.

Ford Advanced Vehicles was set up at Slough, with designer Roy Lunn and ex-Aston Martin team manager John Wyer as technical director and general manager. The basis of the GT40 was a steel monocoque with square-tube stiffening, and fibreglass body panels. When the first GT40s raced in 1964 they were undeniably fast, albeit fragile, particularly at Le Mans: when they reached maximum speed on the Mulsanne Straight the nose was prone

to lift. Despite Phil Hill and Bruce McLaren setting a new circuit record at Le Mans of 211.25km/h (131.29mph), all retired.

The following year the effort was split up: development work on the Mk 2 version was carried out by Kar Kraft near Dearborn, and engine work by Shelby-American, who swapped the Ford aluminium four-cam Indy engine for a 4.7-litre (287-cubic-inch) cast-iron Fairlane lump on the basis that it would be reliable. A ZF gearbox was substituted for a Colotti box, while cast alloy wheels replaced the wire spoke ones fitted earlier. The Slough-based operation under John Wyer built an open-top version of the Mk 1 GT40.

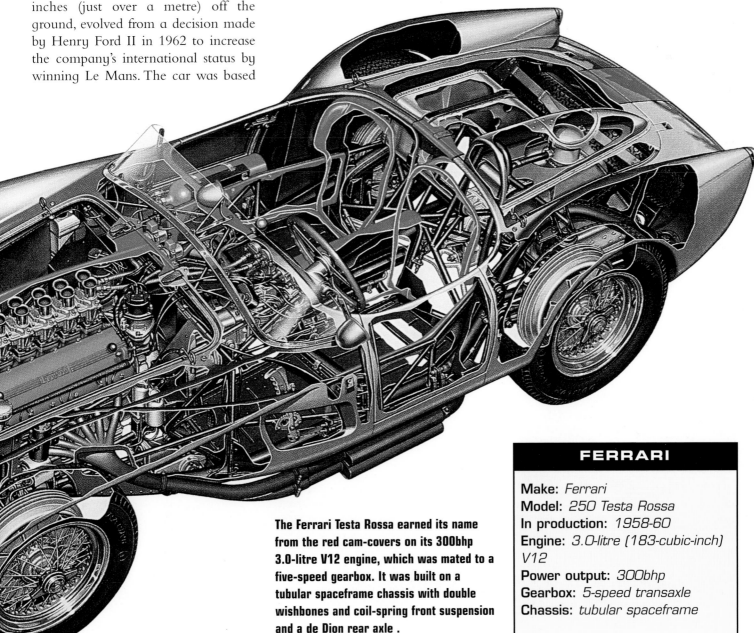

The Ferrari Testa Rossa earned its name from the red cam-covers on its 300bhp 3.0-litre V12 engine, which was mated to a five-speed gearbox. It was built on a tubular spaceframe chassis with double wishbones and coil-spring front suspension and a de Dion rear axle .

FERRARI

Make: *Ferrari*
Model: *250 Testa Rossa*
In production: *1958-60*
Engine: *3.0-litre (183-cubic-inch) V12*
Power output: *300bhp*
Gearbox: *5-speed transaxle*
Chassis: *tubular spaceframe*

When racing car aerodynamics were in their infancy, Jim Hall's Texan Chaparral firm pioneered the adjustable rear aerofoil with the 7.0-litre (427-cubic inch) Chevrolet-powered Chaparral 2F.

The idea was to reduce weight by taking off the roof, but it made the chassis more flimsy.

At Le Mans in 1965, Ford entered a pair of 7.0-litre (427-cubic-inch) Mk 2 cars – basically the Ford Galaxie engine in NASCAR format, mated to a Ford T-44 four-speed gearbox – and the chassis was configured quite differently to accommodate the bigger engine and oil tank. The Mk 2 was altogether a more formidable-looking car, and it was fitted with stabilisers to calm down its waywardness. Six 4.7-litre (287-cubic-inch) GT40s were also entered, but despite the benefit of numbers all had retired by midnight for

one reason or another, and the race was won by Jochen Rindt and Masten Gregory in Luigi Chinetti's NART Ferrari 250LM.

Eric Broadley, meanwhile, had gone back to designing Lolas, and his next offering was the stalwart Lola T70, which provided Aston Martin and John Surtees with a chassis to try a 5.0-litre (305-cubic-inch) V8 in 1967. Normally powered by the 5.9-litre (360-cubic-inch) Chevrolet V8, the Lola T70 Mk 3 and 3B was the mainstay of the sports GT category during the late 1960s, and its open-top version proved its worth in the CanAm series.

And despite the threat from Ford, Ferrari had to concentrate on the new 3-litre (183-cubic-inch) Formula 1 in 1966, so its entries were restricted in sports prototype racing. The Scuderia now raced the Tipo 330P3, powered by the 420bhp 3967cc (242.1-cubic-inch)

engine with Lucas fuel injection and mated to a five-speed ZF gearbox. The chassis was a multi-tubular frame with a bonded fibreglass underbody, moulded round the tubing. The body was fabricated by Piero Drogo with four headlamps in vertical pairs, and the cars were built in both open and closed forms. The contemporary Dino was the 206S, which looked like a scaled-down version of the P3 with a 2.0-litre (122-cubic-inch) V6 engine.

At Le Mans in 1966, Ford fielded a grand total of eight 7.0-litre (427-cubic-inch) Mk 2 prototypes entered by Shelby, Holman & Moody and Alan Mann Racing. Ranged against them were two works Ferrari P3s driven by Parkes/Scarfiotti and Bandini/ Guichet, with a third P3 loaned to the North American Racing Team (NART) and driven by Rodriguez/ Ginther, backed up by four 365P2 cars entered by other private teams. It was not Ferrari's day: Parkes/Scarfiotti crashed, Bandini/ Guichet retired with a blown head gasket, and Rodriguez/Ginther retired with gearbox problems. The result was a clean sweep for Ford, three of the 7.0-litre Mk 2 GT40s crossing the line abreast. The authorities did not allow a dead-heat, so Bruce McLaren and

The Autodelta-built Alfa Romeo T33/2 was powered by an aluminium-alloy 2.0-litre (122-cubic-inch) V8 engine developing 315bhp, and was frequently a class winner as well as placing 4th, 5th and 6th at Le Mans in 1968.

Chris Amon took the honours from Hulme/Miles and Bucknum/Hutcherson. None of the five regular GT40s finished, however, but the highest-placed Ferrari was the 275GTB of Pike/Courage in eighth place.

Ferrari fought back the following year with the new 330P4 car, retaining the 3967cc (242.1-cubic-inch) engine in modified format, with twin plugs per cylinder and four separate coils that raised power output to 450bhp at 8000rpm. It also had a wider track and shorter wheelbase, and the lines were cleaned up, making it one of the most beautiful sports racing cars of all time. Everything about it was right: its engine was both flexible and powerful, and it handled well and was nicely balanced. It could also last 24 hours.

At Le Mans in 1967, there were seven 7.0-litre (427-cubic-inch) Fords, each superbly prepared and painted a different colour. Shelby-American Mk 4s were entered for Gurney/Foyt and McLaren/Donohue, while Hawkins/Bucknum drove a Mk 2A. Holman & Moody Mk 4s were driven by Bianchi/Andretti and Hulme/Ruby, and they had a Mk 2 for Gardner/McClusky. In addition, a Holman & Moody-prepared Mk 2A was entered by Ford-France for Schlesser/Ligier. Ferrari entered three works P4s with a fourth on loan to Equipe Nationale Belge, and there were three privately entered P3/4s. In practice the Ford Mk 4s were plagued by cracking windscreens; indeed, one car's windscreen actually cracked while it was stationary in the pits. They simply flew in replacement screens from the States. Still Ford suffered mechanical attrition. Lloyd Ruby crashed his car, which earlier in the race had set a new lap record, and during the early hours of the Sunday morning Jo Schlesser reported that there were Fords all over the road, and he had been forced to hit the bank to miss them. Andretti had a brake lock-up as he went into the Esses, smashing into the bank, and McClusky hit the bank trying to avoid him. Schlesser missed both cars, but rammed the

bank himself. At the end of the 24 hours, Foyt/Gurney, with their Shelby-American Mk 4, were the winners at 213.18km/h (132.49mph), leading home two P4 Ferraris. The other Shelby-American Mk 4 of McLaren/Donohue came home in fourth place.

With the imposition of a 3.0-litre (183-cubic-inch) limit for prototypes and a 5.0-litre (305-cubic-inch) limit for competition sports cars for 1968, the face of endurance racing changed. Ferrari withdrew, as did the Chaparral and works Ford teams. For two years racing was fought out between Porsche and the superbly prepared and carefully developed 4.7-litre (287-cubic-inch) Ford GT40s of John Wyer's Gulf-sponsored team, which won Le Mans two years in succession. The 1969 victory provided one of the closest finishes in the history of the race, with the GT40 of Jacky Ickx leading the Porsche 908 of Hans Hermann across the finishing line by just under 50 metres (160ft).

SKEWERING THE PORKER
Although the 4.5-litre (275-cubic-inch) Porsche 917 appeared during 1969, few people appreciated its potential. The decision of both Porsche and Ferrari to build 5.0-litre (305-cubic-inch) competition sports cars for 1970 not only frustrated the intention of the FIA to restrict the speed of prototypes (because they actually made Formula 1 cars appear slow), but provided two years of

The 2.0-litre (122-cubic-inch) flat-six engined Porsche 910 of Gerhard Koch/Rudi Lins heads a works 2.2-litre (134-cubic-inch) eight-cylinder 907 at the Nürburgring 1000kms in 1968.

the most exciting racing ever seen.

The original 917 was not particularly sophisticated, but a development of existing Porsche practice. The flat-12 engine was based on the flat-eight of the excellent 907 and 908, which were derived originally from the Carrera 6 of 1966 and 910 of 1967. The air-cooled 917's mighty flat-12 engine was originally 4.5 litres and featured a magnesium alloy crankcase with twin overhead camshafts per cylinder bank. There were two valves and plugs per cylinder operated by twin distributors, with Bosch fuel injection. Transmission was by five-speed all-synchromesh gearbox in unit with the final drive. The 917's spaceframe chassis was similar to that of the 908, fabricated from aluminium alloy tubing with 60-litre (13.2-gallon) fuel tanks in the side members, but such was its thirst they were sufficient for less than an hour's racing. Front suspension was by wishbones and coil-spring/damper units, with wishbones, radius arms and coil-spring/damper units at the rear. Again, this was very similar to the layout of the 908. By 1969, the 917's fibreglass body had rear spoilers fitted that were actuated by rods connected to the rear suspension.

The most highly evolved version of the Ford GT40 was the 7.0-litre (427-cubic-inch) Mk IV, which won the Le Mans 24-Hours in 1967. Entered by Shelby American and driven by A.J. Foyt and Dan Gurney, this car featured a blip in the roof to accommodate the latter's lanky frame.

FORD

Make: *Ford (Kar Kraft-built)*
Model: *GT40 Mk IV*
In production: *1967*
Engine: *7.0-litre (427-cubic-inch) Ford V8*
Power output: *485bhp*
Gearbox: *4-speed Ford T-44*
Chassis: *epoxy-bonded and riveted aluminium honeycomb with tubular subframes*

The 1968 Le Mans-winning 5.0-litre (305-cubic-inch) Ford GT40 of Pedro Rodriguez/Lucien Bianchi in the pits during a driver change. This car outlasted two other JW Automotive-built GT40s as well as the works Porsches, and clinched the Manufacturers' title for Ford.

I was fortunate enough to see these cars race at the annual BOAC 1000km (620 miles) enduro at Brands Hatch several years running, and there was nothing to eclipse them for sheer spectacle, especially in the hands of Pedro Rodriguez and Jo Siffert. At the time they really outshone Formula 1.

At the 1969 Le Mans race, Porsche had a six-car entry with two 917s and four 908s, the long-tailed version performing best on the long Mulsanne Straight. For 1970, John Wyer was lured from the Mirage project and engaged to run the works Porsche team with Gulf Oil Corporation sponsorship. David Yorke, the former Vanwall Grand Prix team manager, acted as team manager, and John Horsman of Aston Martin became deputy managing director of J.W. Automotive

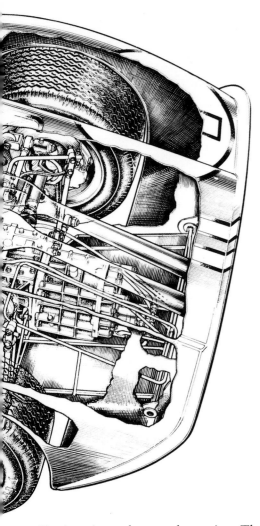

Engineering, who ran the project. The 917's handling problems were cured by fitting the short, uplifted tail used throughout 1970.

The 917s now faced formidable opposition from the new Ferrari 512S 5.0-litre (305-cubic-inch) competition sports cars raced by the works and private teams. The Porsche 917s were lighter than the Ferraris and had better aerodynamics, but although they could match the Ferraris on power, they were not as reliable. On the other hand, the Ferraris were not as well developed and lacked drivers of the same calibre as Porsche, apart from Jacky Ickx. The simple truth was that Ferrari was trying to compete in Formula 1 and endurance racing, and was over-stretched. Porsche dominated the 1970 season; Ferrari achieved only one championship race win.

Le Mans was a three-sided battle as the Gulf team faced opposition from Ferrari as well as other works-support-ed Porsche entries. J.W. Automotive entered three 917s, two of which were powered by 5.0-litre engines and one with a 4.5-litre (275-cubic-inch) unit, all with the short-tail body and small angled spoilers. Porsche Konstrucktionen also had three 917s, two with 5.0-litre engines and one with a 4.5-litre unit; the Porsche Salzburg entry was a long-tail car with a maximum speed of 354km/h (220mph), and the Martini International Racing team had one 917 as well. The Ferrari opposition comprised no fewer than ten 512Ss. Of the Gulf cars, Rodriguez/Kinnunen retired early with a broken fan drive-shaft, Hailwood crashed his 917 into Facetti's stricken Alfa Romeo T33, and Siffert missed a gear change and over-revved the engine. The Ferraris fared no better, and the race was won by the Porsche Salzburg entry, in a striking psychedelic mauve and green colour scheme, driven by Richard Attwood

By 1971 the 5.0-litre Porsche 917 was an established winner, and experimental versions included the suitably liveried 'Pig', which had a shorter, rotund body with twin-tail fins and an aerofoil, plus louvres in the front wings.

and Hans Hermann.

For 1971, Porsche continued to race the 908 and 917, and the 908 was the favoured weapon at circuits like the Targa Florio where nimbleness counted. A great deal of effort had gone into aerodynamic development and the definitive Lang version featured a wider body, long smooth tail, rear wheels enclosed and twin tail fins bridged by an aerofoil. This body configuration was only used at Le Mans, however. The second version featured a short tail with twin tail fins and louvres in the tops of the front wings, and because of its nickname, the 'Pig', it was liveried in the cuts of meat one gets from a pig. It won the 3-Hour

race at the Le Mans test weekend, driven by Kauhsen/van Lennep.

The Gulf team's main opposition came from the Martini Racing team. The other serious contender that year was Alfa Romeo's Autodelta team, who had at last sorted out the 3.0-litre (183-cubic-inch) V8-engined T33 prototypes, and scored several class wins and outright victory whenever the Porsche 917s failed. At Le Mans, six Porsche 917s were entered by the Gulf and Martini teams. After the first six hours the Gulf cars occupied the first three places, but they succumbed to mechanical problems, then Joest crashed the Pig, and the Martini-entered 917 of Helmut Marko and Gijs van Lennep took the lead during the early hours of Sunday morning. It was never headed, the Gulf-entered 917 of Attwood/Muller came second, and Porsche won the championship by a comfortable margin from Alfa Romeo.

With 5.0-litre (305-cubic-inch) competition sports cars banned at the end of 1971, the 917s were no longer seen in international long-distance racing. The 917 programme was reckoned to have cost around DM15 million; the actual cost of the 43 competition cars was DM350,000 each. In 1969 a

Spyder version of the 917 was built for Jo Siffert to race in the North American CanAm series. By 1972 Porsche had developed a turbocharged version of the 5.0-litre engine, and this had a staggering power output of 1000bhp. Porsche then signed a three-year contract with Roger Penske Racing for Mark Donohue to drive the turbocharged 917-10. Donohue came second in the first CanAm round, but was injured in a testing accident and temporarily replaced by George Follmer, who won the CanAm championship that year. Donohue was back to take the title honours in 1973, by which time the 917's engine capacity had been increased to 5.5 litres (336 cubic inches). A fuel-consumption restriction on turbocharged cars stifled Porsche's chances in CanAm in 1974, but the 917-10 turbos with 4.5-litre (275-cubic-inch) engines carried on in the European Interseries Championship until the end of 1975.

MATRAS ON TOP

With the imposition of the 3.0-litre (183-cubic-inch) limit in 1972, Ferrari enjoyed a season of outright success with its superbly balanced 312P. Its high standard of preparation was

The Renault assault on the 1977 Le Mans event centred on the 520bhp turbocharged 2.0-litre (122-cubic-inch) V6 Alpine A442, with Jabouille and Laffite seen here leading Ickx's Porsche 936 and Stommelen's Porsche 935 coupé.

largely down to Ermanno Cuoghi, formerly with the Gulf team, but by then joint chief mechanic at Ferrari. Peter Schetty was team manager, and they hired some of the world's best drivers, including Jacky Ickx, Clay Regazzoni, Ronnie Peterson and Brian Redman.

But Ferrari did not enter Le Mans, and Matra MS670s occupied the first two places, Graham Hill and Henri Pescarolo taking the win. By 1973, the Matra MS670Bs were vastly improved, and all year the French cars were serious challengers to the Ferraris (Pescarolo won Le Mans again). By 1974, the Matra was unopposed, apart from its own occasional weaknesses (Pescarolo won his third Le Mans on the trot).

When Matra withdrew its MS670Cs from racing at the end of 1974, it left the field clear for Alfa Romeo to clean up. Autodelta ran two T33 TT12s in 1975, for Andrea de Adamich/Carlo

Masterminded by Jean Todt, Peugeot's V10-powered 905 LM won the 1992 Le Mans enduro with Derek Warwick/Yannick Dalmas/Mark Blundell sharing the wheel. The rear wing is separate from the 905's enclosed body.

Facetti and Arturo Merzario/Jacky Ickx/Brian Redman; Henri Pescarolo and Tino Brambilla piloted the third car entered by Willy Khausen. The Alfas won at Dijon, Monza, Spa-Francorchamps, Enna-Pergusa and the Nürburgring. For some years after that, long-distance racing languished in the doldrums, with Porsches claiming many victories.

PORSCHE RESURGENCE

Porsche's main weapon for the second half of the 1970s was the open-top mid-engined 936, and it provided Jacky Ickx with his third Le Mans win in 1976. The Alpine Renaults faded, and only the Gulf could sustain a challenge. The same model won again the following year, crewed by Barth/Haywood/Ickx, after the first serious tussle with Alpine Renault. The mainstays of the grids were the Group 4 and IMSA specification Porsche 911

The 1989 Le Mans winning Sauber C9 Group C car was powered by the 5.0-litre turbocharged Mercedes-Benz V8 engine, pictured with Jochen Mass at the wheel in a Japanese round of the World Sports Prototype series in 1990.

Carreras, similar-looking 934s and flat-nose 935s, all sporting vastly over-grown wheel arches and tea-tray spoilers. The Martini and Kremer teams ran Group 5 935s, which looked even more extreme.

By 1978, though, the Alpine Renaults were uncatchable, even though the 936/78s had twin turbo engines now. The car of Barth/Wolleck/Ickx came second at Le Mans that year, followed by the Martini team's older 936/77 driven by Haywood/Gregg/Joest, and the flat-nose 935s were also well on the pace, coming fifth, sixth and seventh, and cleaning up the IMSA and Group 5 categories. The Martini 935 of Schurti/Stommelen was nicknamed 'Moby Dick' because of its whale-like profile, caused by its aerodynamic front and rear bodywork additions.

The 1979 Le Mans was won by the Kremer team's 935 K3 Group 5 car featuring a flat nose, Kevlar bodywork and high rear wing. It was driven by Klaus Ludwig and the Whittington brothers, Dale and Bill, and won by seven laps. Actor Paul Newman partnered Rolf Stommelen and entrant Dick Barbour to second place in an IMSA Porsche 935.

SAUBER-MERCEDES

Make: *Sauber*
Model: *C9*
In production: *1998-90*
Engine: *5.0-litre (305-cubic-inch) turbocharged Mercedes-Benz V8*
Gearbox: *Hewland*
Power output: *720bhp*
Tyres: *Michelin*

The 1989 Nissan R89C Group C1 prototype was a Lola design that replaced its previous March-sourced chassis. It was powered by the 3.2-litre (195-cubic-inch) twin-turbo V8, and driven by Julian Bailey and Mark Blundell with another two similar cars running at Le Mans.

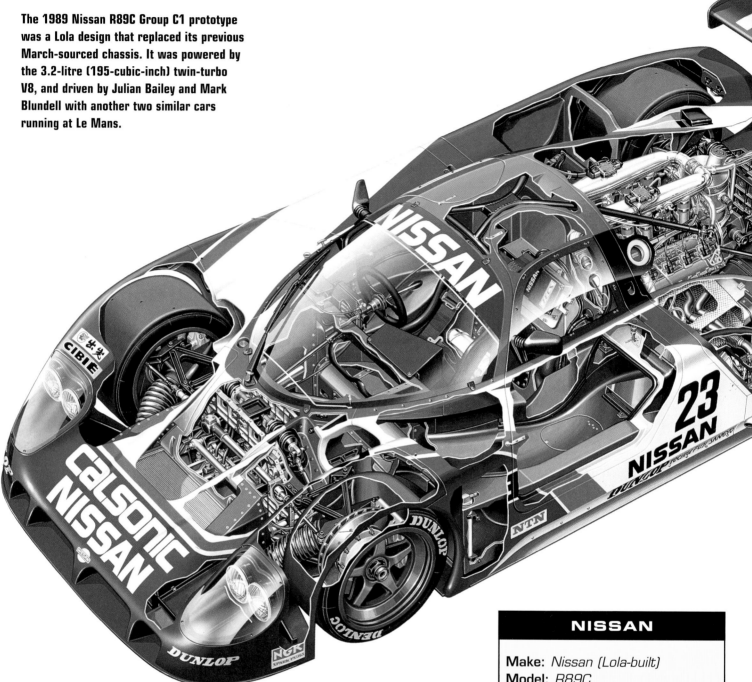

NISSAN

Make: *Nissan (Lola-built)*
Model: *R89C*
In production: *1989*
Engine: *3.2-litre (195-cubic-inch) Nissan twin-turbocharged (Weslake-built) V8*
Power output: *up to 950bhp*
Chassis: *composite monocoque*

It was rare for privateers to get a look in at the podium by this time, but in 1980, Jean Rondeau and team-mate Jean-Pierre Jaussaud won Le Mans in Rondeau's own car. The race had been led for much of the time by the Martini Porsche 936/80 of Ickx/Joest, and it was also notable for being the first appearance of the front-engined Porsche 924 Carrera turbo. Barth/Schurti came sixth and Rouse/Dron 12th overall.

This was just a blip in a remarkable series of Porsche wins at Le Mans. There was yet another victory in 1981 for Jacky Ickx, partnered by Derek Bell, in the very streamlined 936/81, powered by the development engine for Porsche's contemporary Indycar. It finished four laps clear of Rondeau. For 1982, there was a switch to the Group C prototype category, and Porsche's new closed-top 935 model marked a new era in sports car racing, setting the trend for the rest of the decade. There was a fuel consumption

limit, but despite this Ickx and Bell won the 50th Le Mans in the new car powered by the previous year's engine, and still covered a greater distance in the 24 hours. The 956s of Mass/Schuppan and Haywood/Holbert came second and third.

Porsche 956s were again dominant in 1983, the Rothmans cars coming first and second, with the Andrettis, father and son, placing third in a Kremer 956. Similar cars occupied nine of the first 10 places. Although no official works cars appeared at Le Mans in 1984, 956s still managed to occupy the first eight places. And for the next three years Porsche were triumphant at Le Mans, until a new contender arrived on the scene to break the Weissach stranglehold.

GREEN MACHINE

British racing green was back. The Silk Cut Jaguar team, run for the Coventry manufacturer by Tom Walkinshaw's TWR Racing at Kidlington and managed by Roger Silman, fielded the new Jaguar XJR-6, powered by the normally aspirated V12 engine. It was first raced in August 1985, and the following year had been developed into a real contender. The XJR-6 now

The 1999 Le Mans-winning BMW V12 LMR typifies the styling of modern sports racing cars and ALMS runners, ranged against contemporary Audi, Reynard, Lola, Panoz, Courage and Cadillac chassis, as well as aging Riley & Scott and Ferraris.

generated up to 70 per cent more downforce than the new Porsche 962s and the atmospheric V12 engine produced enough power and was economical on fuel.

However, at this early stage in the car's career it was still unreliable, suffering misfires, poor fuel pick-up, minor transmission failures and detached oil lines. Jaguar had its sights set on the drivers' and teams' titles, and TWR ran a full programme of all nine races, taking 12 finishes from 20 starts. Drivers were Eddie Cheever, Derek Warwick, Jean-Louis Schlesser, Gianfranco Brancatelli, Jan Lammers, Martin Brundle and Win Percy. The high point of 1986 was its win at Silverstone, with near misses at Monza, Brands Hatch, Jerez and the Nürburgring.

That year also saw the beginnings of another major player entering the scene. The Kouros Mercedes was fielded in five races by Peter Sauber, and at the wet Nürburgring it

outpaced everything else due mostly to good aerodynamics, Goodyear tyres and its twin-turbo, low-boost, 5.0-litre (305-cubic-inch) V8 engine. Mike Thackwell and Henri Pescarolo won after the Jaguars had failed. Another team at the end of its Group C involvement was Lancia, whose open-top sports cars were blindingly quick on their day in the hands of Sandro Nannini and Andrea de Cesaris. The Martini Lancia LC2 squad was run by Cesare Fiorio, and at Monza and Silverstone in 1986 Andrea de Cesaris started from pole position. But the programme was wound up after the death of test driver Giacomo Maggi. Both Nissan and Toyota had Group C cars, Nissan's built by March Engineering and Toyota's by the TOM's team. Mazda ran its triple-rotary-engined GTP at Silverstone, Le Mans and Fuji. Apart from the works Porsche 962s, one of which won Le Mans, 1986 also featured the Brun Motorsport team, which won the teams' title, and

Reinhold Joest's team, which centred its programme on the Klaus Ludwig/Paolo Barilla car that had won Le Mans in 1984 and 1985. This remarkable 956 had started 54 races and returned 43 top three finishes.

In 1987, Jaguar triumphed in FIA sports car racing. It was the team to beat for the first time in three decades. With new 7.0-litre (427-cubic-inch) V12 atmospheric engines and prodigious downforce, the Tony Southgate-designed XJR-8s were always impressive, and they carried off no fewer than eight of the ten rounds of the world championship series, claiming the teams' title and placing four drivers at the top of the drivers' championship. No other international sports car team had done that since the introduction of

On the parade lap for the 1989 Le Mans 24-Hours are Jaguar XJR9LM of Lammers, Gilbert-Scott/Tambay, the Porsche 962 of Jelinski/Raphanel/Winter, the Sauber-Mercedes C9/88s of Cudini/Jabouille/Schlesser and Acheson/Baldi/Brancatelli, with the yellow Spice SE89C1 of Belm/Spice/St James.

the FIA World Championship in 1953. Yet the 1987 Le Mans 24-Hour fell once again to Porsche.

The TWR team entered three cars for its second Le Mans in 1988, and secured the first three places on the grid. But around midnight Win Percy burst a tyre at over 320km/h (200mph); although the XJR-8 was totally wrecked, the cockpit cell did not even distort, and the driver was unhurt. Another Jaguar retired with a cracked head, while the third car limped home in fifth place, but one of the drivers, Raul Boesel, went on to become 1987 world champion with five victories to his credit.

Already the writing was on the wall for Porsche's flat-six turbocharged 962, constructed on an aluminium monocoque design that was now pretty dated. The Jaguars, on the other hand, used an advanced composite chassis, and its relatively narrow V12 unit allowed the use of F1-type ground-effect aerodynamics. To an extent, Porsche's ability to respond to Jaguar was handicapped by its inability to develop a new works racing car, because that would alienate its loyal

customer teams who would then be saddled with outdated cars.

For 1989, there were three major players: Jaguar with its XJR-9, Porsche still running the 962, and Sauber Mercedes with its C9/88s, running turbocharged V8 engines mated to Hewland gearboxes. Other contenders were Aston Martin, back at Le Mans for the first time as a works entry for 30 years, and the three Japanese makes: Mazda, Nissan and Toyota. The new kids scored, the new Silver Arrows of Sauber Mercedes coming home first, second and fifth, but Jaguar was back the following year with the all-conquering 7.0-litre (427-cubic-inch) XJR-12 driven by Martin Brundle, John Nielsen and Price Cobb.

NEW NAMES
The surprise winners at La Sarthe in 1991 were Johnny Herbert, Volker Weidler and Bertrand Gachot driving a rotary-engined Mazda 787B, its sister car finishing sixth. The Mercedes C11s were the fastest cars in the race, though, and the Schlesser/Mass/Ferté car led for the majority of the 24

hours. The Jaguar XJ-12s may have been overweight and thus heavier on fuel, but they still managed second, third and fourth places.

The following year the engine capacity was 3.5 litres (214 cubic inches), and, again, using Le Mans as the yardstick for the championship, the result was a win for Peugeot's 905LM V10 (the 905s had been on the front row the previous year), with Derek Warwick, Yannick Dalmas and Mark Blundell at the wheel. Second was a Toyota TS-010, with another Peugeot third and a Mazda MXR-01 fourth. In 1993, Peugeot made it a one–two–three after the promised head-to-head

The Brun Team's Porsche 962 3.0 flat-six turbo running at Suzuka in 1989, driven by Tiff Needell/Derek Bell/Costas Los. The rear-wing supports rise steeply from the engine cover to form a significant part of the car's overall design.

with Toyota's TS-010s failed to materialise (the Japanese cars had transmission failure).

The regulations favoured GT cars for 1994, and Porsche was back in the guise of a Dauer 962LM, which the pundits believed was not exactly a GT car. There was an exciting finish to the race as Eddie Irvine, driving a SARD Toyota CV94, pipped Thierry Boutsen, in another Dauer Porsche, for second place after a close match during the final laps.

The 1995 event fell to another newcomer, McLaren's F1 GTR, and the second half of the 1990s came to be dominated by the GT1 and GT2 categories, at the expense of open-top sports cars. By 1999, however, the American Le Mans Series (ALMS) challenge was revising the status quo, and cars such as the BMW LM, Lola's B98/10, the Riley & Scott Ford, and Ferrari 333SP were prominent, and other marques may prosper in 2000.

The works-backed Jöest Team's Audi R8Rs came 1st and 2nd in the Sebring 12-Hours in 2000, opening round of the American Le Mans Series. Latest incarnation of the Silver Arrows theme, the winning R8 was driven by Biela/Pirro/Kristensen.

For 2000, challengers included Reynard's 2KQ and the Northstar-powered Cadillac, which was based on a Riley & Scott chassis, R & S having enjoyed successes in the Daytona 24- and Sebring 12-Hour races, but despite Oldsmobile backing for its first Le Mans attempt in 1996, there was no joy in France. Other privateer R & S teams were under-funded compared to the other top works teams. An all-new carbon-fibre monocoque replaced the Mk III, but R&S retained the car's innovative double-rocker suspension that proved so successful at the gruelling Daytona and Sebring circuits.

At the Daytona 24-Hour in early 2000, an ORECA Dodge Viper came first after a mighty battle with the works Corvette CR-5, which came second. Another ORECA Viper was third, and the fourth-placed Dyson Racing R & S-Lincoln Mk III was the first sports racer home, and it had been the race leader for most of the time.

The gauntlet had been thrown down by the GTO brigade, and it remained to be seen whether the sports racing cars could overturn the GT muscle-car steamroller.

LE MANS 24 HOUR

1923 André Lagache/René Léonard (3.0 Chénard et Walcker): 2209km (1372.94 miles), 92.05km/h (57.21mph)

1924 John Duff/Frank Clement (3.0 Bentley): 2076.90km (1290.80 miles), 86.53km/h (53.78mph)

1925 Gérard de Courcelles/André Rossignol (3.4 La Lorraine): 2233.50km (1388.13 miles), 93.06km/h (57.84mph)

1926 Robert Bloch/Andrè Rossignol (3.4 La Lorraine): 2551.86 km (1585.99 miles), 106.32km/h (66.08mph)

1927 Dr J. Dudley Benjafield/Sammy Davis (3.0 Bentley): 2369.30km (1472.53 miles), 98.71km/h (61.35mph)

1928 Woolf Barnato/Bernard Rubin (4.4 Bentley): 2668.70km (1658.61 miles), 111.20km/h (69.11mph)

1929 Woolf Barnato/Tim Birkin (6.6 Bentley Speed Six): 2843.22km (1767.07 miles), 118.47km/h (73.63mph)

1930 Woolf Barnato/Glen Kidston (6.6 Bentley Speed Six): 2930.04km (1821.03 miles), 122.09km/h (75.88mph)

1931 Lord Howe/Tim Birkin (2.3 Alfa Romeo Sports 8C): 3017km (1875.08 miles), 125.71km/h (78.13mph)

1932 Raymond Sommer/Louis Chiron (2.3 Alfa Romeo Sports 8C): 2953.40km (1835.55 miles), 123.06km/h (76.48mph)

1933 Raymond Sommer/Tazio Nuvolari (2.3 Alfa Romeo Sports 8C): 2499.76km (1553.61 miles), 130.97km/h (81.40mph)

1934 Luigi Chinetti/Philippe Etancelin (2.3 Alfa Romeo Sports 8C): 2886.32km (1793.86 miles), 120.26km/h (74.74mph)

1935 John Hindmarsh/Louis Fontes (4.5 Lagonda Rapide): 3006.14km (1868.33 miles), 125.26km/h (77.85mph)

1936 Race run as the French Grand Prix (winner: Raymond Sommer, 3.3 Bugatti)

1937 Jean-Pierre Wimille/Robert Benoist (3.3 Bugatti T575): 3287.24km (2043.03 miles), 136.97km/h (85.13mph)

1938 Eugéne Chaboud/Jean Tremoulet (3.8 Delahaye): 3180.25km (1976.54 miles), 132.52km/h (82.36mph)

1939 Jean-Pierre Wimille/Pierre Veyron (3.3 Bugatti T57C): 3354.04km (2084.55 miles), 139.76km/h (86.86mph)

1949 Lord Selsdon/Luigi Chinetti (2.0 Ferrari 166 Mille Miglia): 3133.53km (1947.50 miles), 132.39km/h (82.28mph)

1950 Louis Rosier/Jean-Louis Rosier (4.5 Talbot-Lago): 3464.37km (2153.12 miles), 144.34km/h (89.71mph)

1951 Peter Walker/Peter Whitehead (3.4 Jaguar C-Type): 3610.42km (2243.89 miles), 150.44km/h (93.50mph)

1952 Hermann Lang/Fritz Riess (3.0 Mercedes-Benz 300SL): 3732.99km (2320.07 miles), 155.59km/h (96.70mph)

1953 Tony Rolt/Duncan Hamilton (3.4 Jaguar C-Type): 4087.18km (2540.20 miles), 170.30km/h (105.84mph)

1954 Froilan Gonzalez/Maurice Trintignant (4.9 Ferrari 378 Plus): 4060.28km (2523.48 miles), 169.19km/h (105.15mph)

1955 Mike Hawthorn/Ivor Bueb (3.4 Jaguar D-Type): 4134.49km (2569.60 miles), 172.28km/h (107.07mph)

1956 Ron Flockhart/Ninian Sanderson (3.4 Jaguar D-Type): 4034.05km (2507.18 miles), 168.09km/h (104.47mph)

1957 Ron Flockhart/Ivor Bueb (3.8 Jaguar D-Type): 4396.16km (2732.23 miles), 183.18km/h (113.85mph)

1958 Phil Hill/Olivier Gendebien (3.0 Ferrari 250 Testa Rossa): 4101.04km (2548.81 miles), 170.88km/h (106.20mph)

1959 Roy Salvadori/Carroll Shelby (3.0 Aston Martin DBR1/300): 4347.28km (2701.85 miles), 181.13km/h (112.57mph)

1960 Olivier Gendebien/Paul Frère (3.0 Ferrari 250TR60): 4216.61km (2620.64 miles), 175.62km/h (109.15mph)

1961 Olivier Gendebien/Phil Hill (3.0 Ferrari 250TR61): 4475.61km (2781.61 miles), 186.48km/h (115.90mph)

1962 Olivier Gendebien/Phil Hill (4.0 Ferrari 330TR1/LM): 4450.30km (2765.88 miles), 185.42km/h (115.24mph)

1963 Lodovico Scarfiotti/Lorenzo Bandini (3.0 Ferrari 250P): 4560.71km (2834.5 miles), 190.02km/h (118.10mph)

1964 Jean Guichet/Nino Vaccarella (3.3 Ferrari 275P): 4050.69km (2517.52 miles), 195.59km/h (121.56mph)

1965 Masten Gregory/Jochen Rindt (3.3 Ferrari 250LM): 4676.11km (2906.22 miles), 194.83km/h (121.09mph)

1966 Bruce McLaren/Chris Amon (7.0 Ford GT Mk 2): 4842.04km (3009.35 miles), 201.75km/h (125.39mph)

1967 Dan Gurney/A.J. Foyt (7.0 Ford GT Mk 4): 5231.78km (3251.57 miles), 213.18km/h (132.49mph)

1968 Pedro Rodriguez/Lucien Bianchi (4.7 Ford GT40): 4451.93km (2766.89 miles), 185.50km/h (115.29mph)

1969 Jacky Ickx/Jackie Oliver (4.7 Ford GT40): 4996.93km (3105.61 miles), 208.20km/h (129.40mph)

1970 Richard Attwood/Hans Hermann (4.5 Porsche 917K): 4606.81km (2863.15 miles), 185.52km/h (115.30mph)

1971 Helmut Marko/Gijs van Lennep (4.9 Porsche 917K): 5334.16km (3315.20 miles), 222.25km/h (138.13mph)

1972 Henri Pescarolo/Graham Hill (3.0 Matra Simca 670): 4529.43km (2815.06 miles), 195.43km/h (121.46mph)

1973 Henri Pescarolo/Gérard Larrousse (3.0 Matra Simca 670B): 4852.90km (3016.10 miles), 202.20km/h (125.67mph)

1974 Henri Pescarolo/Gérard Larrousse (3.0 Matra Simca 670B): 4605.57km (2862.38 miles), 191.91km/h (119.27mph)

1975 Jacky Ickx/Derek Bell (3.0 Gulf Mirage GR8 Cosworth): 4594.58km (2855.55 miles), 191.44km/h (118.98mph)

1976 Jacky Ickx/Gijs van Lennep (2.1 t/c Porsche 936/76): 4125.30km (2563.89 miles), 198.70km/h (123.49mph)

1977 Jürgen Barth/Hurley Haywood/Jacky Ickx (2.1 t/c Porsche 936/77): 4670.62km (2902.81 miles), 194.61km/h (120.95mph)

1978 Didier Pironi/Jean-Pierre Jaussaud (2.0 t/c Alpine A442B-Renault-Gordini): 5043.44km (3134.52 miles), 210.14km/h (130.60mph)

1979 Klaus Ludwig/Dale Whittington/Bill Whittington (3.0 t/c Porsche 935/K3): 4108.68km (2553.56 miles), 173.87km/h (108.06mph)

1980 Jean Rondeau/Jean-Pierre Jaussaud (3.0 Rondeau M379B-Cosworth): 4607.03km (2863.29 miles), 191.95km/h (119.30mph)

1981 Jacky Ickx/Derek Bell (2.6 t/c Porsche 936/81): 4824.31km (2998.33 miles), 201.01km/h (124.93mph)

1982 Jacky Ickx/Derek Bell (2.6 t/c Porsche 956): 4898.04km (3044.15 miles), 204.09km/h (126.84mph)

1983 Vern Schuppan/Hurley Haywood/Al Holbert (2.6 t/c Porsche 956B): 5046.81km (3136.61 miles), 210.22km/h (130.65mph)

1984 Klaus Ludwig/Henri Pescarolo (2.6 t/c Porsche 956B): 4899.45km (3045.03 miles), 204.15km/h (126.88mph)

1985 Klaus Ludwig/Paulo Barilla/John Winter (2.6 t/c Porsche 956B): 5080.98km (3157.85 miles), 212km/h (131.76mph)

1986 Derek Bell/Hans Stuck/Al Holbert (2.6 t/c Porsche 962C): 4968.69km (3088.06 miles), 207.01km/h (128.66mph)

1987 Derek Bell/Hans Stuck/Al Holbert (3.0 t/c Porsche 962C): 4146.36km (2576.98 miles), 199.61km/h (124.06mph)

1988 Johnny Dumfries/Jan Lammers/Andy Wallace (7.0 Jaguar XJR-9LM): 5330.86km (3313.15 miles), 221.59km/h (137.72mph)

1989 Jochen Mass/Stanley Dickens/Manuel Reuter (5.0 t/c Sauber Mercedes C9): 5263.52km (3271.30 miles), 219.95km/h (136.70mph)

1990 Martin Brundle/John Nielsen/Price Cobb (7.0 Jaguar XJR-12): 4881.34km (3033.77 miles), 203.99km/h (126.78mph) 13.60km circuit incorporating chicanes on Mulsanne Straight

1991 Johnny Herbert/Bertrand Gachot/Volker Weidler (1.3 rotary Mazda 787B): 4915.72km (3055.14 miles), 205.29km/h (127.59mph)

1992 Derek Warwick/Yannick Dalmas/Mark Blundell (3.5 Peugeot 905): 4142.58km (2574.63 miles), 199.29km/h (123.86mph)

1993 Geoff Brabham/Eric Helary/Christophe Bouchut (3.5 Peugeot 905): 5098.52km (3168.75 miles), 214.56km/h (133.35mph)

1994 Yannick Dalmas/Hurley Haywood/Mauro Baldi (3.0 Dauer Porsche 962LM): 4042.10km (2512.18 miles), 195.22km/h (121.33mph)

1995 J.J. Lehto/Yannick Dalmas/Masinori Sekiya (McLaren F1): 4057.25km (2521.60 miles), 168.96km/h (105.01mph)

1996 Davy Jones/Manuel Reuter/Alexander Wurtz (Joest TWR-Porsche WSC95): 4748.64km (2951.30 miles), 200.56km/h (124.65mph)

1997 Michele Alboreto/Stefan Johansson/Tom Kristensen (Joest TWR-Porsche WSC95): 4508.17km (2801.85 miles), 204.15km/h (126.88mph)

1998 Allan McNish/Stephane Ortelli/Laurent Aiello (Porsche 911 GT1): 4773.60km (2966.81 miles), 195.28km/h (121.37mph)

1999 Yannick Dalmas/Jo Winkelhock/Pierluigi Martini (BMW V12 LMR): 4967.55km (3087.35 miles), 207km/h (128.65mph)

GRAND TOURING

Grand touring cars are by definition sleek two-seater coupés (with maybe 2+2 accommodation) with top stylist provenance that offer a high-performance specification but little in the way of luggage space. The archetypal GT competition car is probably the Ferrari 250GTO, the prototype of which ran in the 1961 Le Mans 24-Hour.

Ferrari's GT cars had enjoyed a fair measure of racing success throughout the 1950s, along with Maserati and Alfa Romeo, and this culminated in the 250GT Berlinetta of 1959. Of the 250 units built, perhaps 50 were built as racing GT cars, and they scored wins at the Tourist Trophy at Goodwood in the hands of Stirling Moss, the Tour de France (Mairesse/Berger) and the Paris 1000km (620 miles) at Montlhéry. The 250GTO sprang from the 250GT Berlinetta (the 'O' stood for 'omologato', meaning that it was 'homologated', or officially accepted, for racing), and its engine was brought up to Testa Rossa specification with dry-sump lubrication, six twin-choke Weber carbs and sports-racing camshafts and pistons. The definitive GTO had smoother, more aerodynamic bodywork styled by Pininfarina and built by Scaglietti, and was powered by a Colombo-designed 2953cc (180.2-cubic-inch) V12 engine with single overhead cam per bank of cylinders. Although Ferrari should have built 100, total production amounted to just 40 cars.

Evening pitstop for the Mercedes-Benz CLK GTR of Klaus Ludwig/Ricardo Zonta at Suzuka during the 1998 FIA GT Championship. Power unit for the Lola-built chassis was the 600bhp V12 up to mid-1998, and the 5.9-litre (360-cubic-inch) V8 thereafter. The CLKs won 10 out of 10 races in 1998.

Stirling Moss in the Rob Walker Ferrari 250GT leads a clutch of E-type Jaguars at Brands Hatch in 1961. The short-wheelbase 250GT was developed by Giotto Bizzarini and powered by a 280bhp 3.0-litre (183-cubic-inch) V12 engine.

The 250GTO's competition debut was at the Sebring 12-Hour; driven by Olivier Gendebien and Phil Hill, it came second overall and first in class. Numerous successes followed. At Le Mans, the 250GTOs of Noblet/Guichet and 'Elde'/'Beurlys' finished second and third, ahead of two lightweight E-type Jaguars. In the Tourist Trophy at Goodwood the 250GTOs of Innes Ireland, Graham Hill and Mike Parkes took the first three places. The GTO's competition career continued into 1963 with no modifications, and its run of success included Pedro Rodriguez winning the Daytona 3-Hour race, while at Sebring Penske/Pabst finished fourth overall. In the Targa Florio, Bulgari/Grana finished fourth overall and Noblet/Guichet came second overall at the Nürburgring. At Le Mans, the GTO of 'Beurlys'/Langlois finished second overall behind the winning 250P prototype. Ferrari's fourth successive win in the Tourist Trophy followed, with Hill in a GTO leading home Parkes in a similar car.

The 250GTO evolved into the 250GTO64 in 1964 when Ferrari was unable to get the mid-engined 250LM homologated. The classic 250GTO64 was a much more streamlined car than the classic 250GTO, with a scalloped rear to the cabin top, much like the 250LM would be, with a spoiler at the boot's trailing edge.

THE COBRA

Its chief rival was the Shelby Cobra, a beast of a car if ever there was one. With its origins dimly in the AC Ace chassis into which Carroll Shelby had shoehorned a 4.2-litre (256-cubic-inch) Ford Fairlane engine in 1962, the AC Cobra had graduated to being the Shelby American Cobra in 1965, complete with 7.0-litre (427-cubic-inch) Ford V8 engine. At first, the open sports car was fitted with a hardtop to improve aerodynamics and turn it into a GT car; then, to improve its aerodynamics, Peter Brock designed a streamlined coupé body in aluminium, with long, tapering nose and cut-off Kamm-tail. The Cobra now had a potential maximum speed of 290km/h (180mph) from 350bhp. Still, beneath the skin there lurked an almost prehistoric chassis.

In celebration of Dan Gurney and Bruce Johnson's fourth place at the 1964 Daytona 2000km (1240 miles), the Cobra coupé became known as the Daytona. The cars were made in three factories at first, which resulted in three quite different versions racing at Le

Mans: apart from the Shelby American source, one was built by Carrozzeria Gran Sport at Modena and another by AC Cars at Thames Ditton (the latter causing a stir when it was clocked at 295km/h (183mph) testing on the new M1 motorway in pre-speed-restriction Britain). The Gurney/Bondurant car finished fourth overall at Le Mans, and won the GT category. There were several other promising performances at other venues, but at the 1965 Le Mans, only one of four Daytona Cobras finished, driven by Thompson/Sears to eighth place after a collision caused cooling problems. When the Ford GT40 was homologated in 1966, the days of the Daytona Cobra were over.

Cars like the Cobra and the Ferrari 250GTO are as potent a symbol today as they ever were, and at classic events such as the Nürburgring Old Timer meeting, Laguna Seca, Coys International and Goodwood Revival, the pulses never fail to beat faster at the sight and sound of these fabulous cars duelling seriously in the hands of former Grand Prix stars.

FRENCH TOAST

France's leading producer of sports racing and GT cars was Alpine, formed in 1952 by Jean Redelé, who built his first A106 Alpine in 1954. The Alpine series invariably used Renault power and, like Porsche, its engines were hung out behind the rear axle line. Its prettiest and most effective car was the A110 Berlinette, which was sufficiently adaptable to be a world championship rally winner and a Le Mans racer.

As well as a lineage of single-seater F3 cars that were particularly successful in French and European championships, from 1963 Alpine began to build a separate line of prototypes to contest the World Championship for Makes, with Le Mans its inevitable goal. The mid-engined M63 was as beautiful as it was aerodynamically efficient, and it won the 1000cc (61-cubic-inch) prototype class in 1963. It was based on a curious triangulated tubular parallelogram chassis with fibreglass bodywork. A succession of svelte GTs followed, including the M64, A210, A212 and the open sports prototype A440, which by 1973 ran a V6 3.0-litre (183-cubic-inch) Renault-Gordini engine. On the driver strength were top young Frenchmen like Bob Wolleck, Alain Serpaggi, Christian

Éthuin, Jean-Pierre Jabouille, Gérard Larrousse, Alain Cudini, Marie-Claude Beaumont and veteran Jean Guichet.

As a Renault subsidiary, Alpine made bodies for a number of Renaults, such as the Éspace, at its Dieppe factory. It also made the Alpine GTA road car, which was powered by the PRV Douvrin V6 engine in 2.5-litre (153-cubic-inch) turbocharged and 2.9-litre (177-cubic-inch) normally aspirated format, a rival to Porsche's 911. A one-make series for the GTA included rounds supporting the Grand Prix circus, and privateer examples appeared in domestic championships. In the 1993 German ADAC GT Cup, the Alpine V6 Turbo of Michael Heigert took three consecutive Division 2 class wins at Salzburgring, Ahlhorn and the Nürburgring.

RED MIST
Although the Ferrari F40 had become a major player in the BPR Global GT series and at Le Mans, its smaller 348 and 355 siblings were less evident on the international scene and more visible in national series such as the European Ferrari Challenge and the Dutch/German Ferrari/Porsche Challenge. In 1993, however, the Ferrari 348LM was Maranello's only

representative at Le Mans, run by the British Simpson Engineering team of Robin Smith. Unfortunately, Eddie Irvine in the Toyota Group C racer shoved the Ferrari off the track in the morning warm-up. The following year, Ferrari made its first start at Le Mans in ten years with three cars, which included the rebuilt Simpson 348LM and two Ferrari Club Italia 348GT Competizione, one for Oscar Laurrari and the other for Spaniards Prince Alfonso d'Orléans Bourbon and Tomas Saldana. Only the second one lasted the full 24 hours, the others retiring with clutch and fuel-pump failures. Post-Le Mans, Italians Fabio Mancini and Massimo Monti took their F348 to fifth and sixth overall in BPR races at Spa-Francorchamps and Vallelunga, but by 1995 the car had been superseded by the F40.

For the same reason, the pretty little F355 was never really destined for international racing, although Monti drove MC Motorsport's F355 in just one race in 1995, finishing 15th overall at BPR Monza after starting from 43rd on the grid. The F348 was a mid-engined car powered by Ferrari's 3.4-litre (207.5-cubic-inch) aluminium, normally aspirated V8 driving through a five-speed gearbox. The F355 used the 40-valve V8 engine, and was reckoned to be one of Ferrari's best-ever chassis. Both models have seen action in national and international Ferrari Challenge events.

The F40 epitomised all that Ferrari stood for in terms of image and performance. The last road cars came off the production line at Maranello in 1989, yet in 1996 Ferrari teams were still winning with them against McLaren and Porsche. The F40s had been racing since the late 1980s in Italian sports car events, but, apart from certain American IMSA races, did not debut internationally until the first year of the BPR series in 1994. Anders Olofsson and Luciano della Noce drove their Strandell Racing F40 to victory at Vallelunga that year, and also won the Suzuka 500km (310 miles) in Japan. The French Pilot team

Splash and dash: Mike Parkes' 2nd placed Ferrari 250GT gets a fresh set of tyres and a tank of fuel during the RAC Tourist Trophy at Goodwood in 1961. The 250GT's bodywork was styled by Pininfarina and built by Scaglietti.

of Michel and Alain Ferté and Olivier Thévenin borrowed an F40 from a Luxembourg museum in 1995 and drove with some success, and the Italian Ennea team of Olofsson and Della Noce won at Anderstorp in 1996. A win rate of one a year over three years belied the F40's huge potential, and it was the privately entered cars rather than the fuel-heavy, factory-backed Ferrari Club Italia F40s that were successful.

In its final year, the F40 was prepared by Michelotto as the F40GTE, with revised suspension and aerodynamics, carbon brakes, magnesium sequential gearboxes, increased power and a 100kg (220lb) weight reduction. Jean-Marc Gounon was the top qualifier in 1996 with five poles, and would have

won the last race of the season at Zhuhai had not Porsche's GT1, which was in any case ineligible for points, been present. Ferrari cancelled its follow-up programme for the F50, although it lived on for a while in the French GT series and the international Ferrari/Porsche Challenge.

FULL TILT

With Le Mans successes going back to the 1950s from models including the C-Types, D-Types and XJR Group C cars, TWR transformed the XJ220 road car for a tilt at the new GT category in the 1993 race. Built by the TWR factory at Bloxham in the English Cotswolds, the XJ220 had become a highly prized supercar, using the successful rally-bred Metro 6R4 V6

twin-turbo engine. A customer car had recently won a round of the Italian GT series at Vallelunga, and Tom Walkinshaw was motivated to build a racing version, the XJ220C.

With Jaguar consent, TWR entered three of the big aluminium-monocoque GT cars against the factory Porsches in the GT class, taking advantage of the ACO's more liberal IMSA category regulations. That, sadly, was their undoing. They were warned before the race that the cars could be illegal without catalytic converters,

and the GT-winning car of Nielsen/Brabham/Coulthard was thrown out months after the race, even though IMSA confirmed that emissions equipment was not required. Porsche inherited the win. TWR never ran the XJ220 again, although British teams PC Automotive and Chamberlain Engineering ran two in 1995 at both national and international level; the third car went to the Sultan of Brunei's

museum. PC Automotive ran their XJ220 at the 1995 Le Mans, with James Weaver and Tiff Needell driving, but the engine failed after 12 hours. The following year, Chamberlain ran two cars in the British GT series in which Tommy Erdos finished fourth, and raced in both British BPR rounds. The XJ220C was raced in 1997 by Rob Schirle and Allen Lloyd in the British GT series.

DIABOLICAL LUCK

Lamborghini has never been noted for racing cars, rather as the maker of extravagant road-going supercars, as well as its parent company's tractors. It had, though, been associated with Formula 1 through Lotus, Lola and Larrousse between 1989 and 1993, but without success. Then, in 1995, it licensed a GT project to the British AIM team under the Australian engineer Jeff Amos, who had been responsible for the Group C Tigas and LM Prototype Deboras. AIM took the Lamborghini Diablo SE chassis and turned the 580bhp 5.0-litre (305-cubic-inch) V12 through 180 degrees to allow the use of a Hewland racing gearbox. The car was to have been driven by Andrea de Cesaris and Juan Manuel Fangio II, but its entry in the 1995 Le Mans failed to materialise. Modified Lamborghini Diablo SEs did race in the All-Japan GT series, but without any tangible results.

Gérard Larrousse used his F1 connection with the Lamborghini factory to introduce the Diablo SVR as the base car for the Philippe Charriol Supersports Trophy in 1996. This spectacular one-make series featured as support race for Le Mans in 1996, and there were 32 of these cars involved by 1997. Lamborghini now recognised the market that had been created, and sanctioned the production of the Diablo GT1. It was aimed squarely at Porsche, McLaren and Mercedes, but was almost immediately rescheduled as a GT2 contender after testing at the SAT team's Paul Ricard base. It debuted in the French GT championship's second round at Spa-Francorchamps with Jean-Paul Driot's DAMS team, Emmanuel Clerico and Luigi Moccia finishing fifth and sixth in the two races. With only marginal factory interest, the Diablo was destined to play only a small part in the FIA GT championship.

GRAND TOURER

Although the BMW M3 was originally conceived as a touring car, it soon became used as a GT car in Germany

The definitive Ferrari 250 GTO was first raced in the 1962 Daytona 3-Hours by Stirling Moss, using a dry-sump 3.0-litre (183-cubic-inch) V12 engine with six twin-choke Weber 38DCN carburettors and a five-speed gearbox. The cars of Noblet/Guichet and Beurlys/Elde were 2nd and 3rd at Le Mans in 1962. Derivatives included the 250 GT 'Breadvan' and 250 GT064.

FERRARI

Make: *Ferrari*
Model: *250 GTO*
In production: *1961-64*
Engine: *3.0-litre V12 Ferrari*
Gearbox: *5-speed*
Power output: *300bhp*
Chassis: *multi-tubular space frame*

Headlights ablaze, Roy Salvadori powers the Zagato-bodied Aston Martin DB4GTZ round the curves of Goodwood in 1962. Not really a match for the Ferraris, the DB4GT was superseded by the DP212 series of 4.0-litre (244-cubic-inch) prototype GT cars.

and the USA, matched against the hordes of Porsches which had threatened to swamp national GT championships in the mid-1990s. The M3GTR stood for 'Motorsports, 3-series-engined Grand Touring Racer'. It made its sportscar racing debut in the 1993 ADAC GT Cup, following BMW's withdrawal of its factory cars from the DTM touring car series (the DTM was becoming dominated by touring car prototypes so, although there were still plenty of privateers running BMWs, Munich looked elsewhere). The new GT Cup, with its 40-litres-per-100km (8.8-gallons-per-62-miles) fuel regulation, suited them perfectly, and the GTR was born.

The cars were campaigned by BMW touring car regulars Johnny Cecotto (Warthofer Team) and Kris Nissen (Isert Team). The two 340bhp factory cars dominated the eight-race series, with Honda, Porsche, Ford Escort Cosworth and Calloway Corvette as the chief opposition. The BMW M3GTRs were powered by 3.5-litre (214-cubic-inch) six-cylinder units incorporating variable valve timing for the first time, and they were shod with

Yokohama tyres. Cecotto won all but two rounds; he was beaten by Armin Hahne's Honda NSX at Zolder and by Bruno Eichmann's Porsche RSR at the Nürburgring. Nissen finished in second place six times.

Having virtually cleaned up on the domestic scene, BMW crossed over to the States, where Dieter Quester campaigned the M3GTR in the 1995 IMSA GTS-2 series at Daytona, Sebring and Watkins Glen. He qualified the car on GTS-2 pole for its debut at Daytona, but his best finish was an eighth at Sebring with John Paul Jr. Tom Milner's Prototype Technology Group took over the official US programme in 1996, with factory backing and sponsorship from Valvoline and First Union, and Pete Halsmer took the Valvoline M3 to victories at Sears Point, Mosport and Dallas, and was leading the finale of the 1996 Exxon Supreme GT Championship at Daytona when the car caught fire. His team-mate, Javier Qurios, won the race to give BMW the manufacturers' title. Quester also drove in four races, his best results being third places at Sebring and the Daytona final.

In 1997, Bill Auberlen took the GTS-3 drivers' championship with five wins, including Daytona and Sebring, while Prototype Technology Group's BMWs racked up nine class wins in the 11-race series. In the two events it did not win, BMW was third at Road Atlanta

and second at Las Vegas. The following year, PTG decided to tackle GT2 as well as GT3, and Auberlen won again at Daytona and Sebring. The 1998 drivers' title was won by his team-mate, Brian Simo, by just two points, while BMW claimed the GT3 title yet again with six wins in both the Professional Sports Car and USRRC championships. In GT2, Andy Pilgrim, Boris Said and Marc Duez gave the BMW M3s four wins and a second in six races, but lost out to Porsche in the title chase by just 18 points.

QUALITY CONTROLS

Porsche goes back as far as anyone in GT racing; its 356 finished 20th at the Le Mans 24-Hour in 1951 at an average speed of 118.33km/h (73.54mph), compared with the 150.43km/h (93.49mph) averaged by the winning C-type Jaguar. In 1993, the Porsche Carrera RSR was the factory's first customer GT racer of the decade, built by the company's Weissach competition facility as an alternative to the Supercup 911. The RSR was powered by the 360bhp 3.8-litre (232-cubic-inch) flat-six engine developed in the Carrera and RS models, and it had ABS brakes as original equipment.

The Carrera RSR was first used by Porsche customer teams at the 1993 Le Mans 24-Hour, as well as in the new German GT series. The car's finest moment at Le Mans was when the Larbre entry driven by Dominique Dupuy, Joel Gouhier and Porsche's customer racing manager, Jürgen Barth, won the GT category outright after the Jaguar XJ220 was disqualified.

To celebrate the 911's 30th birthday, Weissach built up a one-off 911 powered by the 962's twin-turbo engine, restricted to a more economical 500bhp. This car was designated the Turbo SLM-GT, and although Hans Stuck put it on GT pole, former rally star Walter Röhrl put it out of the race. However, after the success of the RSR at Le Mans, Barth joined forces with Patrick Peter and Stephane Ratel to form the BPR Organisation, providing a showcase for Porsche racing excellence.

Driven by veteran aces Bob Wolleck and Barth, the LM-GT claimed second place overall in the 1994 Daytona 24-Hour, powered by the same 590bhp 3.2-litre (195-cubic-inch) twin-turbo engine. In the BPR challenge, it was driven to victory at Paul Ricard, Jarama, Suzuka and Zhuhai by Jean-Pierre Jarier, joined at various times by Bob Wolleck, Jesus Pareja, Dominique Dupuy and Jacques Laffite.

Back at Le Mans for 1994, the French Larbre team's RSR won again with Dupuy, Pareja and Palau taking the GT category. They also won the GT2 class in the first BPR race at Paul Ricard with a 3.8-litre (232-cubic-inch) RSR. The RSR was ideal for the GT2 category, and among the dozen examples present was the Bristow Motorsport RSR of Ray Bellm and Harry Nuttall. Team Larbre also won the GT2 class at Jarama, Dijon and Montlhéry. It was also second overall in three of these four events.

By this time, Weissach was preparing to go turbocharged for its next generation of 911 racing cars, and the new GT2 appeared in 1995. Whereas the Carrera RSR body shape was a 911 of

The mighty Ferrari GTO met its match in 1964 in the shape of the AC 'Daytona' Cobra. Inspired by Carroll Shelby, the aluminium-bodied coupé was designed by Peter Brock and featured a cut-off 'Kamm' tail and aerodynamic nose.

the older school, the GT2 was built around the new 993 road-car body. Beneath the skin, though, was a full-blown racer, powered by the M64/81 twin-turbo engine. It was still air-cooled with two valves per cylinder, but with capacity raised to 3.6 litres (220 cubic inches). With GT2 restrictors in place it was still producing 450bhp, while in GT1 Evolution format it mustered 590bhp, with wider 36cm (14-inch) wheels. The Swiss drivers Enzo Calderari and Lilian Bryner had a trouble-free year with their Team Stadler GT2, and finished top GT2 runners and second overall in the series, beating all but the West McLaren outfit. Porsche also experimented with its GT2 Evolution car in the GT1 class, but only won the last event after ten went to McLaren and one to Ferrari, although Jarier and Wolleck managed three consecutive second places at the first three races for Larbre team.

WEAK LINK?

The GT2 Evo's weak link proved to be its transmission, and after its 1994 success, Porsche found that it no longer had a car to beat McLaren or Ferrari, or even Lotus, and eased off to concentrate on its GT1 programme. The German Roock Racing team became Porsche's principal GT2 customer in the 1996 BPR series, and between Roock and Konrad Motorsport,

Porsche notched up eight class wins in 11 rounds, fending off a strong challenge from Marcos. The Roock team also won the GT2 class at Le Mans.

The BPR Global GT series metamorphosed into the FIA GT Championship in 1997, and the Porsche GT2 teams were initially penalised by reduced air restrictor sizes, offset by the 1996 inlets. The 911 GT2 continued to be the category's mainstay though, and all season competition was fierce between Porsche, Chrysler and Marcos. Despite Roock's drivers, Bruno Eichmann and Claudia Hurtgen, winning four times and coming second three times, the rumbling Vipers came through with Justin Bell clinching the drivers' title by one point. At Le Mans, however, Haberthur's 911 GT2 beat the Chryslers, and in the States, Larry Schumacher was crowned Professional SportsCar GT2 champion over Austrian Franz Konrad. In the UK, the national GT championship was also won outright by Steve O'Rourke's EMKA 911 GT2.

By 1998, the latest version of the 911 won the GT2 category at both Daytona and Sebring, and with the expansion of the French GT championship and the Ferrari/Porsche Challenge, the GT2's future was assured. Weissach engineers increased power output to 485bhp, fitted twin-plug heads to improve ignition efficien-

cy and lower fuel consumption, and fitted a new boost-pressure control. Other aspects such as aerodynamics and air intakes were also improved, while plastic panels and a smaller oil cooler made for additional weight saving. More new FIA regulations meant doing away with the ABS brakes.

By now, Chrysler was the dominant vehicle, taking all but one of the GT2 victories in 1998. Porsche beat the Vipers just once when Eichmann and Sascha Maassen took the honours at the Hungaroring, while in the British GT championship the Oftedahl Viper won six of the nine races and the remainder went to Lotus. The picture was brighter in France, where the winning team of Jean-Pierre Jarier and François Lafon took their Sonauto 911 GT2 to the title ahead of the Larbre

The Shelby Daytona Cobras of Johnson/Payne and Schlesser/Grant racing at Le Mans in 1965. Although three out of four Daytonas retired, the surviving car of Sears/Thompson came 8th overall, and Shelby went on to win the 1965 GT Championship.

team's 911. In the USA, Larry Schumacher was SportsCar champion for the second year running in his 911 GT2, with John O'Steen as co-driver.

Back in 1995, to get on terms with the powerful McLarens Porsche needed to build something similar themselves, a road-car derivative that could even win the Le Mans 24-Hour outright in a straight fight with prototypes. The regulations dictated that a road car with full EEC type approval had to exist before a racing version could be accepted, and this was to prevent a return to the characteristics of Group C cars. To this end, Porsche designer Norbert Singer developed the mid-engined Porsche GT1, which was launched at Le Mans at the 1996 test weekend in May. To make the point crystal clear, there was a road-going model in the paddock. Ownership was a different matter, requiring something like a lottery jackpot win to stand even a chance of acquiring one.

Departing from a 30-year tradition of having its engine hung behind the rear axle line, the GT1 was the first Porsche 911 to have its engine

mounted in the middle of the chassis. It was powered by the 600bhp four-valve 3.2-litre (195-cubic-inch) flat-six twin-turbo unit, now with water-cooling, and was also equipped with ABS brakes and power steering. The 911 GT1 was based on the 993 body shape, in fact hardly recognisable as a 911 at all. It looked sensational, and raised the game another notch. It did not disappoint in the performance department either, and won the GT category of the Le Mans 24-Hour at its first attempt.

Although the factory declared it would not compete against its own customers outside Le Mans, Porsche AG entered the car for Hans Stuck and Thierry Boutsen at Spa-Francorchamps and Brands Hatch, and it won both events by a lap. At Zhuhai, Ralf Kelleners and Emmanuel Collard won as well. In 1997, the Porsche was deprived of its ABS and power output, reduced by 60bhp as the FIA tightened regulations, and at the first two races the 911 GT1 was soundly beaten by McLaren as well as being threatened by the new Mercedes-Benz CLK. The works team missed out the Helsinki

round in order to concentrate on development, but was penalised by the FIA
for failing to compete in a race. Then,
when it really mattered, Porsche's
endurance experience came to the
fore, and the two factory cars led Le
Mans for 16 hours until Wolleck
crashed the leading 911 GT1.
Kelleners' car then caught fire with just
two hours to go, handing the GT1
victory to the Gulf McLaren. There
was some consolation from the fact
that Porsche scored outright victory for
the second year with the Joest TWR-
Porsche sports car, but at the
Nürburgring the 911 GT1 was
outpaced by the Mercedes CLK and
McLaren, which had got its larger
restrictors back. Even a couple of
customer cars beat the factory cars. In
fact, Porsche did not manage a GT1
victory in international racing at all in
1997, with Mercedes and BMW
McLaren dominant in the FIA GT
championship.

In the USA, Andy Pilgrim drove the
Rohr Porsche team's new 911 GT1 to
four consecutive victories at the end of
the season. Pilgrim also won the GT1
category of the Daytona 24-Hour in
the team's twin-turbo 993, which was
sufficient to lift the American drivers'
and manufacturers' GT1 titles. At
Zhuhai in China, John Greasley drove
his Blue Coral 911 GT1 to victory in
the non-championship GT race,
staging a repeat performance of the
factory's 1996 success.

While Porsche fared little better in
the FIA GT series in 1998, the factory
effort was augmented by two
Zakspeed cars. Once again Mercedes-
Benz dominated the championship,
with 10 wins out of 10 races, despite a
Herculean effort by Allan McNish and
Yannick Dalmas in the Porsches to
earn pole positions at Oschersleben
and Silverstone. The 911 GT1s were
the only turbocharged cars in the
series, so Porsche AG's Herbert
Ampferer asked for permission to move
the air restrictors further away from
the turbocharger inlets to improve performance. The FIA declined, and
instead slapped a 50kg (110lb) weight
penalty on all three factory teams.
Mercedes CLK-GTR performance
was not affected, and neither was
Chrysler in GT2. The second place
scored by Michael Bartels and Armin
Hahne in the second race at
Silverstone in the Zakspeed car was
scant compensation for Porsche.

Outside the FIA category, the 911
GT1 did well. The car of Allan
McNish, Jorg Muller, Uwe Alzen and
Danny Sullivan won the Daytona 24-
Hour, serving as a taster for Le Mans.
There, the former Opel Lotus
champion and F3000 driver McNish
was partnered by Stephane Ortelli and
Laurent Aiello at the wheel of the
winning works' 911 GT1, giving the
marque its 16th Le Mans victory. The
second Weissach GT1 was second,
driven by Muller, Alzen and Wolleck. In

the autumn, Porsche entered the Petit
Le Mans race at Road Atlanta hoping
for outright victory in the absence of
Mercedes-Benz. McNish took pole
position and led for the first five hours,
but the car was eliminated comprehen-
sively when it became airborne with
Dalmas at the wheel. In a spectacular
back-flip, it was completely wrecked,
and Dalmas was exceedingly lucky to
walk away (the following year it
would be the turn of the Mercedes
CLKs to emulate this terrifying
scenario). Meanwhile, the Champion
team restored some of Porsche's tar-
nished ego when Thierry Boutsen won
the drivers' and manufacturers' titles in
the new USRRC GT1 series.

AMERICAN PIE
The ZR-1 Corvette Team USA entry
for the 1995 Le Mans 24-Hour was an
all-American attempt to dislodge
Porsche from victory in the GT class in
the French classic. Unfortunately, the
project came to fruition at the very
moment McLaren had taken control of
international GT racing.

The car was conceived and built by
Doug Rippie Motorsport at its
Plymouth, Minnesota base. Bob Riley
(of Riley & Scott) and GM's own engineers were put into the programme
and Goodyear worked with the team
to perfect the handling of the spaceframe-chassis, carbon-fibre-bodied
Corvette GT. Doug Rippie was well
known for his racing engines, and had
developed the Chevrolet V8 with Lotus
and MerCruiser. The fuel-injected V8
developed some 560bhp out of 6.3 litres
(384 cubic inches). The drivers were
John Paul Jr, Chris McDougall and
James Mero, but the car was never
competitive. It qualified last out of the
48 cars in the race and blew its engine
after 57 laps. Ironically, rival Callaway
Corvettes finished ninth and 11th

The Alpine Renault A310 was powered by a 2.8-litre V6 engine and more commonly used as a rally car. The Decure/Therier/ Cochise A310 GTP pictured at Le Mans in 1977 ran out of water after 16 hours — something its sponsor couldn't tolerate.

overall, and second and third in the GT2 category.

Callaway is perhaps better known in golfing circles, as the producer of the Big Bertha driver. But since the BPR series started in 1994, his became known as one of the quickest GT2 cars. Built by American engine and turbocharging expert Reeves Callaway at his team's Leingarten base in Germany, the Callaway was the latest of a line of Corvette-based supercars. In 1993, Callaway contested the ADAC GT Cup with its nearly-standard Corvette in the hands of Herbert Schorg and Boris Said III, and it proved to be competitive against BMW, Porsche and Honda. Said came fourth at Zandvoort and fifth at the Salzburgring. For 1994, the team prepared its Corvette Supernatural, with bodywork by Paul Deutchmann and engineering by Max Bostrom. It was based on a tubular chassis frame

clad with carbon-Kevlar bodywork, and was powered by a 450bhp 6.2-litre (378-cubic-inch) aluminium Chevrolet V8 motor in GT2 form. Driven by Said, the Callaway stormed ahead in the first year of the BPR series, taking three consecutive GT2 wins at Spa, Vallelunga and Suzuka. At Le Mans, it was the quickest GT2 car and dominated the class until sidelined by a fuel leak.

In 1995, Callaway also involved the Agusta Racing team based at Silverstone, and Almo Copelli was fastest in pre-qualifying for Le Mans and took GT2 pole for the race. But it was Callaway Competition's own entry of Frank Jelinski, Enrico Bertaggia and Johnny Unser which was quickest in the race, fighting with Honda for the GT2 win throughout the 24 hours (Honda won the class by two laps). There was no further success, and by 1998 Callaway was no longer on the international scene.

Chevrolet came out with a new Corvette, the C5-R, in 1999, developed by US tuners Pratt & Miller, with the intention of running at Le Mans in 2000. It will contest American GT1 races, but, ultimately, Le Mans 2000 is the target.

BATTLE OF VIPERS

Chrysler had high hopes of success in GT racing with its new baby. Based on its stunning Dodge Viper GTS Coupé, its GT1 car was never on the same level as McLaren, Porsche, Lotus and Ferrari, despite hiring the Le Mans-winning French ORECA team, which had brought success for Mazda in 1991, and bringing American technology to Europe. Chrysler insisted that its racing programme was an extension of its road-car programme, thereby misjudging the strength of the opposition, which was becoming more akin to Group C.

The Viper weighs in at 1150kg

The Ferrari F40 was first campaigned in the BPR International GT Championship in 1994, having previously raced in the Italian Supercar series and certain IMSA events. This Pilot Team car of Ferté/Ferté/Thevernin is competing at Jarama in 1995.

(2535lb) thanks to its heavy front-mounted Dodge V10 truck-derived engine, which develops some 600bhp in GT2 format. Because of its prodigious thirst, it balances fuel stops for outright speed in endurance racing. Privateer Dodge Vipers had already been seen racing at Le Mans in 1994 and 1995, with occasional BPR excursions as well, but it was not until 1996 that Chrysler announced a full factory pro-gramme, using its domestic Canaska-Southwind team for IMSA racing and Le Mans, and ORECA to run at Le Mans and the BPR series. In its first season the car finished in the top 10 at Le Mans, and Chrysler promptly quit GT1 and moved into GT2.

Chrysler's decision to stay with its production-based cars was justified when its ORECA-run Vipers took both the 1997 and 1998 FIA GT2 titles. The first one was with Justin Bell, son of sports car legend Derek, and the second involved Pedro Lamy and Olivier Beretta. In both years Chrysler also clinched the teams' championship. At Le Mans in 1997, one car was destroyed by fire, one crashed, and gearbox problems delayed the third factory car, which eventually was placed fifth in the GT2 category. For marketing purposes, Bell was stood down as a full-time factory driver for 1998, alternating drives with the son of another motor sport hero, the American David Donohue. Bell was teamed with Donohue at the 1998 Le Mans 24-Hour, to give Chrysler the coveted GT2 prize.

There were further laurels in the British GT championship, where Richard Dean and Kurt Luby won six of the eight GT2 rounds, including an outstanding victory at a wet Silverstone, to claim both the outright and GT2 title for Chrysler in their Oftedahl Motorsport entry. Around eight Vipers, including two factory cars and six privateers, were in action in 1999, and at season's end the FIA GT champions were Karl Wendlinger and Olivier Beretta, having notched up a sixth victory in the series at Zhuhai in the works Viper by a narrow margin

from the Chamberlain Viper of Christian Vatan and Christian Glasel.

HURRY UP HARRIER

The Harrier marque was established in 1995, and by 1996 had proved to be a GT1 front runner, beating McLaren on three occasions in the capable hands of Win Percy.

Harrier was founded by designer Lester Ray and David Fidgeon, and Harrier Racing produced its LR9 mid-engined, spaceframe, road-going GT cars in the late 1980s. The first LR9 used the 2.5-litre (153-cubic-inch) Alfa Romeo V6 engine, subsequently replaced by the more powerful four-cylinder Ford Cosworth RS500 turbo engine. It was raced in the 1993 British GT series, and a Spider version was built for the 1994 Le Mans 24-Hour, crewed by Rob Wilson, Dave Brodie and William Hewland, who was the son of the gearbox builder. It was retired after 45 laps with front suspen-sion failure, and the following year Richard Austin formed Harrier Cars and took over the race programme. The LR9C was then driven to two British GT victories in 1995, followed by three wins at Brands Hatch, Oulton Park and Silverstone in 1996, making it more successful at this level than Porsche and Renault, with two victories each, and McLaren, with one.

The Harrier's main problem was that its Cosworth engine was by this time

The ubiquitous Porsche 911S even qualified as a Touring Car in the late 1960s, and in the early 1970s in the GTS category they made up the bulk of the field in endurance events. This 2.2-litre (134-cubic-inch) 911S is running in a GT Championship race at the Norisring at Nuremberg in 1971.

outclassed by the McLaren V12, Porsche flat-six turbo and Lister Jaguar V12 powerplants, and the intention was to upgrade to the 3.5-litre (214-cubic-inch) Judd V10 unit.

LISTER PORT

In the 1950s, the Lister Jaguar, with its rotund, Frank Costin-penned body shape, was a highly competitive car on the British and international sports car racing scene. It was not a success at Le Mans however: although Brian Lister's team ran five cars between 1958 and 1963, 15th place was their best finish. After that Lister entered Sunbeam Tigers at Le Mans, but that was not a successful venture either.

The marque was reborn in 1993, and Lister introduced its Jaguar V12-powered production-based Storm GT, with input from former Lotus and TWR designer Tony Southgate. It was powered by the Group C XJR V12 unit, developed by TWR and winner of Le Mans in 1988 and 1990. The Lister Storm was a front-engined GT car in the classic tradition, and the alumini-um-monocoque car was first entered at

Le Mans by Laurence Pearce, who owned the company in 1995. Drivers were Geoff Lees, Rupert Keegan and Dominic Chappell, but it retired at the six-hour mark with transmission failure. The same car, now sponsored by Newcastle United Football Club, went to Daytona in 1996 for the 24-hour race, but its challenge ended when Kenny Acheson was dramatically rolled over. The next car was lighter and stiffer, and it was entered for the 1996 Le Mans 24-Hours with Lees and Needell joined at the wheel by Anthony Reid. The Lister Storm came in 18th overall, and 11th in the GT1 class. The team also raced in a number of BPR rounds during 1996 and proved to be front runners against McLaren, Ferrari and Lotus, running third at the Nürburgring and Spa-Francorchamps before retiring and disputing second place at Brands Hatch when a head gasket failed.

PORSCHE

Make: *Porsche*
Model: *911 RSR*
In production: *1974-75*
Engine: *2.1-litre (128-cubic-inch) flat-six turbo air-cooled*
Gearbox: *five-speed*
Power output: *up to 510bhp*
Chassis: *seam-welded unit construction coupé*

The new Storm for 1997 had major chassis and body modifications, and the car did well to finish the Daytona 24-Hours. The second car was rolled in the opening British GT championship round, but the Lister squad came back to win the third round at Donington Park, with Ian Flux and Jake Ulrich at the helm. Both Listers were on the pace at Le Mans too, having qualified well, and they ran reliably until being eliminated by accident damage before six hours had elapsed. Lister then ran in selected FIA GT championship rounds for the rest of 1997, but without success.

In 1998, an evolution carbon-fibre GTL version was constructed, but an electrical failure put paid to its chances in the Daytona 24-Hours, and it was banned from Le Mans because it did not match its original homologation papers. Pearce elected to concentrate on the British GT series, and Julian Bailey and Tiff Needell took two wins in GT1 at Snetterton and Silverstone and four other podium placings to finish second behind the McLaren of Steve O'Rourke and Tim Sugden. For the following year, Lister reverted to the original 1996 aluminium-chassis Storm GT for the new FIA GT championship for GT2 cars, the world series and Le Mans' new GTS category.

LOTUS POSITION
Although Lotus founder Colin Chapman vowed he would never

return to Le Mans after the factory Lotus 23 was refused entry in 1963 after a homologation row over wheel nuts, his successors felt no such constraints. In 1993, a Lotus sports GT car was again seen at La Sarthe (the Lotus 49 F1 cars had raced there when the French Grand Prix was held on the Bugatti circuit at Le Mans in 1967) when Chamberlain Engineering ran a pair of GT2 Esprit S300s with turbocharged four-cylinder engines. Neither car finished, but the works-supported Chamberlain team took wins in the British GT series and ran in selected BPR races.

In 1994, Chamberlain was back at Le Mans, but again the cars failed to finish, one after 28 laps with a failed stub axle and the other as the result of a crash at 59 laps. For 1995, Lotus Racing, run by former Lotus F1 directors George Howard-Chappell and Ian Foley took control of the project and ran two S300s Esprits. Still running in GT2, the lightweight Lotus benefited from chassis development and became a potential McLaren beater. At the BPR meeting at Donington Park, Alex Zanardi and Alex Portman were headed for fourth

A Martini Porsche Carrera RSR Turbo, running in the Group 5 category prepares to leave the Nürburgring pits in the 1974 1000kms race. This was the beginning of the turbo era, and the 2.1-litre Porsches developed between 450- and 510bhp.

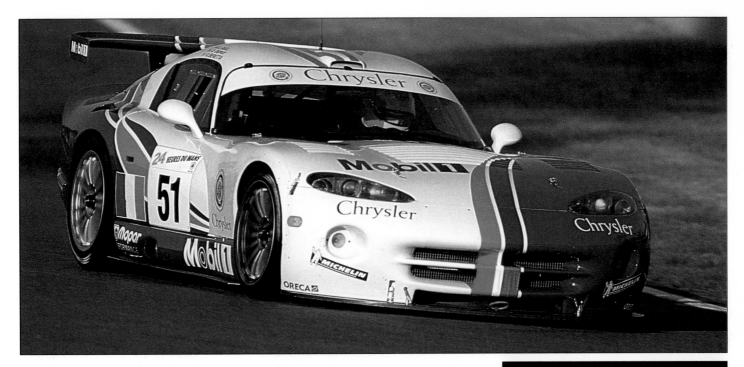

overall when the transmission failed. Then, at a wet Silverstone meeting, they took the GT2 car to a brilliant fourth overall behind the Harrods McLaren and two Ferrari F40s.

Lotus Racing graduated into the GT1 category in 1996, and the operation was taken over by the former European 2.0-litre (122-cubic-inch) sports car, GT and touring car champion Toine Hezemans. The Dutchman provided a cash injection into Lotus Racing, and this enabled the team to develop the Lotus Esprit V8 Turbo, with a two-car team for Jan Lammers and Perry McCarthy, and Toine's son Mike Hezemans with Alex Portman. The car was lightweight, handled well and was extremely quick. It led at Jarama, at Silverstone Lammers and McCarthy finished second to McLaren, and they placed fifth at Spa-Francorchamps, but largely minor problems to do with brakes, oil pumps and overheating brought a string of retirements.

By the 1997 season, Group Lotus was financially stable with the might of new owner Proton behind it, and Lotus Racing was able to forge ahead with the new GT1 car. It was based directly on the new Elise road model, using the Richard Rackham-designed monocoque chassis that was composed of aluminium extrusions and sheet,

The V10-powered Chrysler Viper was the most successful GT2 car in the late 1990s and took the first three places in the GTS class at the Sebring 12-Hours in 2000. Here is the ORECA Team car of Wendlinger/Belloc/Beretta at Le Mans in 1999.

bonded and riveted in a novel process by Hydro Aluminium in Denmark. The chassis was widened to match the track width required for the GT1 racing car, and carbon-fibre body panels were produced in-house. The cars were built at Ketteringham Hall. But just three months after intensive testing of the 560bhp V8 twin-turbo-powered Elise GT1 began, it was revealed that FIA regulations were being changed to penalise turbocharged cars because of protests from another manufacturer, and the Lotus faced a minimum 50bhp power loss with the proposed restrictors. Appeals to the FIA proved fruitless, so the team had to fall back on the Tony Rudd-designed 600bhp 6.0-litre (366-cubic-inch) 32-valve V8 unit destined for the Corvette ZR-1.

Two works Elise GT1 Lotus Racing cars and one Italian GBF Benetton car raced at Hockenheim, headed by the Lammers/ Hezemans GT1, but all three suffered alternator problems. The third car retained the V8 twin-turbo engine, which was noticeably slower with the FIA restrictors, but GBF per-

CHRYSLER

Make: *Chrysler*
Model: *Viper GTS-R*
In production: *1994-2000*
Engine: *normally aspirated DodgeV10*
Gearbox: *six-speed*
Power output: *600bhp*
Chassis: *carbon-fibre/tubular subframes*

severed with it, with Italian engineering input. At Silverstone, Lammers led briefly in a confused and rain-swept second round, but all three cars retired with transmission problems. They then concentrated on the development of a six-speed sequential Hewland gearbox for Le Mans, but it was to no avail. Giroix's works car failed to qualify, and Lammers had oil-pump failure at one-third distance. There was a result, however, at the Nürburgring, where Lotus and GBF fielded five cars between them. Lammers/Hezemans brought the Elise into 11th place, five laps down on the winning Mercedes, and the GBF car of Boldrini/Stretton came 15th.

There were no further placings during the remainder of the 1997 season and the project was grinding to a halt. Toine Hezemans took over the entire Lotus Racing programme for

1998 when funding from the parent company failed to materialise, and he immediately set about swapping engines to run the Chrysler Viper V10 unit. He also renamed the cars 'Bitter' after the German tuning company (possibly, it was also a reflection of his feelings about his former colleagues' employers). However, the cars were plagued by transmission problems, and despite the efforts of Lammers and Mike Hezemans they rarely managed more than a few laps before breaking down or catching fire. By mid-season, Hezemans had abandoned the programme, although one of the cars was refitted with its V8 twin-turbo engine for Dutch rallycross champion Hans Te Pas to run in the British GT series.

Meanwhile, Lotus was itself concentrating on building and marketing versions of its wonderful little sports car. The Elise Sport had already had a one-make series devoted to it in Italy, and it was intended that this should support the BTCC in 2000. The Motorsport Elise was fitted with a 1795cc (109.5-cubic-inch) transverse, mid-mounted, four-cylinder Rover K-series twin-cam engine developing 203bhp, and coupled to a Quaife straight-cut, close-ratio, five-speed gearbox.

MARCOS CORE VALUES

Along with a number of specialist sports car makers that survived the 1950s and 1960s, Marcos remains one of Britain's most respected institutions. Founded by Jem Marsh and Mike Costin, Marcos staged a comeback in sports car racing during the 1990s. Top-class drivers such as Jackie Stewart, Jackie Oliver and Derek Bell started their careers driving Marcos GTs in the 1960s, but more recently Marcos has been a GT2 front runner, both in the BPR series and at Le

With the 911 GT1, Porsche virtually recreated a Group C sports prototype, but in spite of some excellent performances it proved more successful in the US GT1 series. Here, the 2nd placed car of Uwe Alzen/Jorg Muller is refuelled and re-shod at Silverstone during a round of the FIA series in 1998.

Mans, as well as winning the 1995 British GT championship outright. In the latter series it was pitted against McLaren and Porsche with its smaller-engined LM500.

The current Marcos LM600 encapsulates the Marcos attitude very well. Its aggressive-looking, composite bodywork covers a tubular-frame chassis with a big front-mounted Chevrolet small-block V8 power unit of 6.0 litres (366 cubic inches) that develops 520bhp, combined with a manual five-speed Hewland STA gearbox. The LM600 was developed from the Mantara road car, and until the arrival of the Viper GT in 1997, the Marcos racer was the fastest GT2 car. The Marcos LM600 racing programme was run by Dutch touring car and sports car veteran Cor Euser in 1995 under the Marcos Racing International banner. Euser and Thomas Erdos notched up three BPR wins in 1996 from five pole position starts, and they even led at Le Mans until sidelined by an engine failure. Retirements suffered at Hockenheim, Silverstone and Nürburgring were also engine-related, as Marcos tried to find more speed in the cars. A second place at Helsinki, a fourth at Spa-Francorchamps and a third at Laguna Seca in California were at least some consolation.

The Chevrolet V8 motor was duly improved, but although Marcos achieved a series of pole positions and third places at Hungaroring, Suzuka and Homestead, little success came their way in 1998. Their second place

at Donington Park was discounted when the FIA declared their fuel, tainted by traces of pump fuel from a test session, illegal. Euser and Becker were a lowly 13th in the GT2 series, but continued to compete strongly in 1999 when the FIA's GT championship was run exclusively for GT2 cars.

ROAD RACER

McLaren's position of dominance in Formula 1 made the prospect of a supercar from the same stable seem particularly awesome. Known, confusingly, as the F1, it was not the first road-going supercar to bear the McLaren name: founder Bruce McLaren had built a GT version of his all-conquering M6 CanAm cars and used it daily to see if a production version would work (sadly, he was killed before it could become a reality).

Just like Bruce's M6GT, the modern McLaren F1 encapsulates everything GT racing stands for. It is a road car built for the race track, and in 1999 it still held the title of the world's fastest production car with a 372km/h (231mph) top speed. Designer Gordon Murray and McLaren supremo Ron Dennis bent to pressure from racing driver owners such as Ray Bellm, Lindsay Owen-Jones and Thomas Bscher and built a racing version of the 6.0-litre (366-cubic-inch) BMW V12-powered, three-seat F1 supercar. Murray and his race engineers, under former Spice team manager Jeff Hazell, turned the supercar into one of the most successful GT racers, the F1 GTR.

Ranged against opposition like the Porsche 911 twin-turbos and Ferrari F40s, the 640bhp McLaren was an instant success. It won its debut outing at Jerez in February 1995 with Bellm and Sala driving the Gulf car, and they won again two weeks later at Paul Ricard. At Monza, it was the turn of the West Competition car of John Nielsen and Thomas Bscher to spray the fizz. From then on, the BPR series was fought out between these two crews, Nielsen/Bscher taking the title with just two wins and five second places, while Bellm/Sala garnered five victories. Ferrari won just one of the 12 BPR races, and a Porsche GT2 won the Paris 1000 at Montlhéry (which the McLarens had boycotted, complaining that the track was too bumpy). The other three wins went to the Harrods McLaren of Andy Wallace and Olivier Grouillard. A semi-works car, entered by Lanzante Racing for a Japanese customer, won the 1995 Le Mans 24-Hours outright, although the triumph was tempered by criticism from privateer teams who had been assured that no one would get works backing.

For the 1996 season, McLaren improved the suspension and fitted carbon brakes, and the cars shed 100kg (220lb) of weight by the fitting of a

The Lister Storm was a strong contender in GT1 in the late 1990s. The Jaguar V12-powered aluminium chassis GT2 car came good in 2000, Bailey/Jamie Campbell-Walter winning the inaugural FIA GT race at Valencia.

Pit stop for the works' Lotus Esprit S300 GT2 of Alex Zanardi/Alex Portman in the Donington round of the 1995 BPR series. For 1996 Lotus Racing developed a pair of twin-turbocharged V8-powered GT1 Esprits with Dutch backing.

magnesium gearbox. The McLarens were virtually unstoppable. The Gulf racing car was handled by Bellm, now paired with James Weaver, winning the first two races at Paul Ricard and Jarama, then Wallace and Grouillard won at Silverstone. For the Le Mans race, BMW put its Team Bigazzi Fina squad into the race alongside the Gulf, West and Harrods teams, but the Porsche 911 GT1 had arrived, and swept all before it. The top-scoring McLaren was the West car of Nielsen/Kox/Bscher, which came fourth overall, with the Gulf car fifth and Harrods sixth. The Mobil McLarens managed a one-two in the GT category behind the Joest TWR Porsche, and in Japan, McLaren claimed the 1996 GT championship title with David Brabham and Nielsen in charge. McLaren did win further BPR races, but only when the Porsche factory cars were absent. Bellm and Weaver had the most wins, and took the title from Nielsen and Bscher. By the end of 1996, the remarkable McLaren F1 GTR had won 17 out of 23 BPR international

GT races, and it had won both that year's championships.

FULLY COMMITTED

Designer Gordon Murray had already committed to improvements to the F1 GTR when Porsche's radical 911 GT1 arrived on the scene in mid-1996, to be followed by the equally radical Mercedes CLK-GTR for 1997, when the BPR series evolved into the first FIA GT championship. For 1997, Murray came up with an 'Evolution' version of the F1 GTR, with a long tail and considerably modified aerodynamics. The transmission now extended to a sequential gearbox, and there were eight-piston brake callipers. The engine was reduced to 5990cc (365.5 cubic inches) to take advantage of the less severe FIA restrictors for engines below 6.0 litres, and it won its first three races at Hockenheim, Silverstone and Helsinki, followed by Spa and Mugello, although by then it had become a full BMW Motorsport factory team. Drivers J.J. Lehto and Steve Soper looked set for the FIA GT title until the late-starting Mercedes steamroller picked up speed. However, at the 1997 Le Mans 24-Hours the Gulf team beat the BMW, Porsche and Nissan factory teams, giving McLaren the GT honours just as the Gulf corporate name departed from the scene. In the

British GT series, Gary Ayles and Chris Goodwin gave their new Parabolica F1 GTR a debut win at the Silverstone opener prior to an FIA GT campaign.

In 1998, Thomas Bscher and Geoff Lees were the sole McLaren representatives in the former's Davidoff F1 GTR, but really the F1's day was over, and it was never particularly competitive against the new Mercedes-Benz and Porsches. They managed a fifth place at Hockenheim and two sixths at Silverstone and the A1-Ring. In the British GT championship, the 1997 champions Steve O'Rourke and Tim Sugden swapped their Porsche GT2 for one of the Gulf McLarens for 1998, and won the series with two victories and three second places. They took their EMKA car to Le Mans, and brought in American Bill Auberlen as third driver to claim an amazing fourth overall surrounded by a dozen factory teams, as well as finishing third in the fiercely competitive GT category. That was the racing F1's swan-song; by 1999, the road car, too, was out of production.

IMSA SUCCESS

In the 1970s, the Datsun 240Z brought GT motoring to a wider public, and it was a successful racer in the US IMSA series, as well as at club level. Under the Nissan corporate identity, the marque achieved its 200th sports car victory in the IMSA category in 1996.

During the late 1980s, David Brabham and Nissan virtually controlled the IMSA GTP series, taking the drivers' title four years running, while Nissan took the GTP manufacturers' championships in 1989, 1990 and 1991. The Clayton Cunningham team was running tube-frame-chassis 300ZX Twin-Turbos, and in 1992 and 1994 Steve Millen and Nissan took the GTS-1 titles. Two years later, Cunningham Racing repeated NISMO's 1992 success with outright victory in the 1994 Daytona 24-Hours. The winning car was the GTS Nissan 300ZX Twin-Turbo of Millen, Gentilozzi, Leitzinger and Pruett, and the team followed this up with outright victory in the Sebring 12-Hours. Where else could they head next but Le Mans? Cunningham entered the 1994 Le Mans with a pair of GTS cars driven by Millen, Johnny O'Connell, John Morton, Paul Gentilozzi, Eric van de Poele and Shunji Kasuya. One qualified ninth and the other 12th, which was no disgrace considering their aerodynamics were inferior to the Group C Toyotas, Porsche 962s and Courages. Gentilozzi's Daytona-winning car was damaged by fire, but the Millen car finished fifth overall and claimed the GTS class win.

In 1995, Cunningham ran the same Nissan 300ZX cars without turbochargers, forced induction now outlawed by IMSA GTS-1 rules. The V8-powered Infiniti was driven by Millen, O'Connell and Morton to victory in the GT class at the Sebring 12-Hours, but by this time it was clear that the Nissan was no longer a front runner against Oldsmobile.

MARKET FORCE

In order to gain market credibility, the Japanese manufacturers needed to

Business end of the AMG-prepared Mercedes-Benz CLK-GTR revealed during a pit-stop at the 1997 FIA GT series. Based on the proven Class 1 Touring Car technology, the C-class-derived 600bhp 6.0-litre V12 engine was mated to a six-speed sequential gearbox.

achieve monumental success in international motor sport. To that end, Nissan set about an assault on Le Mans. Although this goal has thus far eluded them, they have twice won the equally demanding Daytona 24-Hours. Nissan spent two years racing its R89C and R90C Group C cars, and then developed its Nissan Skyline GTR for GT racing, and ran it twice at Le Mans. Although this powerful twin-turbo model had dominated the Japanese GT championship, it never matched the pace of the McLarens, so Nissan elected to follow the Porsche route in 1996 by producing a GT1 supercar.

The project to build the chassis was handled by Tom Walkinshaw's TWR concern, based on its past successes with Jaguars and contemporary attainments with the TWR-Porsche, with which Reinhold Joest's team won in 1996 and 1997. TWR's solution was the closest a GT car could be to a Group C racer, and the Nissan R390 GT1 was reminiscent of the Dauer Porsche GT of 1994, only lower and sleeker. Nissan's in-house NISMO set-up built a new 3.5-litre (214-cubic-inch) twin-turbo V8 unit for the car, married to a transverse six-speed sequential gearbox located at the rear of the car, but this was to be its Achilles' heel. The best drivers were hired _

Martin Brundle, Riccardo Patrese, Jorg Muller, Eric van der Poele, Erik Comas and Kazuyoshi Hoshino – but when the crack squad reached Le Mans, all three R390 GT1s were beset by gearbox problems due to inadequate soldering of the oil coolers. In the race itself, one car was crashed, another's gearbox failed, but the third car made it to the finish line in twelfth place, which was fair enough on its first Le Mans attempt.

For 1998, Nissan focused doggedly on Le Mans. TWR had made considerable improvements to the R390 GT1, but the Nissans were still out-qualified by Mercedes-Benz, Porsche and Toyota (the quickest Nissan was John Nielsen's, and that was 10th on the grid). In the race, all four TWR-run R390s finished in the top 10, the highest-placed being third. Thereafter, Nissan elected to handle race preparation itself, and for 1999 produced the open-top R391, which from the front looked not unlike a cross between a Panoz and the Bluebird land-speed record car. A Nissan engine would also power a privately entered Courage.

RETRO RACER

In the 1950s and 1960s, the archetypal North American sports racing car was built by Briggs Cunningham and Carroll Shelby, and indeed the Shelby

Roof intake directs air into engine compartment

Air enters through front grill and is directed up to pass through horizontally mounted radiator

After passing through radiator air is ducted out through bonnet

Side intake directs air into engine compartment

Air is also ducted through to brakes to cool them

LOTUS

Make: *Lotus*
Model: *Elise Sport*
In production: *2000*
Engine: *1.8-litre (110-cubic-inch) transverse mid-mounted four-cylinder*
Gearbox: *five-speed Quaife straight-cut*
Power output: *203bhp*
Chassis: *bonded and riveted aluminium extrusions*

Cobra was for a brief period the dominant GT car. Then in the mid-1990s, the retrospective designs became fashionable once more with the Dodge Viper, TVR Cerbera and Marcos LM600 being prominent. Retro meant nothing to Morgan, who continued to race an updated version of its ash-framed Plus 8 model from the 1970s.

In 1997 the Panoz appeared, and this was yet more radical than any of the others. It was designed by Nigel Stroud with a carbon-composite monocoque and was built by Reynard. The man behind the project was American entrepreneur and Road Atlanta circuit owner Don Panoz, and it was at his insistence that the Ford Mustang engine was used. This was to be the Rousch version, a proven IMSA and NASCAR winner, developing 600bhp in normally aspirated trim and coupled with an X-Trac six-speed sequential gearbox. The Panoz GTR-1s were run by two of Europe's top teams, the 1995 BPR champions Dave Price Racing and 1995 Formula 3000 champions DAMS. However, its ultra-low nose meant that it was not an easy engine to cool, and that proved to be the Panoz's main problem area.

Its debut at the 1997 Sebring 12-Hours with the DAMS squad was hindered by overheating, which brought about its eventual retirement,

Based on the successful road-going model, the Lotus Elise Sport was launched in 2000 with its own one-make Autobytel Championship. Power came from a 1.8-litre (110-cubic-inch) Rover-based K-series engine developing 203bhp.

but Panoz's first FIA GT championship race was not a complete débacle, in spite of one of the Dave Price Racing team cars catching fire on the warm-up lap. The other, driven by Wallace and Weaver, survived several excursions into the scenery to finish 10th, while the DAMS car's engine blew up. At Le Mans, two DPR and a single DAMS GTR1 were entered, but all retired, a couple with engine failure and the third because of a fire. At the Nürburgring, the DPR cars finished in 13th and 14th places, but the only FIA GT points were gained by a third place at Sebring at the end of the season. However, in the USA, Andy Wallace had already won three SportsCar GT

With its roots in Club racing in the early 1960s, Marcos remained a worthy contender in GT2 in the late 1990s. The Chevrolet V8-powered LM500 was British GT champion in 1995, and the Euser/Erdos LM600 took three wins from five pole positions in 1996.

races at Road Atlanta, Watkins Glen and Sears Point in the DPR-run Panoz Competition car to confirm its road-racing potential.

For 1998, Panoz Motorsports was based at Road Atlanta circuit, and former Jaguar engineer Tony Dowe was hired. Panoz Motorsports ran the American programme while DAMS took care of the FIA series. David Brabham and Eric Bernard drove in the 1998 FIA GT series, while Wallace concentrated on the US series. The Brabham/Bernard car was fifth at Oschersleben and third at Hockenheim and Dijon, and apart from transmission

failure at Donington, they were in the points seven times. At the 1998 Le Mans the DAMS cars qualified 11th and 18th in race week, and former Daytona winner O'Connell was brought in alongside Bernard and Christophe Tinseau. That car retired at two-thirds' distance with transmission failure, while the Brabham/ Wallace/Jamie Davies car managed an excellent seventh place overall. The Panoz GTR1 proved very fast in the USA, and Wallace led at Daytona before being shunted off by his former co-driver James Weaver. Wallace won the GT1 category in the Sebring 12-Hours, as well as Las Vegas, Lime Rock, Mosport, Sebring and Laguna Seca, and he amassed enough points to give Panoz the SportsCar GT1 title before the end of the season. Wallace/ Brabham won the drivers' championship at Laguna Seca, leading the inaugural ALMS Petit Le Mans at

Road Atlanta until engine failure after eight hours ended their run.

As Panoz Motorsports and DAMS concentrated on their European and North American campaigns with the conventional Ford V8-powered GTRs, Dave Price Racing worked on the Panoz Q9 Hybrid project. Under deceleration, a powertrain controller converted the air-cooled, permanent-magnet, brushless Zytec DC motor into a generator to recharge the 300-volt Varta nickel-metal hydride battery pack, which provided 30 per cent of the car's 690bhp under hard acceleration. It was the first time an electrically

The Gordon Murray-designed McLaren F1 won the 1995 Le Mans 24-Hours outright at its first attempt. Powered by a 6.0-litre (366-cubic-inch) BMW V12 engine mated to X-trac transmission, the F1 was also the world's fastest production car – at 372km/h (231mph).

assisted car had run at Le Mans, and they only managed to give it a shake-down run on the local airfield before Le Mans pre-qualifying. James Weaver was 16 seconds off the pace of the leading Porsche, but the Q9 was carrying 160kg (352lb) of extra weight with its batteries and electric motor. The hybrid Panoz was eventually debuted at Road Atlanta's Petit Le Mans 1000km (620-mile) event in October, driven by Nielsen, Tinseau and Doc Bundy. The Q9's performance was consistent, qualifying 12th and finishing 12th, even though the suspension had broken because of the car's extra weight. Having proved the technology worked, it was a concept that could prove its worth during an even longer endurance event such as Le Mans.

TVR

Make: *TVR*
Model: *Speed Twelve GT1*
In production: *1998-2000*
Engine: *7.7-litre (470-cubic-inch) V12 TVR*
Power output: *600bhp*
Chassis: *tubular spaceframe/carbon fibre/Kevlar*

MILLION-DOLLAR SPORTS CAR

In the mid-1990s, Mercedes-Benz had devoted most of its racing energies to its single-seater engine programme via Ilmor, and its overt on-track presence to the Class 1 ITC. When the highly technical championship collapsed, the AMG competitions department was left with much expertise, a huge investment in equipment and nothing to do with it.

Soon enough, Mercedes-Benz followed Porsche, McLaren and Lotus into international GT racing. AMG produced the C-Class coupé in time for the first race of the 1997 FIA GT championship in mid-April after getting the go-ahead only the previous November. Discounting Sauber, it was the first mid-engined Mercedes-Benz, based on much of the Class 1 ITC technology. The chassis was built by Lola Composites in Huntingdon, and the production-based, normally aspirated 6.0-litre (366-cubic-inch) V12 engine produced 600bhp, transmitted via a sequential-shift six-speed gearbox.

The CLK-GTRs were the closest yet to Group C prototypes and ran well first time out, with Bernd Schneider on pole. At Hockenheim in official qualifying, Schneider hit the top speed of 321.11km/h (199.57mph). Development problems were overcome, and a third car was built for the FIA series, excluding Le Mans. They naturally hired top drivers including Klaus Ludwig and Sandro Nannini, and they dominated the fourth round at Nürburgring with a one-two finish a lap clear of the McLarens. The CLK-GTRs also came first and second at the A1-Ring and Donington Park; Schneider won at Suzuka, and Klaus Ludwig won at Sebring and Laguna Seca. Mercedes and Schneider ended up winning their respective championships, with Ludwig second in the drivers' category.

For 1998, the former ITC team Persson Motorsport was accorded

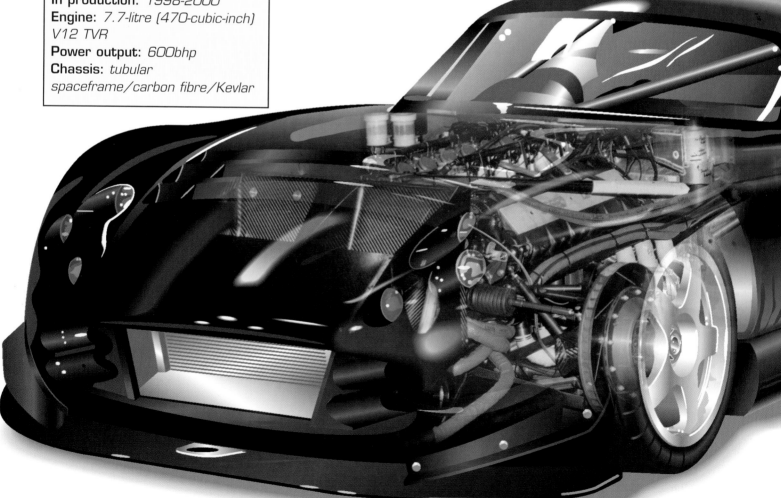

semi-works status to run two of the 1997 cars, while upgraded AMG GTRs were fettled for Schneider, Australian Mark Webber, Ludwig and the Brazilian Ricardo Zonta, for the two races prior to Le Mans. Ludwig/Zonta won the opening Oschersleben round, and Schneider/Webber won at Silverstone. AMG switched to the CLK-LM after the Le Mans 24-Hours, although Persson continued to run the CLK-GTRs for the rest of the season with Jean-Marc Gounon/Marcel Tiemann and Christophe Bouchut/Bernd Maylander. Apart from a second placing for the former pairing at Oschersleben, neither car achieved a podium finish for the rest of the season, although they were perfectly reliable.

Le Mans success has always been the draw for the major manufacturers, and Mercedes-Benz wanted another taste of the success it had enjoyed in 1991 when

TVR has always showcased its roadgoing products with extravagant models, and the Speed 12 was no exception, taking the marque into the GT1 category. Powered by TVR's own modular 7.7-litre (470-cubic-inch) V12, the Speed 12 took up where the GT2 Cerbera left off in 1999.

Michael Schumacher, Karl Wendlinger and Fritz Kreuzpointner had driven their Mercedes C11 twin-turbo V8 to fifth place overall in the French classic. The same engine had won Le Mans in 1989, and was derived from the M119 S-class production unit. Now deprived of its turbochargers and enlarged from 4.9 litres (299 cubic inches) to 5.9 litres (360 cubic inches), it formed the basis of the 1998 Le Mans car. The chassis of the Le Mans contender was still based on the CLK, but the front end featured a lower profile, with air intakes inside the front wings and a boot space, as required by the regulations of the Le Mans organisers, the ACO.

COURAGEOUS DECISION

The Silverstone round was the final race for the AMG-run CLK-GTR V12. From Le Mans onwards, and for the rest of the 1998 GT series, it was replaced by the CLK-LM V8, and this was a particularly courageous decision, given that both cars had failed early on at Le Mans. At Le Mans, Schneider claimed pole ahead of Porsche, Toyota, Nissan and the open sports racers from Porsche, BMW and Ferrari, only to experience engine failure just 19 laps into the race. Bouchut's car failed for the same reason only an hour later. They did not miss a beat thereafter, however, apart from an accident at Dijon when Webber was sidelined by a puncture. By the end of the season, Mercedes had won 10 out of 10 races, taking first and second places at six of them. Schneider was denied a second successive title when Webber went off at Homestead, handing the championship to Ludwig and Zonta. This was rather fitting, as it was Ludwig's last season, the German stalwart retiring after 29 years of racing.

For 1999, the FIA Sports Prototype championship was designed to match the GT1 supercars against open sports racing cars.

COLOGNE COMEBACK

The Toyota GT-One was built by the Japanese manufacturer's Toyota Team

Europe rally division, based in Cologne, rather than its official factory race shops, TOM's or SARD. The car's single purpose was to win Le Mans, and the solution TTE produced was a high-tech GT car that was more akin to a Group C prototype.

Its carbon-composite monocoque was drawn up by the former Peugeot designer André de Cortanze using CAD systems exclusively. The GT-One was powered by the same 3.6-litre (220-cubic-inch) V8 twin-turbo unit that had taken Eddie Irvine, Mauro Martini and Jeff Krosnoff to second place at Le Mans in 1994. The car was aerodynamically advanced, with under-car radiator intakes of which Toyota TTE was protective during Le Mans pre-qualifying. The GT-One ran impressively in testing and Martin Brundle came close to being fastest in the Toyota in 1998. His best time was just fractions of a second off Allan McNish's factory Porsche on pole. And Toyota was serious about success as Brundle headed an impressive line-up of driver talent waiting its turn in the pits: Thierry Boutsen, Ukyo Katayama, Toshio Suzuki, Geoff Lees, Emanuel Collard, Ralf Kelleners, Eric Helary and Keuichi Tsuchiya.

Brundle led the race until slowed by a wheel-bearing problem. Then Boutsen took over in the second-fastest Toyota, shared with Lees and Kelleners, and they disputed the lead for the next 17 hours. They were still out in front of the two works Porsche GT1s with 80 minutes of the race left when the gearbox failed, leaving Porsche with a clear passage to victory. While Brundle had crashed out of contention, Toyota Team Europe's third GT-One crewed by Suzuki/ Katayama/Tsuchiya finished in ninth place.

It had been an excellent debut, and Toyota and Nissan had contrived to shift the parameters of Le Mans cars further away from the original concept of GT1 and closer to Group C. In order to cater for this type of car, the Automobile Club de l'Ouest instituted a new GT prototype category for 1999.

Designed by Nigel Stroud, the Panoz GTR-1 won the 1997 Sports Car GT1 title. The Dave Price Racing Team car is driven here by James Weaver/Andy Wallace at the Austrian A-1 Ring in 1997.

TOWER OF POWER

Back in the 1950s, Britain's backyard motor racing industry catapulted the likes of John Cooper, Colin Chapman and Brian Lister into the limelight. Not so well known was Trevor Wilkinson, the man who gave his name to the TVR.

Spurred on by Lotus successes in the small-capacity classes, TVR set its sights on Le Mans, and with ex-Triumph competitions manager Ken Richardson in charge things ought to have gone better. Three works-prepared TVR Mark IIA Granturas competed in the 1962 Sebring 12-Hours, and another three took part in the 1962 Tulip Rally, leading their class for a while. But the anticipated success was not forthcoming: at Le Mans, all three cars were beset with overheating problems. Only one TVR actually started, and that retired after three laps. It was a similar story in the RAC Tourist Trophy.

TVRs, especially the monstrous Griffith, were also campaigned in UK and US club events, with Gerry Marshall the race fans' favourite in his 4.7-litre (287-cubic-inch) Griffith. The concept of the Griffith was similar to that of the AC Cobra: shoehorn a massive American lump into a taut spaceframe chassis with wishbone suspension all round and you are bound to get a result (a close inspection of the scenery more likely).

PANOZ

Make: *Panoz*
Model: *GTR-1*
In production: *1997-2000*
Engine: *4.6-litre (281-cubic-inch) Rousch-developed Ford V8 Mustang*
Gearbox: *X-Trac six-speed sequential shift*
Power output: *600bhp*
Chassis: *Reynard-designed carbon fibre*

By the early 1990s, Blackpool-based TVR had changed hands a couple of times, and under the guidance of its owner Peter Wheeler (and his dog, Ned) a renaissance began that included the one-make Tuscan Challenge, which was hugely spectacular and based on the same formula as the 1960s Griffith. Big, Rover-based V8 engines in spaceframe chassis and full

Frenchman's creak: the Panoz GTR-1 of DAMS drivers Eric Bernard/Frank Lagorce is checked over in the pits garage at Nogaro, France. Visible is the car's Roush-developed 600bhp Ford V8 Mustang Cobra engine.

22-car grids could only be massively entertaining, but Wheeler, a self-confessed fan of 1950s sports racing cars, wanted more. Surrounded by a talented team of engineers headed by John Ravenscroft, he launched the TVR Cerbera GT in 1994.

Using an advanced spaceframe chassis designed by Nigel Stroud to include an integral roll-cage and pushrod suspension, the Cerbera was powered by TVR's own modular V8 AJP engine. This unit started out at 4.5 litres (275 cubic inches), but the 1999 GT2 race version expanded to 5.0 litres (305 cubic inches), pumping out 410bhp with GT2 restrictors in place. In 1995, Techspeed started to race the Cerbera, with Mark Hales driving, and then TVR took up the race programme for 1996 under racing manager John Swinscoe. The improved and lightened car brought instant results, with Hales and F3000 racer Phil Andrews driving to a number of second places in the British GT championship in the first half of the season, eventually topping the podium with GT2 wins at Snetterton and Silverstone. They also entered BPR races when the series visited Britain.

Then, long-time TVR racer Colin Blower took over the Cerbera competition programme while the factory concentrated on building its spectacular Speed 12 GT1 version. In 1997, Blower and Jamie Campbell-Walter won outright at Donington in the GT2 Cerbera, despite the slight inconvenience of the car being on fire at the time. The race had to be stopped, and the positions at the end of the previous lap formed the basis of the results. However, they only managed a fifth and an 11th place in a year characterised by retirements.

The new Speed 12 was powered by TVR's own 650bhp 7.7-litre (470-cubic-inch) V12 engine, and things augured well for the FIA GT championship and Le Mans. But back at the Blackpool factory there was pressure to produce road cars, and the Speed 12 was only seen in UK events. At Snetterton, in only its second race, it came fourth overall to the two Listers and the McLaren, followed by seventh and ninth in its next two races with Bobby Verdon-Roe, teamed with either John Kent or Martin Short (all noted TVR Tuscan dicers). With no FIA endurance championship held in 1999, the Speed 12 project was put on the back-burner in favour of the 600bhp Cerbera V10 to run in the FIA GT series, although it was scheduled to come out of the closet for 2000.

FUTURE PROSPECTS

The 67th staging of the Le Mans 24-Hours should have been remembered as one of the all-time great races. It never quite lived up to expectations, despite the unprecedented number of manufac-

turers going for outright victory.

The race was partly notable for the series of aerial accidents that befell the AMG Mercedes team. Three of the Silver Arrows CLK-GT racers took off at over 320km/h during the course of the meeting. Given that Mercedes began a self-imposed 30-year exile from motor sport after one of its cars flipped into the crowd at Le Mans back in 1955, the implications if someone had been killed or seriously injured in 1999 were extremely serious. The moment Mercedes-Benz withdrew after Peter Dumbreck's car somersaulted in the fifth hour, it became a straight fight between BMW and Toyota.

The Schnitzer BMW and Toyota teams were the pre-race favourites, but the battle in the final hours was waged between the tortoises from the respective marques, after the hares had long been retired. Victory finally went to the BMW V12 LMR of Yannick Dalmas, Pierluigi Martini and Jo Winkelhock. The Japanese-crewed Toyota GT-One

would have run it close but for a tyre blow-out in the final hour after Ukyo Katayama was pushed over the kerbs by a privateer BMW.

The FIA GT series in 2000 comprised privateers and small marques such as Lister and Marcos, but the departure of the ORECA Chrysler team encouraged new entrants, including five customer Chrysler Vipers, four Lister Storms and a team of Ferrari 550 Maranellos. Ranged against them were a number of Porsche 911 GT3-Rs and Ferrari 360 Modenas in the new secondary class, making the FIA GT series look respectably healthy.

A new Ferrari GT racer was unveiled in February 2000, known as the 550 Millenio and built by Italtechnics to be run by the Swiss FIRST racing team. It was straight out of the mould of its exalted forebear, the Ferrari 250GTO. While it was in no way as radical as the contemporary Audi, BMW or Panoz sports racers, in a way, the wheel had come full circle.

IMSA GTP CHAMPIONSHIP

Year	Driver	Car	Year	Driver	Car
1971	Peter Gregg/Hurley Haywood (USA),	Porsche 911S			Chevrolet/Porsche
1972	Hurley Haywood (USA),	Porsche 911S	1984	Randy Lanier (USA),	March-Chevrolet
1973	Peter Gregg (USA),	Porsche 911S	1985	Al Holbert (USA),	Porsche 962
1974	Peter Gregg (USA),	Porsche 911RSR	1986	Al Holbert (USA),	Porsche 962
1975	Peter Gregg (USA),	Porsche 911RSR	1987	Chip Robinson (USA),	BF Goodrich Porsche 962
1976	Al Holbert (USA),	Porsche/Chevrolet Corvette	1988	Geoff Brabham (AUS),	Cunningham Nissan
1977	Al Holbert (USA),	Chevrolet	1989	Geoff Brabham (AUS),	Cunningham Nissan
1978	Peter Gregg (USA),	Porsche 935	1990	Geoff Brabham (AUS),	Cunningham Nissan
1979	Peter Gregg (USA),	Porsche 935	1991	Geoff Brabham (AUS),	Cunningham Nissan
1980	John Fitzpatrick (GB),	Porsche 935	1992	Juan Manuel Fangio II (RA),	AAR Eagle-Toyota
1981	Brian Redman (GB),	Porsche 935/Lola-Chevrolet	1993	Juan Manuel Fangio II (RA),	AAR Eagle-Toyota
1982	John Paul Jr (USA),	Porsche 935/Lola-Chevrolet	1994	Wayne Taylor (ZA),	Scandia Kudzu-Mazda
1983	Al Holbert (USA),	March-Porsche/March-	1995	Fermin Velez (E),	Scandia Ferrari
			1996	Wayne Taylor (ZA),	Riley & Scott-Oldsmobile

INDEX

PICTURE CREDITS

Action Plus: 17 (t) (DPPI), 23 (DPPI), 29 (DPPI), 36 (t), 39 (t), 44, 48 (DPPI), 61 (DPPI), 98 (DPPI), 111 (DPPI), 118 (both) (DPPI), 120 (DPPI), 132 (DPPI), 145 (DPPI), 163 (DPPI).

Audi UK: 147 (t).

Benson & Hedges Jordan: 10 (b).

Burmah-Castrol: 64 (t), 84, 88, 96, 103 (b), 130-131, 133, 143 (b), 147 (b), 152.

Ian Catt: 26 (t), 85 (b), 86 (m), 87, 136, 138 (both).

Ford Motors/John Tipler: 25 (t), 26-27, 28, 90, 140, 157, 158.

G.P. Library: 10-11.

Jaguar Racing: 35.

LAT Photographic: 106-107, 113.

Lister Cars Limited: 67 (b).

Ludvigsen Library Limited: 156.

McLaren/www.mclaren.net: 6-7.

Linzi Smart: 109, 110.

Sutton Motorsport Images: 12 (b), 33, 46-47, 49, 50 (both), 51, 52-53, 56 (both), 58, 59, 62-63, 64 (b), 65, 70, 71, 77, 78 (both), 79, 89, 92 (b), 93, 97, 100-101, 102 (both), 103 (t), 104 (both), 105, 112, 114-115, 116, 117, 119, 121, 122, 123, 124, 125, 126, 127, 128 (both), 141, 143 (t), 146, 150-151, 153, 156, 160 (b), 164, 166, 167, 169 (both), 172 (both).

John Tipler: 8 (both), 9, 16, 18, 21, 30, 31, 32, 36, 67, 42, 45, 55, 57, 86 (b), 108, 139, 142, 159, 160 (t), 161, 162.

Vauxhall Motorsport: 82-83.

Williams F1: 14-15.

ARTWORK CREDITS

Richard Burgess: 24-25, 34, 38, 39 (b), 54, 66-67, 69, 91, 94-95, 95, 168, 170-171.

Tony Matthews: 11 (tr) (Renault), 12-13 (Renault), 18-19, 20-21 (Maserati), 22-23 (Cooper), 42-43, 68 (Ilmor Engineering), 74-75 (Lola Ford), 76-77 (Valvoline Inc.), 80-81(DH Enterprises), 136-137 (Brandon Wang), 144-145 (Lola).

Orbis Publishing: 17 (b), 134-135, 154-155.

John Tipler: 40-41, 85 (t), 92 (t), 140-141.